Rethinking Information Work

*A Career Guide for Librarians and
Other Information Professionals*

G. KIM DORITY

LIBRARIES
U N L I M I T E D
A Member of the Greenwood Publishing Group
Westport, Connecticut • London

Library of Congress Cataloging-in-Publication Data

Dority, G. Kim, 1950–
    Rethinking information work : a career guide for librarians and other
    information professionals / by G. Kim Dority.
      p. cm.
    Includes bibliographical references and index.
    ISBN 1–59158–180–X (pbk. : alk. paper)
    1. Library science—Vocational guidance—United States. 2.
Information science—Vocational guidance—United States. 3. Career
development.   I. Title.
  Z682.35.V62D67   2006
  020.23–dc22   2006023752

British Library Cataloguing in Publication Data is available

Library of Congress Catalog Card Number: 2006023752
ISBN: 1–59158–180–X

First published in 2006

Libraries Unlimited, 88 Post Road West, Westport, CT 06881
A Member of the Greenwood Publishing Group, Inc.
www.lu.com

Printed in the United States of America

The paper used in this book complies with the
Permanent Paper Standard issued by the National
Information Standards Organization (Z39.48–1984).

10 9 8 7 6 5 4 3 2

This book is dedicated to all the students I have had the opportunity to teach, and to learn from—you are our future. It is dedicated also to the extraordinary community of friends and colleagues who for me have always been the best part of being an LIS professional.

Contents

Introduction

In 1999, I began teaching a class in the University of Denver MLIS program on alternative career paths for library and information science students. The class had never been taught before. That fall, a small but intrepid (and stunningly patient) group of students began to develop together an understanding of what we needed to learn.

We discovered that although our focus was alternative career paths, that is, what other career opportunities might be available to library and information science (LIS) professionals, that was only part of the equation. Students also needed to step back from their existing lives and jobs and expectations in order to understand who they were, and what might bring them joy in their professional lives. They needed to have more realistic information about the various career choices in order to understand whether or not specific options might fit with their skills and personalities and life circumstances. They needed to be coached on strategy, on figuring out how to approach a given goal by creating a plan of action. And they needed to learn that not only were they capable of achieving their goals and dreams, they had an obligation to themselves to at least try.

Over a period of many years and many students (equally patient), we ended up creating a body of knowledge around strategies, solutions, and information resources. But in every class, the most important challenge the students undertake is that of rethinking information work.

Most students arrive with a practice- or discipline-focused mindset. That is, I know how to catalog, therefore I'm a cataloger. Or I know how to do research, therefore I'm a reference librarian. Or I come from a family of teachers, therefore I'm destined to become a school librarian.

But just as we rethink how we envision the universe of possible information work, we need to rethink how we envision what we are capable of, what we expect from ourselves, what we expect *for* ourselves. What is important to us? Is it salary, benefits, serving the public good, working in an intellectually stimulating environment, living close enough to the library to be able to bike to work?

Equally important, who do we want to be, and how do we want others to think of us? Over the years, different words and phrases have begun to define our preferred self-image, words such as ...

Energy. Innovation. Thought leadership. Impact. Engagement. Passion. Excitement. Self-Confidence. Participation. Entrepreneurial. Collaboration. Improvisation. Dynamic action. Joy. Contribution. Laughter. Politically astute. Change agent. Connected. Adventurous. Smart. Resilient.

Each of these characteristics will be necessary for LIS practitioners in the coming years as the profession continues to be driven by new circumstances we can guess at now, as well as those we can't even imagine. We know the roles of public, school, and academic librarians will shift in response to demographic changes, technology advances, and funding issues, but what other disruptive changes are hiding in the wings? We know that fewer and fewer businesses are establishing and/or maintaining "traditional" corporate libraries, but what about the large number of information-based roles that are opening up in their stead? For independents, how many new and different ways are there to earn a living in an "information-based" economy? The opportunities are essentially limitless, which is exhilarating on a good day – and often overwhelming on other days, especially for students!

There are a number of excellent guides and online resources available to help you explore the library profession, and you will find them recommended throughout the following chapters. The goals of this book, however, are a bit different. The first is to introduce you to the incredibly broad and diverse range of professional situations for which your LIS skills might be applicable, including traditional librarianship. When you have a better sense of how very many options are open to you, you'll be much less likely to stay stuck in a job that isn't good for you, and to instead find the job (or career path) that brings you joy.

The second goal is to help you get to where you'd like to be. This involves systematically sorting out the options, providing you the tools and coaching you need to figure out which ones are best for you, and then helping you lay out a strategy for achieving the career you dream of. Essentially, this is a process of self-discovery, decision making, and action based on a philosophy of empowerment and choice.

Energy. Innovation. Thought leadership. Impact. Engagement. Passion. Excitement. Self-Confidence. Participation. Entrepreneurial. Collaboration. Improvisation. Dynamic action. Joy. Whether we choose to work in traditional libraries, nontraditional environments, or as independents, these are the characteristics for which we want to be known. We have *huge* contributions to make to the lives around us, to the communities we live in, to the broader world with which we engage.

No matter what career paths we decide to pursue, all LIS professionals should be able to participate and contribute in the ways that most closely align with who they want to be in the world. It is my hope that this book helps you do exactly that.

1
Rethinking Information Work

*... each of us has a picture of what we want to do
before we die. How close we get measures the
quality of our lives.*
—Mihaly Csikszentmihalyi

We do information work.

We may work with the public answering reference questions, work in corporations creating competitive intelligence reports, work for nonprofits doing development research, or work for clients doing industry trend analysis (among myriad other options). But in all cases, we are working with information on behalf of others.

When most of us graduate with our master's degree in library and information science, we view our possible career paths within the framework of jobs we might land within the traditional spheres of librarianship. Many of us head off for positions as school, public, or academic librarians, while a relative few go after special library jobs. And these are terrific career paths if they fit your skills, interests, aptitude, financial requirements, and life stage at the time you follow them.

These traditional paths of librarianship can provide extraordinary, richly rewarding careers. However, for those whose interests or professional circumstances dictate other choices, it's reassuring to know that the traditional path is but one of *many* open to information professionals. That familiar MLIS designation signifies that we possess a stunningly diverse skill set, one that can be deployed in an equally stunning number of places, positions, and opportunities. The challenge comes in rethinking how we frame what we know, and *what we know how to do.*

1

In my career "doing information work" has given me the opportunity to set up a special-collection library for a nonprofit, write several books, create web content to support marketing and public-information campaigns, create a virtual library for online students, evaluate manuscripts for publishers, create an executive information service for a CEO, head up an LIS graduate program on an interim basis, create a course in alternative career paths for LIS students and professionals, do freelance research projects for a broad range of clients, and establish a consulting business focused on information strategy for businesses, government agencies, and nonprofits.

Many friends and colleagues have had equally diverse careers. Take Christine Hamilton-Pennell, nationally known expert in the sustainable economic-development practice known as "economic gardening." Christine has built a career that includes research work related to school libraries and at the Colorado Department of Education, teaching at the graduate level, freelance research, marketing consulting for libraries, developing web-based continuing education courses, developing a multimedia product, running a special library, and co-authoring a long-running online Internet review site. She has been a presenter at national conferences on the topics of competitive intelligence, planning and community development, and economic development, and currently works as the Economic Intelligence Specialist, Business/Industry Affairs, for the City of Littleton, Colorado.

Christine has done just about every type of information work available. Some of it has been within what we think of as "traditional librarianship," while other projects have been well outside of it. In all circumstances, however, she has built—and then expanded—on a core group of skills central to being an *information professional*, which includes being a librarian.

It's easy to assume that what we know is "librarianship." We may know cataloging, or readers' advisory services, or bibliographic instruction, or how to build a dynamic academic library portal. In fact, today's graduates probably know at least a good bit about each of these aspects of librarianship, as well as much more. They know how to "do librarianship."

But they—and we—also know something equally valuable. We all know how to do *information*. As LIS professionals, we know how to find it, evaluate it, organize it, maintain it, present it, and put it in play. We can create information and deploy it, align it with strategic goals, and use it to support individual, organization, or community development. And this is just for starters.

LIS professionals are managing complex information projects, designing community information systems, taking the lead on extraordinarily sophisticated digitization initiatives, running GIS projects, helping launch cutting-edge information products and services, and creating online communities of practice.

They're taking school libraries onto the web, embedding bibliographic instruction in online learning courses, and experimenting with virtual reference via podcasting. They're answering questions 24/7 for online, for-profit companies, organizing data networks for online auction businesses, and doing collection development for database developers. LIS professionals can be found throughout the nonprofit, for-profit, government, and library worlds—sometimes, but not always, being called librarians.

If we reframe our skill set from "librarianship" to the larger and more encompassing "information work," then we have choices that can respond to changes in job markets, personal financial requirements, living arrangements, and other professional and life circumstances. We may be information professionals who happily choose to spend our entire careers in the library field, in traditional libraries. But if budgets continue to be cut, staffs continue to be downsized, and jobs become scarce in times of economic crisis, information professionals can *always* deploy their skill sets in new directions should they need or want to.

And therein lies the key to a dynamic career. The more broadly you consider your career and your professional skills, the more numerous—and rewarding—your career opportunities.

Change Happens

Things change.

No matter how much our directors love us, no matter how great a job we do, circumstances, and management, change. Budgets get cut, people move on, organizations' priorities (and staffing needs) change.

Our working environments may change overnight, as the previously wonderful boss moves into the executive ranks, bringing in the replacement supervisor from hell. A flexible work schedule that fits you perfectly may be replaced with a more restrictive one that reflects the new management focus on a "tight ship." Or a change in leadership style at the top may result in fewer opportunities for growth and initiative throughout the rest of the organization.

Or the nature of the work we do and how we do it changes. Disruptive technologies such as digitization, the Internet, RSS feeds, blogs, instant messaging, and podcasting have changed forever what we mean by information collection, management, and dissemination. Our students are growing up in an integrated digital surround of information, communications, entertainment, and learning—and take for granted their 24/7 availability. Those of us who grew up before these technologies came online and went mainstream now find ourselves in a professional landscape bearing little resemblance to the one we trained for. As has been pointed out by industry guru Barbara Quint, Google now fields more searches in a few *days* than the total received by the world's libraries in a *year*.[1]

Or the nature of libraries within their constituencies changes. This isn't necessarily a diminishment of the role of libraries, but may take them in new directions that push staffers outside their comfort zones. Perhaps expectations of what libraries are and can do rise as technologies advance. Or libraries may be asked to be critical lifelines for underserved populations, often without preparation or training (or, frequently, funding). Or perhaps corporate libraries are asked to take on the more critical roles of analysis and strategic intelligence provider for their organizations—an unfamiliar and sometimes daunting responsibility for some traditional corporate librarians.

Or the nature of those leading the profession changes. We've got a passionate, smart, and dedicated group of "next-gen" librarians pushing to step into leadership roles in a profession not necessarily known for embracing innovative new ideas, especially if accompanied by body piercings and purple hair. Like the next generation of library users, many of these individuals have grown up in the electronic information surround, and their easy familiarity with emerging technologies is critical to the profession. Yet finding opportunities for these exciting new voices to be heard, and to mainstream these professionals into leadership roles, may require a willingness to rethink how libraries exist in the world.

Or we change. We outgrow a job we once loved, yearning instead for a new challenge. We leave a job to follow a significant other to the opposite side of the country. We decide to seek part-time work to spend more moments laughing with our toddler. We discover a passion for history, and begin to wonder about archives work. We realize belatedly that working on the reference desk is not the best job match for an introvert. We find that being able to afford a mortgage might be nice after all.

The reality is that we can't rely on an employer to pledge undying fealty—that is, lifetime employment—to us, because just like us, they have no idea what the future will hold. They may need to close our department, lay off staff because of mergers, cut our hours because of funding shortfalls, or transition us into positions that suit the organization's needs rather than ours. *None of this is personal*—it's simply how organizations (including libraries) work.

Things change, life changes, we change. And approached with the right attitude, that can be terrific. The trick is to find a way to create a career that can match us change for change, can keep up with our growth, can continue to offer us new opportunities and new challenges. The key is to understand that, in the long run, we are all self-employed.

And believe it or not, this is good news. Because if we understand that regardless of our current employment situation we are solely responsible for the well-being of our careers (and paychecks), that means we can take control. We can focus not on lifetime employment but on lifetime *employability*.

Lifetime Employment vs. Lifetime Employability

Lifetime employment means hanging on to a job, any job, rather than risk pursuing more fulfilling career choices. Lifetime *employability* involves continually developing new ways to contribute and grow professionally, and seeking out opportunities to do so.

In 1989, British organizational management specialist Charles Handy published a landmark book, *The Age of Unreason* (Harvard Business School Press). In it, he charted the effects of discontinuous change on Western economies and those who work within them. Especially applicable to information workers was Handy's description of portfolio workers, those individuals whose careers were built on their portfolios of projects rather than on decades-long work for one employer. William Bridges expanded on Handy's thesis with his *Jobshift: How to Prosper in a Workplace Without Jobs* (Perseus, 1995), a practical guide to creating a career based on ever-expanding skills rather than on finding an employer willing and able to guarantee a job for life.

Handy, Bridges, and many others have made the point that in an era of school and municipal budget cutbacks, corporate downsizing, mergers and acquisitions, and outsourcing and offshoring, the only job security lies within ourselves—and our ability to improvise our careers.

What does it take to ensure employability? First and foremost, it requires a sense of loyalty to your own professional goals. Although professional integrity mandates that we do our very best jobs for our employers and/or clients, we nevertheless must keep our own career goals moving forward at the same time.

The easiest way to practice this "enlightened self-interest" is to have your own career agenda firmly in place. This includes the strategies, tools, processes, and information resources that will support you as you—

- respond to new opportunities within your library, organization, or community;
- expand your skills to keep up with new technologies, disciplines, and processes;
- demonstrate your ability to transition from an area of lessening opportunity to one of greater demand;
- document a track record of initiative, innovation, and increasing responsibility; and
- develop a career that reflects who you are, what you value, and how you want to contribute, for as long as you want to do so.

Although information professionals are charting career paths in a work environment increasingly unpredictable, they're proving that lifetime employability is an achievable goal.

They're setting and executing research agendas, initiating new services built on emerging technology capabilities, participating in strategy teams, and applying their skills to information-business products, services, and start-ups. "Info pros" are being drawn into a brave new world with few road markers, fewer still established career paths to follow, and little guidance as to how to survive in this new workplace. Bottom line: we're making it up as we go along.

Although occasionally (okay, often) unnerving, improvising a career in such a dynamic environment can also be incredibly rewarding, in every sense. No path to track means you're free to chart your own best route. No job description means you can create your own definition of how you contribute. No footsteps to follow means no assumptions of what can or can't be done—and the freedom to set expectations high enough to challenge yourself. And no rigid pay grade means you can negotiate compensation that appropriately reflects your individual level of contribution.

What does it take to design a resilient career, one that allows you to successfully navigate the opportunities available to information professionals today—and tomorrow? And for that matter, what *is* a resilient career?

A resilient career is one that enables you to work for as long as you'd like, at work that you love, with an appropriate level of compensation and benefits. Ideally, it will offer you the level of challenge you thrive on, opportunities for learning and growth, and rewards of value to you, whether emotional, social, intellectual, or financial. And, when necessary, it should provide you with enough professional independence to leave an unhealthy work situation for a healthy one.

If we work at it, all of these goals are achievable. Through a combination of self assessment, strategies, tools, processes, information gathering, and attitudes, you can design a career that closely reflects the type of professional life you'd like to have.

By creating your own professional agenda, you'll be able to focus your time and career "energy" on moving toward your goals ... no matter where or how you're currently working. By rethinking information work as the broadest possible application of your skills, and then choosing how you will deploy those skills for the greatest personal reward, you can redefine your universe of career possibilities.

Career Competencies

What does it take to start moving your career in a direction that brings you work that will sustain you, financially and intellectually, for tomorrow and for a lifetime? As we'll see, it takes strategies and tactics, supported by tools and information. But first and foremost, it takes attitudes, expectations, and assumptions that work *for* you rather than against you. Among these are—

An understanding of who you are, who you can be, and who you want to be. Self-knowledge is a powerful tool. Without it, you can have no meaningful direction; yet with it you can consistently identify what will support (or detour) you on your path. Self-knowledge comes from exploring your preferences, thinking about what jobs, environments, and types of work make you happiest, and understanding what determines success for you.

Having a better understanding of yourself in the context of your career also makes it easier to distinguish between your own goals and desires and the expectations others may have for what your career should be about. Not that they don't always have the best of intentions, of course. . . .

A determination to accept reality. Yep, librarians should be paid more. Yes, they should be treated with the respect their role in society deserves. And there definitely should be more good, rewarding job opportunities and more potential for career growth in the profession. The reality is— salaries are probably not going to improve much in the foreseeable future. The general public rarely appreciates the extraordinary benefits libraries deliver at the level we would hope. Landing full-time jobs in traditional library settings may continue to challenge recent MLIS grads.

Neither wishing nor whining is going to change these realities. Only by facing them can you make useful choices and trade-offs among the options that *do* exist. That may mean living on a lower salary, moving to a different city, working in different environments where there's more flexibility, or higher pay, or more opportunity for growth. The key is, choices based in reality are the only ones that will actually get you unstuck.

A focus on solutions rather than obstacles. There are a million ways to say no: *we've never done that, we tried it before and it didn't work, that's not how we do things.* Or the famous and ever-popular *I can't see how that would work, who's going to pay for it, not my responsibility,* and my personal favorite, *are you nuts???* When someone poses a new challenge (okay, problem) for you to deal with, it's easy to focus on all the potential obstacles and raise these as reasons not to move forward. But a solutions focus gives you the opportunity to use (and demonstrate) your analytical skills, your ability to think strategically, your project management capabilities.

By taking the initiative instead of ducking under the desk, you become a professional who has contributions to make, and value to add. And your career efforts will focus not on the obstacles blocking your way, but on the solutions moving you forward.

An understanding and acceptance of change. We'll explore the impacts of change in greater depth in Chapter 8, but for now, the most important thing is to simply accept that change is nonnegotiable, and your goal is to focus on the energy rather than the fear inherent in change.

In order to do this, you'll need to explore how you react to change. This will help you become comfortable with your "change process," and consequently more confident in dealing with the ongoing changes of the LIS profession.

A willingness to adapt skills to the environment. Whether in a business, a public library, an association information center, a government agency, or any of the other environments LIS professionals find themselves in, your ability to move easily among them depends in large part on your flexibility. Can you adapt to the language of your organizations, align your processes to support theirs, develop systems that use your knowledge to suit new goals?

How well you read environments and how effectively you transfer your skills to them determine how readily you succeed in new opportunities. The world is not going to adapt to us, we will need to be willing to adapt to it.

A willingness to look for opportunity. Opportunities are all around us, yet if not paying attention to them, we'll miss most of the moments when our careers—if not our lives—could have opened up.

French biologist Louis Pasteur asserted that "chance favors the prepared mind," and careers are no different. If your mind is focused on finding or creating opportunities, then you will be positioned to move quickly with new solutions or products or services when an opening arrives. Just as chance favors the prepared mind, opportunity favors the prepared skill set.

An ability to anticipate. The old assumption was that librarians waited to be asked. Their role was a passive, reactive one. No longer. LIS professionals must have an eye out for what will be needed next, and be there in advance. Often your most effective role is scout, riding ahead of the troops to see what's coming over the horizon. Your research and analysis skills uniquely equip you for this spot; you need only claim the ground.

"I think success lies at the intersection of preparation, determination, and opportunity," suggested Edward B. Stear in his *Online* article "Predicting the Future Is Important, Navigating the Future Is Essential."[2] Add to that intersection a focus on anticipating the needs of your clients, customers, colleagues, and communities, and you have insured a key role for yourself as an LIS professional, no matter what your career path.

A willingness to take risks. All growth involves risk. Every new opportunity demands that you move from what you know into the unknown, with all its potential risks. It's critical to accept the complementary relationship of risk and reward; doing so often determines whether or not you can continue to move toward your goals.

It's often said that men make decisions driven by a desire for gain, whereas women's decisions are based on a fear of loss. If we remain mired in a bad situation based on this latter choice, then we've already lost. So learning how to take risks in such a way that you're not paralyzed by fear means you'll have the confidence necessary for large (and well-thought-through) risks later.

A commitment to continuous learning. We graduate with an MLIS based on the information (and learning?) universe—and its tools—of that moment. Within a few short years the tools and technologies of that universe have changed, or unforeseen opportunities have taken our careers in new directions. Continuous growth calls for continuous learning; without it, we're stuck with yesterday's solutions.

Staying abreast of new ideas, processes, technologies, and tools is one of the most effective ways to ensure ongoing career resiliency, as well as your continued ability to contribute strategically to your organization.

An enthusiasm and willingness to engage in the work. Enthusiasm generates energy. Positive engagement communicates itself to everyone around you and allows you to work at a high level of effectiveness while also motivating your colleagues.

Bottom line: being an enthusiastic contributor makes people want to work with you. It's easy to fall into habits of boredom or disengagement or negativity, but consider the signals you're sending—is this really how you want to be known?

An ability and willingness to continually reinvent ourselves. This last point comes from renowned information entrepreneur Mary Ellen Bates, who listed it among the key traits that she'd like to see among newly graduated LIS students.[3] Mary Ellen exemplifies the success that comes from this level of adaptability: her career includes being an information broker, columnist, book author, business consultant, seminar speaker, guest lecturer, and international keynoter. She has grown into these roles by continually reinventing herself, and what she is capable of.

SLA's Personal Competencies List

The Special Libraries Association (SLA) provides another interpretation of "Personal Competencies" as part of its highly regarded *Competencies for Information Professionals of the 21st Century*. This list includes, among others, the following attributes:

- Seeks out challenges and capitalizes on new opportunities
- Creates partnerships and alliances
- Builds an environment of mutual respect and trust; respects and values diversity
- Employs a team approach; recognizes the balance of collaborating, leading, and following
- Takes calculated risks; shows courage and tenacity when faced with opposition
- Plans, prioritizes, and focuses on what is critical
- Thinks creatively and innovatively; seeks new or "reinventing" opportunities
- Recognizes the value of professional networking and personal career planning
- Balances work, family, and community obligations
- Remains flexible and positive in a time of continuing change
- Celebrates achievements for self and others.[4]

Designing Your Career

Okay, you're in charge—where do you start? We'll explore each of these steps in greater depth in the following chapters, but essentially you'll explore questions, gather information, assess answers, establish agendas, and create strategies to execute your plans. This isn't necessarily a step-by-step plan of attack so much as an ongoing, iterative journey whose direction is determined solely by you: by your immediate life circumstances, by your dreams for the future, and by your willingness to invest yourself in their realization.

As you work through your career design process, you'll—

Do some information-gathering. For once, it really *is* all about you. Aside from a cursory Myers–Briggs assessment, few of us have taken the time to really explore who we are—or want to be—in terms of all the aspects of our careers. Your first step will be to spend some serious time asking yourself lots of questions and then carefully noting your answers. This will provide a structure of self-knowledge on which to base career choices that support rather than sideline your goals.

Explore the options. The next step is to assess the many career paths open to information professionals, including traditional, nontraditional, and independent. There are dozens if not hundreds of variables here that can shape whether or not a given job or career path fits your needs, so it's helpful to consider the options from as many different angles as possible. This exploration of possibilities can also help you shape a flexible career that fits your life circumstances as they change throughout the decades of your working life.

Once you've developed your information base of self-knowledge and the universe of opportunities, you'll be ready to design your strategies. At this point, you'll want to

Consider your skill set. You'll want to think about repackaging your skill set to most broadly define your capabilities, and the arenas in which they can be deployed. This step is part brainstorming, part word-smithing, and part research—how are jobs described, and how might your skills best be described to align with them?

Consider your learning, professional community, and "positioning" requirements. You'll need to consider expanding your skill set to match market opportunity. Once you've surveyed job postings, you'll have developed a good sense of skill gaps between jobs of interest to you and your existing skill set. This is where your learning process comes in—determining what you need to learn, when and where you'll learn it, and how you learn most effectively. In addition, you'll want to determine how to grow your professional community, and how to present your skills to the world at large.

Identify opportunities. You'll also want to practice identifying opportunities that let you move in new career directions. There are systematic ways to ferret out circumstances that drive new opportunities, whether entrepreneurial or internal to your organization. And if the right opportunity isn't there? Then try out ways to create your own.

After the work you've done asking questions, gathering information, and determining answers, you'll be ready to create your strategies for achieving the career you've envisioned. To get you from here to there, your next step will be to—

Lay out your career map. After you've done your research and brainstorming, it's time to pull together your action plan. Think of goals, strategies, and tactics that will take you from where you are now to where you want to be, and lay them out in a systematic, actionable plan.

Lastly, you'll want to think through how your career fits into the world, how it aligns with your life, and how you'll structure your decisions to drive the outcomes you seek. At this point, your goal will be to—

Figure out your frame. How do you think about your career? Your world? Your life? What are your expectations of yourself, and of your value in the workplace? How do you define success, and how will you know when you've achieved it? Thinking through your answers to these questions will allow you to use the information you've gathered and the strategies you've developed to shape a career path that fits who you are, where your life is, and what the world of information work looks like for you at any given time.

Beginning Your Career Journal

As you work through the coming chapters, you'll be exploring all sorts of career options and opportunities. You'll be approaching things from two angles: the information itself, and your responses to it, in an effort to learn about various career paths as well as how appropriate they might be for you personally. In order to capture all that knowledge, I'm going to ask you to start a career journal.

What is a career journal? It's any sort of book, binder, portfolio, or folder that allows you to capture all of the elements of the journey you're about to set out on. A place where you can record ideas, identify questions and fill in answers, highlight key discoveries about yourself, draw connections, and engage in any other activities that document your findings.

You can organize your career journal in whatever format best supports your creative process. You might want to use a notebook full of lined or blank pages; you might find that you'd rather draw pictures than outline ideas in order to represent your thinking. This is where you'll keep your to-do lists, your descriptions of your perfect job, notes about your highest priorities. The goal is to create a resource that inspires you and motivates you, or in any other way keeps you moving forward toward your goal. It should become an organic document, one that continues to grow with you as your career grows.

Consider this, then, the first assignment for your upcoming career journey. Using a format that reflects your style and preferences, purchase a journal that will be solely dedicated to your career exploration. Consider colored pens and highlighters if you'd like, perhaps use sticky notes to record fleeting thoughts, or paste in pictures if they add meaning to your ideas. Populate your journal in whatever way best reflects how you interact with the world of information and ideas and inspiration.

Throughout this book, you'll use your career journal to write responses to chapter exercises, so that you can refer back to them and continue to build on them. But more importantly, you should use your journal to chart what's uniquely important to *you*.

When you're ready to start using your journal, try out some of the activities suggested below in "Starting Your Exploration," and experiment with writing about the outcomes of your research. Remember, this journal is solely a reflection of you, so how you choose to chart the territory is up to you also.

Starting Your Exploration

As you work through this book, there will be many suggestions for things to think about and ideas to consider. But it's also important to be able to take concrete action as well, to move from internal reflection to external engagement.

With that goal in mind, consider one or all of the following activities to help you get started on your exploration:

- Read through the articles posted at LIScareer (liscareer.com) and the back issues of the *Info Career Trends* newsletter archived at www.lisjobs.com/newsletter. Note any articles that seem especially interesting to you, indicating *why* you find them interesting—is it the environment, the type of work, the service opportunity described? Sign up for the LIScareer information feed and the Info Career Trends newsletter for useful, actionable, and realistic information about the LIS profession and its opportunities. These two resources are simply invaluable for LIS professionals (and students!) exploring career options.

- Go through the job-posting sites listed under "Job Postings" (see Appendix B) and identify jobs that sound interesting to you. Check out what titles are being used to describe them, what responsibilities each entails, and what skill sets are required to get a sense of possible jobs of interest—both traditional and nontraditional—and their parameters. Both the current listings and archived postings are useful here.

- As you read through the articles in the current and archived issues of the *Info Career Trends* newsletter, identify the contributors who have jobs or have discussed topics that interest you. After reading their articles, follow up with the contributors for an e-mail or phone information interview to learn more aspects of their jobs that interest you.

If you're a student, also consider these actions:

- Use your time in the graduate program to get a sense of what different career choices offer in terms of flexibility, salary, challenge, self-direction, and opportunity. Use your course research assignments, ask questions of guest lecturers, explore options with your faculty, and peruse the professional journals in the library or through its LIS databases.

- When you have guest speakers in class, research what they will be speaking about and come prepared with questions. They will appreciate your interest and engagement, and you will establish a professional connection with someone who will probably be happy to counsel you regarding professional choices. Write thank-you notes to express your appreciation for their time and effort.

- Join appropriate professional organizations while you can still take advantage of the student rate, and keep an eye out for scholarships available to students for graduate school tuition, conference attendance, etc. Also, participate and get visible at the local chapter level; this gives you an opportunity to start building your professional community while still in school.

- As you enter the second half of your graduate program, develop and work on a strategy for transitioning from student to employed professional. Your job as a student should be as much about career exploration as about learning LIS skills; explore the profession as it exists, as it may become, and what paths you might like to pursue throughout your career. It's okay if you're not focused on a decision at this point, but you *can* focus on exploring.

Most importantly, for both students and professionals, get comfortable with the idea that you have a right to develop or pursue your own best career opportunities. Yes, we may be in a service profession, but that does not mean that we abandon our own well-being and best interests.

Your Value Statement

As you explore your career options, you'll need to keep one key question always at the forefront of your thinking: what value do you, as a professional, bring? This will determine what paths your career may follow, what opportunities you may have. Your value will be built on your unique competencies, your expertise, and your ability to align these with the strategic goals of your potential employer or client.

In a 2003 *Library Journal* article, writer Andrew Albanese noted that "the challenge for information professionals has far surpassed the static role of information provider.... They must provide solutions." An equally powerful statement came from Dr. James Matarazzo, Dean Emeritus of the Library and Information Studies program at Simmons College in Boston, who pointed out that "The real question is not what you are called, but how do you add value?"[5]

Whether in the traditional library sectors of public, school, and academic, or in the nontraditional LIS career paths, it will increasingly be up to each of us to not just do a job, but to add value to the organization. If we create new programs, design new processes, conceptualize innovative services, or in myriad other ways contribute to the improvement of the enterprise (including our libraries), we are adding value—and building a career.

In *Flow: The Psychology of Optimal Experience* (Harper, 1991), psychologist Mihaly Csikszentmihalyi explains the optimal experience of *flow*, wherein one is completely immersed in a self-directed activity that is so emotionally and intellectually engaging that one loses track of time.

There are many opportunities to work at this level of personal engagement in the LIS profession, but, as with any profession, it will probably take some effort on your part to get there. You need information, strategies, and tactics as well as personal initiative and a willingness to take risks. You need the confidence to stand up for yourself, and a commitment to your goals strong enough to help you over the rough spots.

You have the right to create the career of your dreams. But first, you'll need to get in touch with those dreams, the ones based on who you are at your most authentic, passionate core. That's what we'll explore next.

Resources

Books

de la Peña McCook, Kathleen, Margaret Myers, and Blythe Camenson. *Opportunities in Library & Information Science Careers.* McGraw-Hill, 2001. 160 pp. ISBN 0658016423.
Good job of identifying career choices, including education requirements, salary statistics, and some resources. Especially useful for beginning students and career novices. McCook is a public librarian and library educator known for her writing about the profession.

Eberts, Marjorie and Margaret Gisler. *Careers for Bookworms & Other Literary Types.* 3rd ed. McGraw-Hill, 2002. 128 pp. ISBN 007-1390316.
Think libraries, publishing, writing, research, teaching, and bookselling . . .. The authors include interviews and practitioner profiles, give tips on how to move into specific career tracks, and include a selective list of resources for each career. Brief but good overview of possibilities.

Gordon, Rachel Singer. *The NextGen Librarian's Survival Guide.* Information Today, 2006. 208 pp. ISBN 1573872563.
Intended for librarians in their twenties and early thirties, *Survival Guide* first describes the unique characteristics of this demographic and its issues and opportunities, then considers approaches to graduate school, the job hunt, entry-level positions, and moving forward in one's career. Provides invaluable, practical information—and lots of it.

Kane, Laura Townsend. *Straight from the Stacks: A First-Hand Guide to Careers in Library and Information Science.* ALA Editions, 2003. 192 pp. ISBN 0838908659.
A great resource for its combination of profiles or "spotlights" on real-life practitioners and sample job descriptions (environment, responsibilities, education and training, recommended memberships). Categories include public librarianship, school/children's/young adult librarianship, academic librarianship, nontraditional librarianship (corporate and freelance), and medical and law librarianship. A concluding section describes the job of "library director," with profiles of directors in public, law, university, and university health science libraries.

Nesbeitt, Sarah L. and Rachel Singer Gordon. *The Information Professional's Guide to Career Development Online.* Information Today, 2002. 416 pp. ISBN 1573871249.
Within the parameters of its specified focus, this book does a thorough job of describing ways to use the Internet to find and apply for jobs in the LIS field. Topics are grouped into four broad areas: learning and growing online, professional involvement, education, and employment. Chapters in each of these areas cover their topics with an eye toward their usefulness for career development. Appendixes cover additional resources, and numerous screen shots and graphics supplement the text.

Sellen, Betty-Carol. *What Else You Can Do with a Library Degree: Career Options for the 90s and Beyond.* Neal-Schuman Publishers, 1997. 300 pp. ISBN 1555702643.

Although this book is somewhat out of date relative to the others, its approach is interesting: the entire book is made up of contributed sections (ranging in length from four to twelve pages) from practitioners who talk about their careers and backgrounds. Although dated, still a useful resource.

Shontz, Priscilla K. *Jump Start Your Career in Library and Information Science.* Scarecrow Press, 2002. 208 pp. ISBN 0810840847.
A practical overview of the steps involved in getting your LIS career started. Shontz has included tips, checklists, resources, and personal stories that all add up to excellent advice for recent (or soon-to-be) MLIS graduates and those wanting to energize their existing careers.

Shontz, Priscilla K., ed. *The Librarian's Career Guidebook.* Scarecrow Press, 2005. 592 pp. ISBN 0810850346.
Imagine hanging out with sixty-three of your best friends ... who also happen to be really smart, career-savvy information professionals "from diverse positions, workplaces, and locations." Shontz's contributors offer practical, immediately actionable advice on all sorts of career issues of interest to LIS students as well as to seasoned LIS practitioners.

Periodicals

Info Career Trends. Lisjob.com, 2000– . Monthly. ISSN 1532-0839.
www.lisjobs.com/newsletter
Info Career Trends is Rachel Singer Gordon's bimonthly electronic newsletter devoted to professional development. Each topic-focused issue includes practical advice from successful practitioners supplemented by book reviews and links to relevant articles and websites. A must-read for anyone contemplating career development. The website also provides a content-rich starting point for exploring professional choices. A key resource.

Articles and Columns

DeCandido, GraceAnne A. "New Jobs for Old: Librarians Now," *Leading Ideas: Issues and Trends in Diversity, Leadership, and Career Development*, no. 15 (July 2000).
www.arl.org/diversity/leading/issue14/newjobs
The Association of Research Libraries (ARL) initiated a series of publications that became the basis of the *Leading Ideas* forum, now found on the web at www.arl.org/diversity/leading/index.html. Although no new materials have been added since 2000, the papers are still useful today. In this particular piece, Ms. DeCandido profiles seven successful professionals about how their careers—and their choices—kept pace with new opportunities.

Mort, Mary-Ellen. "The Info Pro's Survival Guide to Job Hunting," *Searcher*, vol. 10, no. 7 (July/August 2002), pp. 42–59.
www.infotoday.com/searcher/jul02/mort.htm
Making the argument that hitting monster job sites is probably not the best way to find your best job, Mort instead explains what she calls the Invisible Job Market, and how to work it. Her "Information

Professionals' Map to Invisible Job Market Resources," which links from the online article, is a must-read.

"Next Gen" column, *Library Journal*
www.libraryjournal.com
An occasional column written by various next-gen librarians that should be a must-read for all librarians, especially those in management and/or leadership positions. These writers represent the future of the profession, and their comments, questions, and insights provide an important window into potential new thinking. Also provides realistic commentary from those "in the trenches" regarding career challenges and issues for those just coming into the profession. Select "New Librarians" from the Browse Topics drop-down menu to view past columns at the *Library Journal* website.

Pergander, Mary. "Working Knowledge," *American Libraries*
www.ala.org/
Check this monthly column for practical information on career issues encountered by professionals in traditional library positions. From ALA site, select Products & Publications > Periodicals > American Libraries.

Wein, Terren Ilana, Marjorie Gagnon, and Maura Barrett. "Job Power: Career Management Resources for Librarians," *Information Outlook*, vol. 7, no. 1 (January 2003), pp. 11–16.
An annotated list of books, articles, and websites that provides a great overview of key resources for the job hunt, including general sources as well as those focused on LIS professionals.

Online Resources

Beyond the Job
librarycareers.blogspot.com/
A blog from Sarah Johnson and Rachel Singer Gordon ("the Library Job People"), Beyond the Job offers professional tips and up-to-date information for librarians wishing to further their library careers. Includes articles, advice on job-hunting specific to the library field, professional development resources, and related links.

Career Articles & Resources
www.sla.org/content/jobs/careerportal/index.cfm
A "members-only resource to assist information professionals in becoming indispensable to their clients and organizations." The site includes articles, web content, and tools to enhance your career development goals. If you're thinking of a nontraditional career path, this resource provides another terrific reason to join SLA —think of this content-rich repository as your own personal career coach.

Career Development
www.sla.org/chapter/ctor/resources/careerdevindex.asp
A highly valuable collection of annotated bibliographies, articles, white papers, education resources, annotated links, salary surveys, and information on alternative career choices. An excellent starting point for beginning your career exploration, from the Toronto chapter of SLA.

Career Planning
www.careerplanning.about.com
Offers general career planning advice and tools, plus a section specific

to library science professionals (Career Planning A–Z > Library Science Careers). Discusses what librarians do, working conditions and employment, training and other qualifications, and job outlook and earnings, all drawn from the *Occupational Outlook Handbook*. "Additional Resources" provides links to ALA, the Medical Library Association, and the American Association of Law Libraries, among others. Not a comprehensive resource, but a good starting point for those interested in traditional library options.

Careers in Libraries
www.ala.org/ala/hrdr/careersinlibraries/careerslibraries.htm
From ALA's Human Resource Development and Recruitment group, this site is a directory of unannotated resource links under the headings General Resources; Librarian (public, school, special); Educational Policies and Competencies; and Support Staff (resources for paraprofessionals).

Guide on the Side: Marie Wallace / LLRX.com
www.llrx.com/cgi-bin/llrx.cgi?function=browseauth2&id=9
Wallace writes a monthly career column for LLRX, a content-rich site focused on law and technology resources for legal and LIS professionals. Her topics are highly eclectic, but are generally focused on career skills. Browse through an archive of all of her columns at the LLRX website.

Indiana University Jobs in Library and Information Science
www.slis.indiana.edu/careers/mls_career_links.html
Annotated directory of links grouped under the categories of MIS (Corporate/Information Science, Nonprofit/Government, Other Opportunities, Alumni Profiles) and MLS (Academic Library, General, Public Library, and School Media Centers). Includes an especially useful (and lengthy) listing of professional associations; students interested in alternative careers should check out the broad range of jobs listed under SLIS Job Successes. A terrific resource for exploring LIS careers.

LibraryJournal.com: Careers
www.libraryjournal.com/community/891/Careers/42799.html
Solid, content-rich collection of career advice and related articles and resources, including JobZone, a jobs listing that organizes its postings by category: academic, children's/young adult, management, public libraries, and technical. *Library Journal* is to be commended for making this valuable information publicly available at no cost; employed LIS professionals should support this effort by subscribing to the print publication. A key resource.

Library Science As a Career
www.libraryhq.com/libcareer.html
Part of the LibraryHQ website created and maintained by Katharine Garstka, MLS, the career page provides resources related to job hunting, education options, types of library career paths, and resources for specializations such as law or health sciences librarianship.

LIScareer.com
www.liscareer.com
Billing itself as "the library & information science professional's career development center," LIScareer.com aggregates articles, resources, and information on career planning, education, job hunting, experience, networking, mentoring, interpersonal skills, leadership, publishing, and work/life balance. Some materials have been created

specifically for the site, others pulled in from a variety of resources both print and electronic. An extraordinarily content-rich tool for those contemplating a library/information-related career, wanting to advance their careers, or make a career change within the field, this is the companion to Priscilla Schontz's *Jumpstart Your Career in Library and Information Science*. A key resource.

Occupational Outlook Handbook: Librarians
www.bls.gov/oco/ocos068.htm
Provides a solid overview of the various aspects of the profession, including the nature of the work, working conditions, employment statistics, education requirements, job outlook, and salary information.

Notes

1.   George R. Plosker, "The Information Industry Revolution: Implications for Librarians," *Online*, 27(6) (November/December 2003): 16–18.

2.   Edward B. Stear, "Predicting the Future Is Important, Navigating the Future Is Essential," *Online*, 22(1) (January/February 1998): 62.

3.   Bates, Mary Ellen, "The Newly Minted MLS: What Do We Need to Know Today?" *Searcher*, 6(5) (May 1998): 31.

4.   *Competencies for Information Professionals of the 21st Century*. Rev. ed. Special Libraries Association, June 2003. Accessed at www.sla.org/content/learn/comp2003/index.cfm on June 24, 2005. Used with permission.

5.   Andrew Albanese, "Opportunity in the Air," *Library Journal*, 128(12) (July 15, 2003): 36–38.

2

Self-Knowledge: Your Career Starting Point

Where the needs of the world and your talents cross, there lies your vocation.

—Aristotle

Who are you, and what do you want to do when you grow up?

Although hopefully it's no longer parents asking these questions, most of us are still wrestling with them (the questions, not the parents) well into our careers. And—given the iffy state of many of our retirement funds—we're likely to be asking them again and again as we change jobs, career paths, and even life goals over the coming decades.

Your career is likely to be knocked about by the disruptive technologies, demographic changes, and social/political issues emerging daily. But actually, that's good news—it means the number and breadth of opportunities that will open up, including ones that are not even on your horizon yet, will be dazzling.

Your challenge, as you position yourself to meet those opportunities, is to start getting a better handle on who you are, and what you want to be *while* you grow up ... over the next ten or thirty or fifty years. And the best way to do that is to start asking yourself lots of questions.

As you go through this process, play close attention to who is driving your responses. Most of us are strongly influenced by the other "stakeholders" or interested parties in our lives—parents, spouses, faculty advisers, friends, co-workers, and others, many of whom have an understandably vested interest in the career choices we make. It's important to be able to distinguish between what you yourself want and what others have convinced you you *should* want. It's important to be sure that *your* agenda is the one in place.

Who Are You?

When Socrates first commanded his student to "know thyself," that guy probably had a lot fewer ways of looking at the issue. Today, knowing yourself can take many paths. What are your aptitudes, i.e., those talents that come to you naturally? What are your skills, your learned competencies? What are the specifics of your personality that you were born with versus those that may have become ingrained after years of coping with various job and life circumstances? What work processes, environments, activities, structures let you bring your best stuff into play?

What values have you developed, what commitments have you made as you moved through your adult life? Do you still like/dislike the things that drove you early in your career, or have you grown in different directions? Have changing life circumstances—perhaps the birth of a child or eighteen years later that youngster's looming tuition payments—affected what you most need from your job right now?

And, as important as all of the rest of these self-assessments, what might you simply *enjoy* doing?

For purposes of putting together careers that are personally rewarding, there are a number of ways to approach these questions. But as you explore these, keep two things in mind. First, few of us are "either/or"; rather, most of our answers will be on a continuum of response. Instead of "I *hate* working alone," your response is more likely to be in the "I'd *prefer* to work as part of a team" range. That's okay—it's still helping you understand your preferences.

Second, your needs, priorities, preferences, and sometimes even values are shaped by your life circumstances and stages. Who you are today may be different than who you are ten years from now (actually, one would hope!). So keep in mind that your resilient career will be based to a great degree on your ability to remain fluid through not just the transitions of the workplace, but also those of your life.

Finding Out About You

So what are some of the tools for self-assessment? Happily, there are many ways to explore, including a diverse collection of tools and approaches.

Myers–Briggs. Probably the best known is the Myers–Briggs personality-types indicator (MBTI). According to authors Tieger and Barron-Tieger in their *Do What You Are* (2001), the Myers–Briggs assessment considers four personality characteristics or dimensions:

- How you interact with the world and where you direct your energy—toward people and the "external world" of relationships, communities, and events (*extroversion*), or toward the "internal world" of information and ideas (*introversion*)?

- The kind of information you naturally notice—do you focus on facts and the clarity of evidence (*sensing*), or prefer to explore the often ambiguous intellectual unknown (*intuition*)?

- How you make decisions—are you the analytic type, relying on logic and objectivity (*thinking*), or are your decisions driven by personal beliefs, values, and feelings (*feeling*)?

- How you prefer to live your life—do you thrive on structure, stability, and plans (*judging*), or are you instead more of a free spirit who flourishes in a spontaneous flow of day-to-day events (*perception*)?

(And in case you were wondering—the "classic" MBTI profile for librarians is ISTJ: introversion—sensing—thinking—judging.)

If you're not familiar with the Myers–Briggs approach, *Do What You Are* provides an excellent and down-to-earth explanation of how to understand both your personality profile and its applications in your career choices. It's a great place to start exploring the inherent characteristics that drive how you relate to the world—and people—around you. Are you an ENFJ, one of those outgoing individuals who loves people? Or an INTP, an intellectual adept at solving problems? (The flip side of understanding your own profile, of course, is that it can help you understand how to work more effectively with others whose profiles are the polar opposite of yours.)

Additionally, the Myers–Briggs conceptual scaffolding provides a great way to think about such questions as whether you, the extrovert, would really be happy with the more solitary life of a cataloger, for example.

Keirsey. A second well-known personality test is the Keirsey temperaments assessment, which reframes the idea of personality types into four temperaments—"traditionalists," "experiencers," "idealists," and "conceptualizers." Like the Myers–Briggs test, the Keirsey approach is another way to understand how we process our environments, and by extension, how we can find a "right fit" in the work we pursue. (Keirsey presented not only his ideas but also their application in *Please Understand Me II: Temperament, Character, Intelligence* [Prometheus Nemesis, 1998], which provides the best starting place for understanding your temperament.)

Temperament becomes important as you consider not just the work that you do, but also the environment within which you do it, as we'll see below when we explore preference filters. For example, a conceptualizer, adept at ideas and innovation, would be less than effective in an administrative role but an excellent contributor in a strategy role. An idealist might be uninspired in most corporate bureaucracies, but bring passion and commitment if leading a nonprofit.

Aptitudes. Another part of "who you are" is what aptitudes or talents you're born with, as opposed to what skills you've acquired. Nearly every career book has some sort of aptitude "checklist," but basically what you're looking for is the cross-point between those things you've always been good at and those you've always enjoyed doing. Someone may have an aptitude for math, or for many of us in the LIS profession, an aptitude for information. (Were you identified as an "information junkie" early on?)

As you explore your aptitudes, however, keep in mind that you're not identifying things that you've learned how to do (for example, being an accountant or a cataloger), but rather exploring intellectual or creative activities for which you have an innate talent and that bring you joy.

Information Aptitudes

One way to get a sense of your aptitudes is to do a sort of "archeological dig" on your life work so far, including paid work, volunteer projects, grad school activities, and any other engagements where you brought your talents to bear in a way that was meaningful and enjoyable to you.

Consider the following beginning list of some possible information aptitudes for you in relation to the work you've found rewarding in the past. Which ones best reflect what you've been engaged in when you had the greatest sense of enjoyment and competence?

- Finding information
- Analyzing and synthesizing information
- Categorizing and classifying information
- Creating information systems
- Visualizing information
- Organizing information
- Sharing information
- Presenting information
- Creating information
- Doing something else with information, that is, _____

How have these aptitudes played out throughout your career, or your graduate studies, or volunteer work you've engaged in? Have your career choices so far reflected these aptitudes? How might they form the core of your professional work going forward? Be sure to note your answers in your career journal, so that you can use them to begin to build your "best career" profile as you move through the book.

Although you'll probably be able to unearth many other general aptitudes, identifying your "information aptitudes" will provide a starting point for building a career based on your natural gifts, the ones from which you derive the greatest joy.

In a broader career sense, you have other aptitudes that play across many professional environments in addition to the library/information marketplace. You may be a natural leader, or have an innate ability to motivate and inspire people, strong powers of persuasion, or an ability to see opportunities before they're evident to anyone else. Although to some extent aptitudes can also be taught as skills to those who don't possess them naturally, for now your goal is to describe those areas of easy intersection between your inherent gifts and where your joy lies. Identifying those aptitudes will help you frame possible career opportunities.

Innate strengths. In an alternative spin on aptitudes, in their popular management book *Now Discover Your Strengths* (2001), authors

Buckingham and Clifton identified thirty-four "themes" or strengths—such as achiever, analytical, deliberative, developer, futuristic, ideation, learner, relator, and strategic—that they believe to be among the most prevalent human strengths. The authors make an interesting point, arguing that our usual way of approaching aptitudes or natural strengths is backward.

Instead of supporting individuals' strengths, managers focus on "fixing" their weaknesses, and consequently miss the opportunity to help people maximize the contributions they could otherwise make. In some ways, we as individuals often do the same thing. We focus all our energy on our perceived failings, while simply taking for granted—or even dismissing—those collections of strengths or aptitudes uniquely our own.

Bottom line: what have you been doing when you've felt most alive? What activities give you energy? What gives you a deep sense of satisfaction and contribution?

Information—People—Systems. Most of us in the LIS profession find that we're inherently adept in one of these three areas; in other words, we're pretty good at it, we enjoy doing it, and we like to figure out how to get better at it. For example, I'm a born information junkie, and thought I'd died and gone to heaven when the Internet showed up.

Colleagues of mine, on the other hand, have made wonderful contributions through their ability to connect with people, doing community outreach, establishing seniors' groups at the library, coaching college students through cool and engaging bibliographic instruction workshops, organizing sixth-grade multimedia library projects. They bring an excitement and energy to these interactions that are amazing to watch. They've completely aligned their LIS skills with their passion for people connection.

Then there are the systems professionals, bless them. They thrive on organizing the world, be it through indexing, cataloging, taxonomies, digitization structures, search engines, metadata schemas, information architectures, or enterprise knowledge management systems (among others). Systems people are able to extrapolate patterns, relationships, and structures from a universe of details and data, using information technologies to create the infrastructures that enable all our work.

Whichever of these three areas most calls to you, they can be practiced in any LIS career path, including traditional, nontraditional, and independent.

Generalist versus specialist. One of the questions most frequently asked by students is whether to specialize in a specific area (say cataloging or government documents) or graduate as a generalist, someone who has a broad range of skills, but is not expert in any. Ask five seasoned practitioners for their advice here, and you're likely to get five well-reasoned, passionate, and completely different answers.

The reason is, there are benefits and disadvantages to both approaches.

Being a generalist means you can easily transfer your skills from one environment to another, and you can pursue many avenues of intellectual curiosity that can be woven into your generalist knowledge base. You tend not to worry too much about your expertise becoming obsolete because its general nature means that it isn't tied to a specific process, technology, or market.

On the other hand, you never feel like you know enough. Since you tend to know an "adequate" amount about a lot of things, you never feel like you know anything in any depth. Keeping current in your field is a constant challenge, because often your "field" covers everything from LIS issues to research tools to business trends to international developments. When hanging out with LIS colleagues who have specialized in some area, you spend a lot of time feeling clueless, trying not to let on that you have *no idea* what all those acronyms they're throwing around really mean.

Being a specialist in any of the various LIS disciplines brings the opposite challenges and rewards. Your skills do not travel as easily, but there are fewer people who can do what you do, so less competition for available jobs. The more tied to a specific process, technology, or market your skills are, however, the greater the likelihood that they may become obsolete during your professional lifetime. You may find yourself going through a challenging learning curve at some point as you transition your core skill to a new "operating system," or move into a related but new LIS discipline to stay professionally viable.

Depending on the professional area, specialists tend to be paid more (especially those in technology fields or at strategy levels). Also, you have the luxury of exploring in depth a single topic, with all its ramifications, applications, and emerging issues. You get the ego boost of being an expert in something, and have a built-in community of colleagues who share your passion (or understand your fixation).

Preference Filters: How Will
You Work?

In addition to understanding your intrinsic aptitudes and strengths, it's useful to also consider your personal *preferences* when it comes to working. There are many ways to think about these, many filters within which to consider your options. These include types of LIS work, types of organizations, your workplace environment, your individual working style, your preferred way of dealing with interpersonal relations, your professional and employment expectations, and job-specific considerations. These are starter filters; you may have several others that are unique to who you are, for example, values filters.

Also, keep in mind that some considerations may be more important to you than others. Consider the following "filters" to be simply examples to start you exploring the criteria that *are* most important to you. Remember that your responses will most likely fall on a continuum that will indicate a preference rather than an absolute, and that some items might be critically important to you while others are not at all. It's the critical ones that need to drive decisions for you.

To track your preferences among these choices, create a four-column page in your career journal that allows you to identify the choice in question, your preference, your reasons why you prefer one option over the other, and how important this criterion is to you. Or, simply photocopy the following pages with your responses to include in your journal.

Organizational characteristics. There are many ways to characterize organizations, having to do with their missions, their markets and constituencies, their size, and similar criteria. Consider the following choices regarding a potential employer, and note which options seem more appealing to you:

- **Library vs. nonlibrary:** For many LIS professionals, working within the library community is central to who they are; for others, the work they do is more important than where they do it.

  Library _____   Nonlibrary_____   Importance_____

  Reason for preference_____

- **Nonprofit vs. for-profit:** Nonprofits may include political and religious groups and professional and trade associations as well as socially beneficial or community-based organizations, but they are usually mission—rather than profit—driven.

  Nonprofit _____   For-profit _____   Importance_____

  Reason for preference_____

- **Education-focused vs. product/service-focused:** Education organizations support and deliver knowledge, whereas product/service-focused organizations generally use information to succeed in a competitive marketplace.

  Education _____   Product/service _____   Importance _____

  Reason for preference _____

- **Technology-focused vs. technology-neutral:** Technology-focused organizations assume and demand a high level of tech expertise, and necessitate an ongoing commitment to staying ahead of the technology curve.

  Tech-focused _____   Tech-neutral _____   Importance _____

  Reason for preference _____

- **Emerging industry/discipline vs. established industry/discipline:** Organizations based on emerging industries and disciplines tend to offer exciting and challenging opportunities, while those in established or maturing disciplines often provide saner workplaces.

  Emerging _____   Established _____   Importance _____

  Reason for preference _____

- **Large organization vs. small:** Large organizations generally bring the tradeoff of stable job expectations vs. rigid management structure, while smaller organizations may tend to be more responsive to new ideas but offer less direction.

Large _____ Small _____ Importance _____

Reason for preference _____

- **Established organization vs. start-up:** Established companies can usually offer superior benefits, while start-ups may be more willing to negotiate other perks such as stock options and flextime in lieu of traditional benefits.

Established _____ Start-up _____ Importance _____

Reason for preference _____

- **Local or community-based vs. national:** Local or community-based groups often invest more in being good community citizens, but are prone to mirror the circumstances of the local economy, whereas national organizations may have less of a commitment to your community but are also less affected by its economic ups and downs.

Local _____ National _____ Importance _____

Reason for preference _____

- **Focused on patrons, customers, students, business colleagues, or clients:** The nature of the working relationship and the expectations of those we work for/with shift based on the organizations we work within; which most appeals to you?

Patrons, etc. _____ Clients _____ Importance _____

Reason for preference _____

Now go through the same exercise for the choices below:

Workplace environment. Working environments can bring out our best abilities to contribute or throw us into a black hole of bad morale. Some of the options include:

- **Structured vs. unstructured:** Do you do your best work in a structured environment, or thrive in its absence? Most traditional libraries offer fairly structured environments, while nonprofit and for-profit start-ups can epitomize "freewheeling."

Structured _____ Unstructured _____ Importance _____

Reason for preference _____

- **Formal vs. casual:** Organizations vary immensely as to their tone and their expectations of employees. Do you feel more comfortable with established standards of dress and behavior or prefer a week of casual Fridays?

Formal _____ Casual _____ Importance _____

Reason for preference _____

- **Hierarchical vs. flat organization style:** This choice is about how decisions are made. Hierarchical enterprises are primarily top-down, flat ones more likely to distribute decision-making responsibilities (which may impact quality and speed of decisions).

Hierarchical _____ Flat _____ Importance _____

Reason for preference _____

- **High accountability/reward vs. more moderate accountability/reward:** The former usually is found in the for-profit world; although it can be financially lucrative, it can also carry a substantial stress factor.

High _____ Moderate _____ Importance _____

Reason for preference _____

- **Project-focused or consistent workflow:** Projects are typical of client work (for example, information brokering), while a consistent workflow is usually found in more traditional, structured environments.

Projects _____ Consistent workflow _____ Importance _____

Reason for preference _____

- **Structured/lots of direction vs. minimal structure/ direction:** Depending on their leadership, jobs in traditional libraries usually offer the most structure and direction, while the opposite end of the spectrum is being self-employed.

Lots of direction _____ Minimal _____ Importance _____

Reason for preference _____

- **Established hours vs. flexible or nontraditional schedule:** If you prefer a traditional eight-hour day, your best choices may be working as a school librarian or for a for-profit or nonprofit. Public and academic librarians are more likely to work evenings or weekends as part of their forty-hour week.

Established _____ Flexible _____ Importance _____

Reason for preference _____

- **Family-friendly vs. family-neutral:** Depending on your life circumstances and what personal responsibilities you are juggling, this may be *the* most important consideration for you.

Friendly _____ Neutral _____ Importance _____

Reason for preference _____

Interpersonal dynamics. Another facet of how you prefer to work is how you prefer to connect with people (or not) in your professional life. Do you thrive on the mix-it-up energy of dynamic groups, or seek out the solace of solitude? Do you enjoy managing staff, or dread dealing with "people issues?"

Note your responses in your career journal, so that you can refer to them when exploring possible job options and career strategies. Be sure to note not just your answers, but also *how important this issue is to you.* As you answer, keep in mind that your responses may change with your life circumstances, but asking these questions is a way to help yourself be aware of where you are now.

Do you ...

- **Prefer formal or informal relations with people at work?** (formal relations are usually more common in larger, more structured, or hierarchical organizations, whereas informal, peer-to-peer relations are generally the hallmark of small or start-up groups)

    Formal _____ Informal _____ Importance _____
    Reason for preference _____

- **Draw energy from people or from solitude?** (if you derive energy from people, the often solitary life of an independent may not be for you)

    People _____ Solitude _____ Importance _____
    Reason for preference _____

- **Like meeting new people, or prefer to stay with people you know?** (meeting new people is a major component of vendor sales jobs, many public library outreach positions, as well as independent information work)

    New people _____ Existing friends _____ Importance _____
    Reason for preference _____

- **Feel comfortable supervising others, or uncomfortable being in a position of authority?** (a critical question if you aspire to management or executive-level positions, where you will be responsible for holding others accountable for their work)

    Supervise others _____ No supervision _____ Importance _____
    Reason for preference _____

- **Prefer working as part of a team (collaborator), or prefer working solo?** (although some independent work involves collaboration, more frequently you're working solo; also, some extremely hierarchical organizations are known for having departmental "silos" that make collaboration difficult at best)

Team work _____   Solo work _____   Importance _____

Reason for preference _____

- **Enjoy contact with the public, or prefer to avoid contact with the public?** (a *very* important question if you are considering any sort or public service work, for example, becoming a reference librarian)

Lots of contact _____   Minimal contact _____   Importance _____

Reason for preference _____

- Thrive on intellectual exchange with colleagues, or prefer to focus on task-specific discussions? (if you thrive on intellectual exchange, consider academic librarianship, where this is an important and ongoing component of the profession)

Intellectual _____   Work-focused _____   Importance _____

Reason for preference _____

Professional/employment expectations. What job requirements are you willing to meet in order to land the job of your dreams? Again, these will change as your life circumstances do; a willingness to travel or work weekends may shift as family obligations show up. But thinking about your responses to these questions will help you determine that some career paths definitely aren't for you. For example, if you find you're not willing to write, publish, and/or volunteer for advancement, then you'll probably not want to target a job as an academic librarian.

As you consider these questions, remember to note your responses in your career journal. Are you . . .

- **Willing/not willing to work substantial extra hours?** (generally, established organizations offer fairly established and reasonable work hours, unless they've recently undergone a downsizing, whereas start-ups are often operating on the assumption of twelve-hour days)

Extra hours _____   No extra hours _____   Importance _____

Reason for preference _____

- **Willing/not willing to work weekends?** (public and academic library jobs, as well as vendor sales, often entail weekend work)

Weekends _____   No weekends _____   Importance _____

Reason for preference _____

- **Willing/not willing to work a schedule that changes regularly?** (as with the question of extra hours, established organizations may offer fairly established and reasonable work hours, whereas start-ups generally operate on a more chaotic schedule)

Changing _____   Standard _____   Importance _____

Reason for preference _____

- **Willing/not willing to undertake more schooling to achieve professional goals?** (academic librarians may need a second master's degree, corporate librarians may consider an MBA or a master's in knowledge management systems)

  More schooling _____ No more _____ Importance _____

  Reason for preference _____

- **Willing/not willing to write, publish, volunteer if necessary for advancement?** (an ongoing requirement of academic librarianship if tenure is involved)

  Willing to _____ Not willing to _____ Importance _____

  Reason for preference _____

- **Willing/not willing to relocate for job?** (in all areas of the LIS profession, your willingness to relocate may substantially increase your odds of landing the job you want at the salary you seek)

  Relocation ok _____ No relocation _____ Importance _____

  Reason for preference _____

- **Willing/not willing to travel for business?** (any sort of vendor sales usually requires substantial travel)

  Travel ok _____ Minimal travel _____ Importance _____

  Reason for preference _____

- **Focused mostly on job or focused more on personal and family time?** (a key consideration with start-ups, whether yours or someone else's, is the intense amount of time they demand; if personal time is important to you, you may want to focus on a more established and reliable work environment)

  Job focus _____ Personal focus _____ Importance _____

  Reason for preference _____

Job-Specific Considerations

For some of us, having a flexible work schedule determines whether or not we'll even consider a job. For others, a solid benefits package is the determining factor. As you consider the following criteria in terms of your own preferences, keep in mind that most if not all of these items can be negotiated as part of an employment package for jobs not in the public sector (public sector jobs often have fairly established parameters that can't be negotiated).

Before you think about negotiating, however, you'll need to know what's most important to you, what's "need to have" vs. "nice to have." As you consider the following aspects, rank them by priority and then note in your career journal your top three "need to haves." That way, you'll be able to quickly identify whether a specific job opportunity offers you "goodness of fit," or can be negotiated in that direction.

Job structure	Very important	Somewhat important	Not important
Full-time/part-time	—	—	—
Allowed to telecommute	—	—	—
Flexible hours	—	—	—
Opportunities for growth (expand knowledge base)	—	—	—
Opportunities for advancement (increased levels of responsibility)	—	—	—
Pay based on performance	—	—	—

Salary requirements	Very important	Somewhat important	Not important
Salary competitive with industry benchmarks	—	—	—
Base salary plus bonus (for sales)	—	—	—
Performance bonuses (individual/team)	—	—	—
Established process, expectations for raises	—	—	—

Non-salary requirements	Very important	Somewhat important	Not important
Health benefits	—	—	—
Number of vacation days	—	—	—
Family medical leave support	—	—	—
Tuition reimbursement	—	—	—
Support for professional development	—	—	—

Opportunity for growth	Very important	Somewhat important	Not important
Presence of formal or informal mentoring program	—	—	—
Support for interdepartmental cross-training and collaboration	—	—	—
An atmosphere of innovation and intellectual openness	—	—	—

Exploring Your Career Preferences

To continue to gather information about what job characteristics might be a match for you, consider the following activities, noting your findings and reactions in your career journal as appropriate.

1. If you haven't done so already, take the MBTI test in *What Type Am I* and determine your personality profile. Talk to your colleagues who seem to enjoy their jobs and ask them about their MBTI profiles to get a sense of how profiles match various types of LIS work.

2. Think through all the jobs you've had so far and assess them against the filters we've identified. What can you learn from your job history? One of the challenges here is to distinguish among all the aspects of a given job that contributed to it being a good or bad experience for you.

3. Make a list in your journal of what you consider to be your innate strengths and weaknesses, and then solicit feedback from your friends, family, or colleagues to see if they agree with your assessment—they may see a strength that you overlook simply because you assume everyone has the same strength. Also, consider when and/or how your strengths, taken to the extreme, may become a liability, or your weaknesses under the right circumstances actually be assets.

4. Interview LIS professionals who are successful and happy in their jobs, with a focus on what they especially like in their work, and how those aspects line up with their personalities to get a sense of how you might approach your own job choices. Ask them what aptitudes and personality characteristics they feel are necessary to perform effectively in their positions. Write up your findings; they'll provide another way to judge the jobs and career paths we'll look at in the coming three chapters.

5. If you're a student, pay close attention to what coursework you most enjoy, and then speak with your instructor about possible career paths based on that type of work. Research those that appeal to you (and consider writing up your findings for the student newsletter).

6. Use your time in grad school to explore the generalist vs. specialist question. Often the choice will become evident for you as you move through your program. You may find yourself gravitating to a specific area of interest (public outreach, school librarianship, information architecture). Or you enjoy sampling all of the different LIS courses, and find that you enjoy the research component of each, or the technology aspects. This process of discovery is one of the most important aspects of being a student, so whenever possible pay attention to where your interests are drawing you.

7. Also if you're a student, whenever the opportunity arises, ask your class guest speakers about their career preferences, and in what ways these have shaped their career choices and paths. In what way might their preferences mirror yours?

8. Finally, consider that past is prologue. Wander back through your childhood, and remember what activities used to delight you. Be as specific as possible. For example, not just "I loved pretending to be Nancy Drew," but "I loved pretending to be Nancy Drew when she would figure out clues and chase the bad guys and help bring them to justice, and then get to ride off to a new adventure." Write those childhood activities down in your career journal, and then take it one step further. Why did you enjoy this? What aspects of a specific activity particularly engaged you, and what applicability might they have to your career? For example, channeling your inner Nancy Drew might mean you thrive on risk-taking, and/or enjoy project work (a new adventure) rather than a set routine.

How Preferences Shape Career Paths

One of the first choices you have in terms of career and personal preferences is the path you choose to pursue your goals. Again, none of these paths is necessarily a lifelong commitment, but simply a choice that reflects your current interests or priorities. However, some options are more suited to certain personality types than others.

For example, someone who successfully works as an *independent* or *freelancer* usually enjoys working alone, has a strong ability to self-manage, is adept at managing multiple tasks and deadlines, and is strong on detail and "learning on the fly." Although many independents—often classic introverts—don't necessarily enjoy the people/social demands of constant marketing, they've learned strategies for getting the job done.

An *entrepreneur* building up a small business, on the other hand, will need to rely on strong leadership skills to motivate his or her team, will need the ability to think strategically, must have no compunctions about working regular ninety-hour work weeks, and will need to be extremely comfortable with risk-taking. Entrepreneurs need to possess strong egos, an enormous amount of self-confidence, and a high tolerance for uncertainty and unpredictability.

An *intrapreneur*, someone responsible for starting up new businesses within existing companies, must possess many of these same skills, although the risk-taking is not quite so extreme because of whose money is at stake (i.e., the company's rather than yours). Generally, an intrapreneur has a higher ability to accept corporate control and restriction than does an entrepreneur, but a similar eye for identifying business opportunities.

Someone targeting an *executive* or *leadership* role within an organization, whether library focused, for-profit, or nonprofit, will need to be strong on strategic thinking, possess excellent people and communication skills, be willing to commit long hours on an ongoing basis, and be willing to take responsibility for outcomes (which they may or may not have control over), whether successes or failures. As with entrepreneurs, strong egos and lots of self confidence are must-haves.

A *management* role, on the other hand, demands the ability to multi-task, to manage people, projects, and priorities, to deal with difficult interpersonal issues, and to diplomatically and effectively manage up as well as down. Effective managers (i.e., those who do a good job of balancing people needs vs. organization priorities) are able to blend the roles of teacher, coach, and team leader to bring out the best in their staff.

An emerging role, which combines the opportunities of entrepreneurship with the social values that motivate many who go into librarianship, is *social entrepreneurship*. Social entrepreneurs are individuals who take a business approach to solving a social problem. Their enterprises may be established as nonprofits, but they are run with an eye toward becoming financially self-sustaining so that they can contribute to the community on a long-term, ongoing basis. Social entrepreneurs need to have the same business and strategy skills, leadership ability, and self-confidence necessary to any chief executive. But they also possess the creativity to envision innovative solutions, the management skills to execute them, and the ability to generate excitement and buy-in among others for their vision.

The point of all your explorations is to try many different pathways to connect with what brings you—or has brought you—joy and a sense of engagement. By writing down your ideas and remembrances and questions and answers in your career journal, you will have begun to build the base of self-knowledge against which you'll be able to evaluate the possible career paths we explore in the next chapters: traditional, nontraditional, and independent.

Resources

Books

Albion, Mark. *Making a Life, Making a Living: Reclaiming Your Purpose and Passion in Business and in Life*. Warner, 2000. 256 pp. IBSN 0446524042.
One of many excellent and useful "find your path" books, Albion's distinguishes itself by its focus on giving as well as getting. Organized by four categories: Who Are You? (find your passion); What Do You Want? (establish purpose); What Can You Do? (develop market value); Where Can You Go? (free your spirit). A great place to start for a values-based career exploration.

Baron, Renee. *What Type Am I? Discover Who You Really Are*. Penguin, 1998. 171 pp. ISBN 096568489X.
A popular treatment of the well-known Myers–Briggs Type Indicator (MBTI) temperament test, *What Type Am I?* walks you through the four categories of assessment: how you relate to the world, how you take in and process information; how you're most comfortable making decisions; and how you approach the circumstances of your life.

Beck, Martha. *Finding Your Own North Star: Claiming the Life You Were Meant to Live*. Three Rivers Press, 2002. 400 pp. ISBN 081293217X.
Reading this book is like having a cup of coffee and a therapy session with your best friend—providing she is exceedingly smart, funny, wise, and compassionate. A life coach, Beck went through her own struggle to

find her path, and her guidance is informed by the lessons she learned as well as the insights she has gained from her clients. A key resource for identifying, describing, and nurturing your dreams, whether personal or professional.

Bolles, Richard Nelson and Mark Emery Bolles. *What Color Is Your Parachute? 2006. A Practical Manual for Job-Hunters and Career-Changers.* Ten Speed Press, 2005. 402 pp. ISBN 1580087272.
Bolles focuses on practical, immediately actionable advice and tactics that are geared to quickly move you from identifying your career goals to successfully pursuing them. A familiar and reliable resource for job hunters and those considering career transitions.

Buckingham, Marcus and Donald O. Clifton. *Now, Discover Your Strengths.* Free Press, 2001. 272 pp. ISBN 0743201140.
Following on the success of Buckingham's first business best-seller, *First Break All the Rules* (Simon & Schuster, 1999), this work asserts that trying to help people correct/improve their weaknesses is a waste of time; it makes more sense to build on people's innate strengths. In combination with its website, the book helps readers identify their unique strengths. Another way to assess your personal characteristics, although as a career strategy, ignoring your weaknesses seems a bit questionable at best!

Jansen, Julie. *I Don't Know What I Want, But I Know It's Not This: A Step-by-Step Guide to Finding Gratifying Work.* Penguin Books, 2003. 288 pp. ISBN 0142002488.
An action-oriented guide jammed with checklists, self-assessment questionnaires, processes to follow, and sound advice on finding the work that will make you happy. As applicable to librarians and other information professionals as to others on this path.

Keirsey, David. *Please Understand Me II: Temperament, Character, Intelligence.* Prometheus Nemesis Book Co., 1998. 350 pp. ISBN 1885705026.
A revision of the third edition of *Please Understand Me* (1978), *II* again focuses on the four temperaments: artisans, guardians, idealists, and rationals. Unusual in that Keirsey takes assessment a step further by identifying not just a single temperament for each of us, but a layered "ranking" of the various temperament characteristics within given personalities.

Laney, Marti Olsen. *The Introvert Advantage: How to Thrive in an Extrovert World.* Workman, 2002. 256 pp. ISBN 0761125892.
Introverts of the world unite! Any book that asks "would you rather be reading books in bed in your pajamas?" immediately gets my attention—and that of many other librarians I know. Laney does a terrific job of explaining not only what makes introverts tick but how they can most effectively create active, engaged lives and careers. A great resource for those of us who fall into Myers–Briggs "I" quadrants.

Lore, Nicholas. *The Pathfinder: How to Choose or Change Your Career for a Lifetime of Satisfaction and Success.* Fireside, 1998. 384 pp. ISBN 0684823993.
Lore does a great job of combining left-brain strategies, goal-setting, and checklists with right-brain Zen exploration. Worth reading just for the great quotes, but also a solid tool for career strategizing.

Sher, Barbara. *I Could Do Anything If I Only Knew What It Was: How to Discover What You Really Want and How To Get It*. Dell, 1995. 336 pp. ISBN 0440505003.
> Sher comes across as your favorite aunt—or at least the one you *wish* you had. Supportive and nurturing, she nevertheless expects you to shape up and really go for those dreams. Especially valuable for identifying assumptions and circumstances that can sabotage you, while motivating you to overcome them.

Sher, Barbara. *It's Only Too Late if You Don't Start Now: How to Create Your Second Life After 40*. Dell, 1999. 352 pp. ISBN 0440507189.
> Sher has written many books on creating your best life (see above), but this one specifically targets those wondering if it's still possible once we hit middle age. An especially valuable resource for those coming into the LIS profession as a second or later-in-life career.

Tieger, Paul D. and Barbara Barron-Tieger. *Do What You Are: Discover the Perfect Career for You Through the Secrets of Personality Type*. 3rd ed. Little Brown, 2001. 416 pp. ISBN 0316880655.
> *Do What You Are* is widely used by individuals not only to identify and understand their Myers–Briggs profile but also to then bridge that understanding to optimum work choices. In other words, if I'm an INTJ, what types of work and work environments are most likely to provide me an opportunity to thrive?

Periodicals

Psychology Today. Sussex Publishers, 1967– . Monthly. ISSN 0033–3107. www.psychologytoday.com
> Broad coverage of psychological topics and issues, including such career-relevant ones as personal motivation, change management, risk assessment, dealing with difficult personalities, understanding personality types, bridging different communication styles, etc.

Utne. LENS Publishing Co., 2002– . Bimonthly. ISSN 1544–2225. www.utne.com
> Formerly known as *Utne Reader* (1983–2002), this alternative publication frequently focuses on quality-of-life, values, and authentic-living issues. Its articles regularly provide an excellent framework within which to explore who you are, what you seek in life, and in what ways you can contribute.

Articles and Columns

Agada, John, "Profiling Librarians with the Myers–Briggs Type Indicator: Studies in Self-Selection and Type Stability," *Education for Information*, vol. 16, no. 1 (March 1998), pp. 57–68.
> Fascinating research on the distribution of Myers–Briggs personality types among a select group of LIS students. Among graduating students, some 33.33 percent were classified as ISTJ, 16.66 percent INTJ, and 8.33 percent each for ENTJ, ESTJ, ENFP, ISFJ, INFP, and INTP. Also, 83.3 percent were classified as introverted, 16.67 percent as extroverted.

McDermott, Irene E., "Know Thyself: Self-Assessment Tests of the Web," *Searcher*, vol. 12, no. 6 (June 2004), pp. 16–20.

A survey of all the testing sites available on the Internet. Although some have more applicability to your career work than others, they're all interesting!

Online Resources

Keirsey.com
www.keirsey.com
An extensive collection of information resources related to the Keirsey temperaments (artisans, guardians, idealists, and rationals) plus role variants within temperaments, such as composer, crafter, performer, or promoter with "artisan." A fascinating, content-rich site.

Motivational Appraisal of Personal Potential (MAPP)
www.assessment.com/
The MAPP assessment comprises "71 triads of three statements" for which you select the statement you *most* agree with and the statement you *least* agree with (one remains blank). The goal is to measure your "potential and motivation" for various types of work, while also profiling your temperament, aptitude, and possible career matches. There are a number of MAPP variations, several of which could be valuable to career exploration, but the assessment evaluation is fee-based—you'll want to check out the cost before determining its value for you.

Myers–Briggs Test
www.myersbriggs.org
A comprehensive collection of information about the Myers–Briggs Personality Type test, including the assessment tools, results interpretations, and information on how to use your results (for example, personality and careers, type and learning, and type in personal growth). An outstanding resource.

Personality Tests and Resources
http://library.stmarytx.edu/acadlib/subject/psych/prsnlty.htm
From St. Mary's University Blume Library, this engaging site groups its two dozen annotated links under the headings of Myers–Briggs-Related Material, Online Psychological Tests, and Other Personality Info.

3
The Traditional Path

I have always imagined that paradise will be a kind of library.
——Jorge Luis Borges

Now that you've explored your aptitudes, interests, and preferences, the next step in designing a career that aligns with them is to consider what options are available. Those fall into the categories of traditional, nontraditional, and independent.

Although it's debatable whether *any* of today's libraries can be described as "traditional," for purposes of this chapter we'll use that term to describe the three major types of facilities-based libraries: public, school, and academic. Although careers in these libraries are as subject to change (and opportunity) as any others, they represent the paths the majority of librarians set out on when graduating from a master's degree program.

There are two ways to think about careers in traditional libraries—by the type of library you might work in, and by the type of work you might do within that library, or others. Generally, however, regardless of what type of library you work in, the work falls into one of three categories: user or public services, technical services, or administrative services.

User services (also known as *public services*) generally includes all of the ways librarians "reach out and touch someone"—that is, reference, research assistance, community outreach, Internet and/or bibliographic instruction, readers' advisory, programs for children, seniors, immigrants, and other special populations, and similar types of activities. Sometimes the circulation (book checkout, reserves, holds, interlibrary loan) function is considered part of user services, sometimes part of technical services.

Technical services includes acquisitions (ordering/purchasing/receiving resources), collection development (deciding which resources to purchase), serials management (subscribing to, checking in, shelving, and binding journals and magazines), processing (including cataloging) materials, shelving, and managing the library's computers and system technologies. Although the library's website is always a collaborative effort, generally its management is considered a tech services function. In addition, systems librarians (sometimes also called automation librarians) usually fall within the purview of technical services.

Administrative services includes process organization, personnel management, budget setting, staff development, external liaison and communication (with mayors, school principals, chancellors, "friends" groups, donors, advisory boards, and assorted other stakeholders), organizational management, and leadership, among other functions. According to the U.S. Dept. of Labor's *Occupational Outlook Handbook*, librarians in this role "oversee the management and planning of libraries: negotiate contracts for services, materials, and equipment; supervise library employees; perform public-relations and fundraising duties: prepare budgets; and direct activities to ensure that everything functions properly."[1]

Each of these job areas differs somewhat—or even substantially—based on which type of library they're performed in. Also, depending on library size, one person might end up covering several bases in public, administrative, or tech services. Also, based on size and system organization, some multibranch public libraries may centralize tech or administrative services in one location, while school libraries that are part of larger school districts may have their tech and administrative services handled at the district level.

What are some of the specifics of these three types of libraries?

Public Libraries

There are roughly 9,000 public libraries in the United States, employing about 123,000 professionals, paraprofessionals, and support staff, according to ALA's "America's Libraries: Some Basic Facts and Figures."[2]

Public libraries are where many of us first fell in love with the *idea* of libraries. The quiet, calm, nurturing environment, the helpful librarian, the world of ideas—and all those books, just waiting to be devoured.

However, today's public libraries are as much about videos and DVDs, Internet instruction, small business resources, English-as-a-second-language tutoring, and exam proctoring for local online students as they are about books. Electronic resources—including e-books and databases—consume a substantial amount of library budgets, and entire categories of new jobs are now tied to dealing with automated systems, regional collaborative networks, and web-based patron interactions.

Public libraries—and the librarians staffing them—are on the front lines of community changes and challenges. A career in *public services* in a public library brings you into contact with a patron base as diverse as your community (with, of course, the same proportion of delightful versus crazy-making people). The opportunity to have an impact on people's lives is substantial, as often you are helping them find and use information to improve their lives.

Tech services roles in public libraries vary based on a number of circumstances, including

- the size of the library and whether or not it's part of a larger system (for example, a branch library, with most cataloging done at the main library)

- the level of technological sophistication of the library (are internal systems automated and integrated with regional networks, or stand-alone? Have they not yet been automated? Will they be soon, and with what budget?)

- the library's funding (which determines, for example, whether or not the library has a state-of-the-art website)

- the library leadership (does the director resist new ideas or constantly press the tech services group for innovative, cool pilot projects using the latest technologies?)

Administrative services in today's public libraries often focus on constantly doing a bit more with a lot less, as libraries have taken increasingly severe budget hits over the past years. This affects the library's processes, its staffing and staff development resources, its collection development priorities, and its ability to meet the community's expectations of what a library should be.

The original "people's universities," public libraries in many communities may also face skeptical city administrators who fail to understand the library's strategic value. Because of this, more and more library directors are taking an active, highly visible communications and marketing role as well.

Salaries and Education

According to the "2005 ALA Survey of Librarian Salaries," salaries earned in 2005 varied substantially based on geographic region (North Atlantic is generally higher, Southeast and Great Lakes/Plains areas are generally but not always lower), size of library (the largest public libraries tend to pay substantially higher salaries), and of course, level of responsibility. In terms of size of library, ALA considers five categories:

- very small public libraries (serving a population of less than 10,000; amazingly, nearly 60 percent of our public library systems fall within this category)

- small public libraries (population ranging from 10,000 to 25,000)

- medium-sized public libraries (population ranging from 25,000 to 99,999)

- large public libraries (population ranging from 100,000 to 499,999)

- very large public libraries (population of 500,000 or more)

With exceptions (check the full report to determine specifics), salary ranges (in the thousands of dollars) generally broke out as approximately

- low- to high-thirties for beginning full-time librarians with an MLS but no professional experience;

- mid-thirties to high-forties for librarians with no supervisory responsibilities;

- high-thirties to low-fifties for library managers and those who supervise support staff;

- mid-forties to high-fifties for department heads/coordinators/senior managers,

Exploring Public Library Careers

To learn more about public library jobs and how they might align with your skills, aptitudes, and preference filters, consider the following activities:

1. Shadow several different public librarians (if possible, in different libraries) for a day each to get a sense of the different types of activities that make up their jobs. Note the following in your career journal:

   • Do these work activities appeal to me? Why or why not?

   • What can I tell about the culture of the organization? Do I think I would thrive in this culture? Why or why not?

   • Does this position focus on people, collections, systems, or administrative processes? Whichever it is, does it seem like an area of expertise I would enjoy learning more about and growing in professionally?

   • Does the person I am shadowing seem to be happy in his or her job? If not, does it seem to be a mismatch between the individual personality and the requirements of the job? Would this be the same or different for me?

2. Read through the profiles in *The Librarian's Career Guidebook* (Scarecrow, 2005) and explore the archives of the *Info Career Trends* newsletter (www.infocareertrends) to read stories and profiles of librarians in the various public library roles. In your career journal, note answers to these questions:

   • What career paths seem most interesting to me, based on the profiles I've read? Why? What questions do the profiles, interviews, and articles raise that I should pursue further, possibly by contacting the author?

   • Imagine that five years from now I were being interviewed, or asked to write an article. What would I want to be writing about? What aspects of public librarianship would I want to be known for, be considered an expert in?

   • Is there discussion of recurring, ongoing problems or issues generic to public librarianship that might be especially problematic for me personally, given what I now know about who I am and what I need? (Needless to say, this is keeping in mind that no job or career is without challenges!)

   • What career options have I discovered that I'd like to explore further, for example public library marketing or community information systems?

3. Read six recent issues of *Public Library* magazine to get a good sense of the state of the profession today. As you peruse the articles, note in your career journal the following information:

   • What articles seem most interesting to me? Am I most engaged by stories about creating a community website, developing new outreach programs, policy issues, management challenges?

- What specifically engages me about the articles? Creating new solutions? Helping others? Contributing to the betterment of a community? Employing technology in innovative ways? Developing team leadership skills?

- Are there practitioners who have written articles that caught my eye who I could contact to learn more from?

- Do there seem to be areas where I believe my unique skills, aptitudes, and insights could contribute? Where and how?

4. After reviewing your responses to the information you've noted in your career journal, answer these questions:

- Based on what I discovered through my previous self-assessment process and what I now know about my preferences and priorities, does public librarianship seem like a career path that could offer me the levels of growth, challenge, security, and engagement that I need to thrive?

- If I still am unsure about this question, what other information would I need to make this assessment?

- How will I gather that information?

- high-thirties to low-sixties for deputy/associate and assistant library directors (with the exception of very large public libraries, where the regional salary means and medians range from the low-eighties to more than $100,000); and

- low-fifties to low-nineties for public library directors (again, with the exception of very large public libraries, where the regional salary means and medians range from a bit under $120,000 to more than $140,000).[3]

Naturally, these salaries are strongly influenced by the state of the local or regional economy; some states and municipalities have been strong public library supporters, others less so. Also, the salary survey is based on information submitted for full-time employees, and consequently doesn't reflect a rise in part-time hiring driven by budget cuts, a situation faced by a substantial number of MLIS graduates just entering the profession. These part-time jobs often have no benefits and a much lower pay rate than do full-time positions, so these employees may find themselves cobbling together a collection of part-time jobs simply to pay rent in the early stages of their careers. The bottom line? There *are* great library jobs that pay decent salaries, but you may need to be flexible about relocation.

A master's degree in library and information science (or some variation of this title) is usually required for professional (rather than support or paraprofessional) jobs in public libraries. Additional skills of value might be subject expertise in an area such as consumer health information or small business resources, second-language proficiency if that language is prevalent in the community, or teaching ability. Strong technology skills are always an asset, and increasingly expected of MLIS graduates now coming into the profession.

Why You Might Love Being a Public Librarian

Holly Deni, Director of the River Vale, New Jersey, Free Public Library, has been a public librarian since 1984. Her enthusiasm for the role of public libraries was reflected in her assessment of the importance of libraries to their communities:

> *Public libraries are one of the cornerstones of enlightened society—they are truly the 'people's university.' As a public librarian, you provide opportunities for lifelong learning and self-exploration to people from all walks of life. Your work can help change lives in significant ways.*

Claudine Perrault, Library Director for the Estes Park Public Library in Estes Park, Colorado, suggested that "public libraries are about human potential—yours and your customers'." It can be a wonderful job for those who are innately curious and like to find information, those who enjoy the intrinsic rewards of connecting people with the information they need, and those who enjoy contributing to the well-being and development of their communities.

In addition, working with the public on a daily basis usually involves a high degree of variety, an excellent environment for those who thrive on diverse human interaction and intellectual challenge.

There is also the sense of purpose and camaraderie that comes from belonging to a respected professional community with a long tradition of dedicated, selfless commitment to values such as intellectual freedom, First Amendment rights, and equality of access. In communities where the role of the public library is respected and supported, this career path can offer the enjoyment of an ever-changing environment, the opportunity to contribute professionally, and a sense of personal reward from helping others.

Rochelle Logan, Douglas County [col.] Libraries' Associate Director of Support Services, confirmed this aspect of public librarianship, noting that "every day I see how the presence of this library contributes to the community. Feeling that my work helps improve the lives of the people in the town and county where I live is very fulfilling." Logan, who was present during the design and building of her town's new public library, said participating in the process meant that she can now "look at this library and say to myself, 'I helped build that.'" And in many ways, this sense of contributing to the building of not just a library, but a community, is one of the greatest rewards of public librarianship.

When asked why he loves his job, Bob Belvin, Director of the New Brunswick Free Public Library, frames the joy—and challenge—of public librarianship this way:

> *I do it because people are paying me to have fun and do good. Fun because every day has a different problem to solve. The doing good part is because most of the public I serve doesn't have a well-stocked library at home nor Internet access. We will make a difference in some people's lives, the question is in how many lives we will influence.*

Public libraries serve multiple roles for those they serve: among other missions, they function as community information centers, as resources for change in their patrons' lives, and, as Holly Deni noted, as keepers of our "shared culture." If this public service mission aligns with your goals and values, few choices could be more rewarding.

School Library Media Centers

There are nearly 94,000 school libraries in the United States employing about 72,000 professionals plus about 92,500 other paid staff. Of those school libraries, about 17,000 are in private schools.[4] Most states mandate a certified school library media specialist at the high school level; many, however, do not require them at the elementary or middle-school level.

School librarians are often the first librarians to touch the lives of our children. They have the potential to shape students' lifelong attitudes and assumptions about libraries and those who work in them. Are you considering a school librarian career path? If so, regardless of what other professional attributes you may have, certainly the most important one will be the ability to take delight in working with kids and teenagers. If that describes you, then school librarianship can be a truly rewarding option.

Unlike most public or academic libraries, where individuals tend to specialize in a given functional area (say serials management or reference), school library media centers generally offer the opportunity to engage in a diverse range of activities. Your day might include any combination of these roles:

- *Teacher*, as you demonstrate the use of reference materials and key topic resources to students

- *Instructional partner*, as you collaborate with a tenth-grade history teacher to develop class assignments interweaving information literacy skills, and scout for cool web resources that can be incorporated into a lesson plan

- *Coach*, as you work one-on-one with students to help them identify, evaluate, and use appropriate information resources for a specific assignment

- *Technologist*, as you demonstrate the use of new communications, research, and website tools to both students and teachers

- *Collection development and acquisitions specialist*, as you draw on your professional resources and faculty input to identify and acquire appropriate materials to support student learning

- *Manager*, as you set priorities, manage projects, supervise clerical help, and interact with school teachers, library volunteers, and administrators

- *Circulation clerk, shelver, and chief bottle-washer*, as you pick up the assorted tasks that remain when aides leave for the day

This multitasking approach is especially prevalent in private schools, which often encompass grades 1–8 in one location. In this case, if there is a school librarian in place, he or she may provide story times for the youngest

Exploring School Library Media Specialist Careers

To learn more about school library media specialist jobs and how they might align with your skills, aptitudes, and preference filters, consider the following activities:

1. Volunteer several days each at two or three local school libraries, preferably at different levels (e.g., elementary and high school). If possible, arrange your volunteer hours when the librarian is engaged in different activities so you can get a sense of the broad range of tasks involved. After each visit, note your answers to the following questions in your career journal:

   - What about these activities might engage or bore me? Would I do them the same way, or would I do them differently? How? Why?

   - What can I tell about the relationships among the school library media specialist, the teachers, the administration (i.e., principal), and the students? Do I think I would thrive in this environment? Why or why not?

   - Does the multitasking, multiple-role nature of this work appeal to me? Would I enjoy organizing everything and thrive on the challenge of staying on top of things, or would I find it too stressful?

   - Does the level of people interaction suit my personality? Would I be comfortable with the increasing focus on electronic and Internet-based resources in school libraries?

2. Sign up for one or two of the school library media specialist electronic discussion groups (for example, LM_NET, CALIBK12) and monitor the online postings for a month or two. Your goal is to get a sense of the questions asked and issues discussed, and then note in your career journal answers to the following:

   - Do these questions and issues engage me? Why or why not?

   - What changes to the profession are being discussed? How might these changes impact a potential career I might have as a school library media specialist?

   - Do school librarians seem to focus their energy and passions in areas that resonate with my skills and aptitudes? Does it seem that the majority of questions are devoted to administration, teaching, new resources, managing relationships, student coaching, or a balance of these? Does the balance reflect my interests?

   - Does there seem to be a general attitude toward change (positive, negative, or neutral), and would I be comfortable with this? Are postings solutions-oriented, and can I see myself contributing to those solutions?

3. After reviewing the responses you recorded to the self-assessment questions of Chapter 2, put together a hit list of

questions that help you understand how school librarianship might align with your professional goals. Based on these, contact at least five school library media specialists and ask them if you can interview them via e-mail. Some starter questions might include the following:

- In general, what percentage of your time do the following activities occupy: library administration, student programs and instruction, working with teachers, working with school administration, resource review and evaluation, other?
- Which activities do you enjoy the most, and why? The least, and why?
- What do you consider to be the most important skills for an effective, successful school library media specialist?
- What do you see as the biggest threats or opportunities to the continued viability of school librarianship as a good career path?
- Would you choose this career again? Why or why not?

Include their responses in your career journal, noting any recurring themes. Consider how their comments align (or not) with what you know about your own strengths and preferences.

4. After reviewing your responses to the information you've noted in your career journal, answer these questions:

- Based on what I discovered through my previous self-assessment process and what I now know about my preferences and priorities, does school librarianship seem like a career path that could offer me the levels of growth, challenge, security, and engagement that I need to thrive?
- If I am still unsure about this question, what other information would I need to make this assessment?
- How will I gather that information?

students, teach basic information literacy skills to fourth-graders, tutor the sixth-graders on Internet navigation, research, and evaluation skills, coach the seventh-graders through their initial efforts in organizing a research paper, and support the eight-graders who are now in the throes of actually *writing* those research papers.

A career in public school librarianship, on the other hand, is more likely to also offer paths into management and administrative technologies. Depending on the size of the school system, for example, you might become a library automation specialist at the district level or a media cataloger at a centralized technical services facility.

Whether in a public or private school media center, however, school librarians have experienced the same impacts from electronic resources as have their public library colleagues. Students are growing up in a digital information surround at home and in their communities, and they expect the same in their libraries. Consequently, more and more of a school librarian's job focuses on evaluating, aggregating, and teaching the appropriate, effective use of nonprint resources.

Salaries and Education

Generally, the salaries of school library media specialists, like those of teachers, increase with years of experience and additional levels of education. Like those of public librarians, school librarians' salaries vary depending on location (for example, large city vs. small town), size of school, and often the affluence of the school district. According to the most recent statistics from *School Library Journal's* "SLJ Spending Survey," elementary school librarians earn an average of $43,000 annually, while their peers in middle and senior high schools earn about $48,000.[5]

The education requirements for becoming a school library media specialist are unusual, in that you can take one of two paths to become certified. The first is to obtain a master's degree in library and/or information science from a school that includes the school library media curriculum and certification among its program offerings. (In addition to the certification, you'll also need a teaching degree for the state in which you plan to work.) The second option, intended primarily for teachers who have decided to transition into the school library profession, is to complete a one-year "school library media certification" program that builds on students' existing teaching credentials.

Each state sets certification standards for its school librarians, so that a school librarian certified in Nebraska would need to be certified again in the specific states to work in, for example, California or Maine.

Why You Might Love Being a School Librarian

Summers off—need we say more?

Seriously though, school librarianship can be a great career choice for those who love working with children who are entering the world of learning, preteens just emerging from childhood, or adolescents whose lives are fraught with all the emotional upheaval of life's toughest transition. It's a profession where your successes can change lives; a good school librarian can help a student find his inner scholar, can connect a high school athlete with her college aspirations, can help kids become savvy, successful navigators of our digital knowledge universe.

It can also be a good career fit if you like to take on multiple roles. The job often includes a bit of everything—although heavy on public services (i.e., student and teacher contact), there's often also a bit of tech services (serials management, collection development, special-item cataloging) and plenty of administrative work. You get to collaborate with teachers, contribute to the learning process, and stay current with emerging information technologies and resources.

Citing his enjoyment of "integrating technology and information literacy into existing curricula," Bill Derry, school library media specialist at Green's Farms Elementary School in Westport, CT, further notes:

I enjoy working with two other classroom teachers and 40 5th graders to run our school television studio to produce a daily live news program. I enjoy the faces and comments of our kindergarten and first grade students when they are treated to incredible literature. I love having authors and illustrators like Patricia Polacco, Dan Gutman, Andrew Clements, Patricia Reilly Giff, Jerry Pinkney that the students treat like famous "rock stars." I appreciate working with the research process (the Big6 and Super3) and watching kids make their own questions for research. It is especially exciting when kids begin to internalize the research process and begin to apply it to independent research projects. I enjoy having parents help with keeping the collection in order, creating displays and working with students on research projects. For me it is the ability to work with students in all grades (K-5), classroom teachers, staff members, administrators and parents to help make a difference in teaching and learning at our school.

Betty Bankhead, Project Director, Colorado Power Libraries, specifically highlighted the excitement inherent in the leadership aspects of school librarianship, noting that "leadership is no longer positional in good schools, and successful school librarians must influence and motivate their colleagues to partner with them to create the next generation of proficient library users." Said Bankhead:

I think being a professional school librarian encompasses the best of three worlds: libraries, education, and entrepreneurship. People who are successful in our field are those who enjoy and excel at the management aspects of library work by being organized, efficient, and cost effective. But, along with that management expertise, they must have the ability and enthusiasm to teach by making information literacy and technology skills understandable and achievable for the school community, which includes both students and adults. And finally, most successful school librarians must be entrepreneurs in that they have to provide the leadership to "create" a strong information management and technology presence within a complex content curriculum.

Linda Corey, who can call on twenty-two years of experience as a library media specialist at each level from prekindergarten through high school, notes the joy that comes from promoting and using "an exemplary collaborative integrated library media program that offers a wide variety of resources and flexible access for all students." Now the District Coordinating Teacher for Library Media Services for Blue Valley Schools in Overland Park, KS, Linda thrives on the teamwork involved in working with the library media specialist, technical staff, administrators, and teaching staff. And although she misses the "daily face-to-face interaction with students and staff," Linda's career path has led her to a position where she now uses her skills to "recruit and mentor new library media specialists, develop curriculum, supervise library technical functions, represent library ideals of freedom to read and intellectual freedom, open new libraries, represent library media specialists at the district level, facilitate the sharing and exchange of ideas and best practices, problem solve and advocate for the program."

Clearly, a career as a school librarian can represent an excellent choice for someone who thrives on a day that includes a highly diverse set of tasks, a lot of people interaction, and a high level of self-direction.

Academic Libraries

The *Online Dictionary for Library and Information Science (ODLIS)* defines an academic library as:

> *A library that is an integral part of a college, university, or other institution of postsecondary education, administered to meet the information and research needs of its students, faculty, and staff.*[6]

The term "academic library," however, encompasses a number of distinct types of higher-education libraries differentiated by the mission of the institution, the nature of its student body, and the size of its collection. One way to categorize academic libraries is by whether they support two-year or four-year degree programs. Another way is whether the library is an *undergraduate* or *graduate library* (i.e., supports undergraduate or graduate students and curricula), or a *departmental library* (for example, a library devoted solely to supporting a business school program and its students). A *college library* may be one of several specialized libraries supporting separate "colleges" within a large university. The role of these libraries is primarily to support the curriculum and course-related research needs of their specific constituencies, including both students and faculty.

An academic library that is considered a *research library*, on the other hand, has a somewhat different mission. A research library is expected to maintain a broad and very deep collection of primary and secondary sources of value to serious scholarly research in a specific topic area or discipline. Such a collection often includes archives of original manuscripts, rare books, personal letters, and similar types of scholarly resources.

A further distinction among academic libraries is whether they are part of a *research university*, that is, one of the major research institutions such as Johns Hopkins University, UCLA, the University of Wisconsin, the University of Michigan, Massachusetts Institute of Technology (MIT), Stanford, or the University of Pennsylvania. This distinction is generally based on the amount of federal and/or private-sector research funds flowing into a given institution on an annual basis, among other criteria.

The official classification system used to categorize types of American colleges and universities is the Carnegie Classification of Institutions of Higher Education, developed by The Carnegie Foundation for the Advancement of Teaching. Although the classification system is currently under revision, see a summary of the existing classification and distribution of institutions at the Carnegie Foundation website (ww.carnegiefoundation. org/Classification/CIHE2000/Tables.htm).

According to *Academic Libraries: 2000* (2003, National Center for Education Statistics), there are 3,527 academic libraries in this country. Of these, 1,379 support two-year colleges, 2,148 four-year colleges and universities. Of the total, 1,566 are in public institutions, 1,961 private.[7] Academic libraries employ approximately 31,000 professional librarians. In addition, many of the proprietary schools (also known as vocational or technical schools or career colleges) and for-profit colleges (for example, University of Phoenix) provide library resources and services to their students.

The states with the highest number of academic libraries (and therefore, theoretically, the greatest number of job openings) are California (341), New York (260), Pennsylvania (211), Texas (183), Illinois (153), Ohio (143),

Florida (120), North Carolina (118), Massachusetts (114), and Michigan (99).[8]

Regardless of the types and sizes of academic libraries, user or public services, tech services, and administrative services generally follow the same outlines of activity. The goals of the library are to select, acquire, and maintain a resource collection that supports the curriculum as well as the research needs of students and faculty; teach students how to effectively use not only that collection but also the myriad other online information resources that exist; work with faculty to integrate advanced information and communications technologies into the learning dynamic; and create and support technology infrastructures that enable each of these goals.

Academic librarians working within the *public* or *user services* arena will find themselves in a strong teaching and coaching role with students (and occasionally faculty). *Bibliographic instruction* (BI) has traditionally been a core responsibility on the reference desk, but today BI is moving into the broader embrace of *information literacy*—teaching students not only how to use the information resources offered by the library, but also how to be effective, informed users of *all* information resources.

In addition, the entire reference interaction is more and more moving into a virtual or digital exchange, requiring new skills of academic reference librarians, including a strong ability to communicate effectively in an online environment. Also, the advent of online courses has seen an increase in the embedding of information literacy assignments into the courses themselves ("at the point of need," rather than in a separate bibliographic instruction session). This trend has resulted in many reference librarians developing a new set of collaborative skills around theories of learning styles, lesson plan development, and instructional design.

In the *tech services* arena, serials management plays a much greater role in the workings of an academic library than in public or school libraries because serials are such a large part of academic holdings. In addition, e-books and electronic journals are changing how collections are developed and managed. Helping to create, manage, and support databases has also grown as a tech-services function. Interlibrary loan (ILL) continues to be an important part of academic library services, although online (immediately available) resources are somewhat lessening the demand for ILL. And depending on the nature of an institution's holdings, "original cataloging," that is, cataloging unusual items from scratch rather than relying on OCLC's cataloging services, may be a large part of the catalogers' jobs.

Administrative services in academic libraries are similar to those in public libraries, although the external communications are more likely to be with chancellors, donor groups, deans, and department heads than with the broader public community. In many academic libraries, the librarians are also part of the larger academic community and its expectations (i.e., tenure-track activities), which changes to some extent how personnel management issues and staff-development initiatives are approached.

Salaries and Education

Academic librarians' salaries, like those of school and public librarians, are based on a wide variety of circumstances. Size, financial well-being, prestige, and geographic location of the institution are all factors, as is whether an institution is publicly or privately funded. But academic librarians often have other job benefits that augment their salaries. For example, they usually have free tuition at their employing institution, often have the

Exploring Academic Library Careers

To learn more about how being an academic librarian might suit your career interests and goals, consider the following activities:

1. Shadow several academic librarians in different departments (for example, reference, collection development, circulation) for a day each to get a sense of the different types of activities that make up their jobs. Note the following in your career journal:

   • Which of their daily activities seems most interesting and enjoyable to me? Does one position seem to align with my skills and aptitudes more than the others, or are there aspects of each that appeal? If so, what are they?

   • How do colleagues interact with each other? Is it a strong collaborative environment or are departments "information silos?" Do I think I would thrive in this culture? Why or why not?

   • What does the person I'm shadowing most enjoy about his or her job? Most dislike? If the person is willing to discuss his or her personality type, do the "dislikes" seem to be a mismatch between job requirements and personality (for example an introvert staffing the reference desk)? Would this be the same or different for me?

   • Would I be comfortable working with students, scholars, and faculty, and their broad range of attitudes about and expectations of the library and librarians?

2. Sign up for one or two of the position-specific (e.g., BI-L, the Bibliographic Instruction Discussion Group or DIG-REF, for public and academic digital reference services) electronic discussion groups and monitor the online postings for a month or two. Your goal is to get a sense of the questions asked and issues discussed, and then note in your career journal answers to the following:

   • Do I think I would enjoy learning more about the issues discussed, and contributing my knowledge and solutions?

   • What seems to be the general level of community morale on the listservs? Are people excited about their jobs, the work they do? Is there a sense of mutual support, are newcomers welcomed?

   • What role does technology seem to play in the disciplines in question, and does this level of technology engagement align with my skills? If my skills are lower, would I be comfortable learning more? If higher, would I be enjoy becoming the technology "guru?

3. Read six recent issues of *The Journal of Academic Librarianship (JAL)* (either in your local academic library or online at their website). Consider the articles' high level of research and

scholarship. As you peruse the issues, note in your career journal the following information:

- Would I enjoy this level of professional scholarship, and find it a rewarding aspect of my career, or would I find it intimidating or too much pressure?

- Do I find the article topics engaging? Which ones most so/least so? Does there seem to be a spirit of openness to new ideas among the contributors, so that new theories and solutions would be welcomed?

- Do there seem to be areas where I believe my unique skills, aptitudes, and insights could contribute? Where and how?

4. After reviewing your responses to the information you've noted in your career journal, answer these questions:

- Based on what I discovered through my previous self-assessment process and what I now know about my preferences and priorities, does academic librarianship seem like a career path that could offer me the levels of growth, challenge, security, and engagement that I need to thrive?

- If I am still unsure about this question, what other information would I need to make this assessment?

- How will I gather that information?

opportunity to seek the job security of tenure-track faculty, and frequently have substantial vacation, healthcare, and retirement benefits packages. Also, for those contemplating upcoming kids' tuition payments, a job in an academic library may also offer the delightful perk of free school tuition for family members.

According to the *ALA Survey of Librarian Salaries 2005*, with exceptions (check the full report to determine specifics), salaries (in the thousands of dollars) generally fall into the following ranges:

- low- to high-thirties for beginning full-time librarians with an MLS but no professional experience at both colleges and universities;

- low- to high-forties for librarians with no supervisory responsibilities at two-year and four-year colleges, mid- to high-forties for those at universities;

- mid-forties for library managers and those who supervise support staff at two-year and four-year colleges, high-forties for those at universities;

- mid- to high-forties for department heads/coordinators/senior managers at two-year and four-year colleges, mid-fifties for those at universities;

- mid- to high-forties for deputy/associate and assistant directors at two-year and four-year colleges; mid-sixties for those at universities, and

- low- to mid-fifties for directors and deans at two-year and four-year colleges, mid- to high-nineties for those at universities.[9]

Education requirements for professional jobs in academic libraries vary by institution, although all require the MLS. The debate is whether or not you need also complete an additional master's degree in a subject area such as life sciences or American literature or social sciences. The argument *against* an additional degree is that the salaries paid to academic librarians are simply too low to expect this level of education, financial, and time investment. The argument *for* the second masters is that it gives you an edge over other job applicants, may convince faculty to respect you more as a peer, helps support tenure efforts, and may be an important asset when applying for administrative and/or management positions. Like so many career considerations, at the very least, a second subject-oriented master's degree may simply open up more and better options for you in the long-term.

Why You Might Love Being an Academic Librarian

If you love ideas, the learning process, and teaching students from 18 to 80 how to become effective users of information resources, academic librarianship may offer you a career of ongoing intellectual and professional engagement. An academic library is a dynamic environment, and in a well-funded one, you'll be on the cutting edge of advances in information and communications technology, working with faculty to design interactive, multimedia assignments that engage and teach students. You'll be exposed to a wide variety of scholarly disciplines, and be challenged to stay abreast not only of the institution's resources but also those of the information universe at large.

Plus, many institutions offer a great work schedule—ten-month contracts, multiple holidays, two weeks off at Christmas and another at spring break. The work hours are flexible, and the rich mixture of on-campus political, arts, and cultural events are inexpensive and easy to attend. And if you're one of those whose idea of heaven is being a perpetual student, it's hard to imagine a more enjoyable career choice than academic librarianship.

When asked what she loved about her job, Allison Cowgill, Co-coordinator of Instruction & Reference Services at Colorado State University, talked about the rewards of "connecting users with the resources that best meet their needs and providing them information on how to access those materials." She also pointed out that "helping graduate students do the research required for their theses and dissertations" lets you know that you're really "making a difference in the outcomes."

Jim Rettig, University Librarian at the University of Richmond and well-known reference expert, cited the intellectual and cultural enrichment to be found on an academic campus. Pointing out that being an academic librarian is "a way to work with really interesting people who are intelligent and bright," he also noted that academic librarians often had opportunities to "work with opinion makers who could help influence outcomes."

Chris Brown, reference librarian and government documents specialist at the University of Denver, sees being able to experiment with the latest technologies as one of the biggest benefits of his job. "Academic libraries are on the cutting edge of new technologies. Opportunities abound to experiment with OpenURL, reference linking, Open Archives Initiative, and numerous other fun activities." But he also enjoyed the people interaction, noting that it's "extremely stimulating to work with students on their research. It's rewarding to see the undergraduate student learn how to find relevant articles in a database. But it's also rewarding to instruct a Ph.D. student in all the databases and reference tools for a very specific area of in-depth research."

And Santiago Canyon College (cal.) reference librarian Linda Dressler says that one of the things she most enjoys in her job is that she gets to work with "a variety of patrons—18 to 80 year olds, men and women, and every race and religion. I even get some high school and junior high students who come here for help with their assignments when their school libraries have little or no information." Dressler also noted how much she enjoys the teaching aspects of her job, which can involve working with everything "from English 101 to Biology 210 to an ESL class."

All of these academic librarians cited the variety of their jobs (in terms of activities, technologies, intellectual challenges, and types of people served), and noted how enjoyable it was to work with service-oriented colleagues who supported the college and/or university goals of research and scholarship.

Types of Jobs Within Public, School, and Academic Libraries

As suggested previously, there are two ways to consider traditional library career paths. One is to categorize by type of library—that is, school, public, or academic. The other is to approach by type of role or activity, including those found among public, technical, and administrative services. As noted, however, a library's size often determines how specialized these roles and activities become. For example, a small public library may have only a library director, a couple of reference librarians who double on the circulation desk, and one hardy soul handling all technical services. A large academic library, on the other hand, is likely to have individual reference librarians dedicated to specific academic disciplines such as humanities, sciences, and business, with a similar breadth and depth of coverage across all of the functional departments.

Also, technology advances and electronic resources continue to blur the lines between and among functional areas, so that the roles of (for example) adult services, user education, and web development will regularly overlap in an ongoing collaboration. However, as a starting point, below are brief descriptions of many of the positions found in traditional libraries. (Given the breakneck pace of change in our profession, all of the job titles, descriptions, and comments noted below should be considered at best a snapshot in time.)

Public Services Roles and Activities

Access services librarian—oversees all the ways in which the library provides access to its collections, including circulation, reserves, interlibrary loan (ILL), and document delivery. Involves management of people and processes, plus strong attention to detail.

Adult services librarian—creates and/or manages programs and resource collections that meet the needs of the library's adult users (as distinct from those of children or young adults). A creative, service-oriented job that involves working with the public and responsiveness to patron input.

Business librarian—in a public library, works with the local business community (or with individuals considering starting a business) by developing and maintaining a collection that supports business information needs and training users on how to most effectively use the appropriate resources. In an academic library, a business librarian has the same responsibilities, but focused on students and faculty in the school's business program or courses. Entails lots of people interaction, broad and deep knowledge of existing business information resources and their uses, as well as constantly monitoring/mastering emerging resources.

Children's librarian—creates and/or manages programs and resource collections that meet the needs of the library's youngest users (as distinct from those of young adults or adults). Especially rewarding for those who love working with children and parents and bring a high level of creativity to their work.

Instructional services librarian—responsible for bibliographic instruction (BI) in academic libraries, or teaching individuals how to locate, evaluate, and use the resources offered in the public library. With the advent of the Internet, this position now focuses on the broader "information literacy" mandate, that is, teaching students and patrons how to use and evaluate *all* information resources effectively, including those of the institution's collection. In a large public library, a similar focus is often called "user education." A great path for those who would enjoy combining a teaching role with their information skills; often involves substantial use of technology-based instructional tools.

Outreach librarian—designs and delivers programs to meet the needs of underserved populations and special constituencies, for example, the visually impaired, non-English-speaking groups, the homebound, or local small business development centers. Usually found in larger public libraries. A great career choice for individuals with strong people skills, who possess a high level of comfort addressing groups, and who are comfortable taking initiative.

Reference librarian—the job that many fall in love with when first considering librarianship. Answers patron or student questions in person, by phone, by e-mail, or via interactive "chat" using one of the new virtual reference software programs. Frequently, the reference librarian may also be called on to help provide user instruction, explain the use of the library's technology, and collaborate on collection development. In larger academic institutions, the reference librarians may have areas of specialization, such as the humanities, sciences, or social sciences. A good option for extroverts who enjoy a lot of people contact, who thrive on the research process, and can patiently coach users through the intricacies of various reference tools.

Readers' advisory services—a service often provided by an adult-services librarian where specific books or authors are recommended to a patron based on his or her reading interests. Readers' advisory services may also include helping to organize and support book clubs, and may also be crafted for children and young adults. For those who know and love genre reading (fiction and nonfiction) and enjoy connecting readers with the books they'll love.

Young adult/youth services librarian—creates and/or manages programs and resource collections that meet the needs of the library's young adult patrons (that is, adolescents in the ninth through twelfth grades). Usually involves collection development work, program design and implementation, and readers' advisory services. Similar to adult services, a great choice for those who love working with teenagers and have a strong sense of creativity.

Keep in mind that all of these roles and activities are increasingly playing out in a digital surround, resulting in job descriptions like digital collections specialist, online business librarian, and e-reference or virtual reference librarian. In fact, no matter what area of public services you might be in, it's a good idea to assume at least part of your job will entail online delivery (and virtual communication skills).

Technical Services Roles and Activities

Acquisitions—manages the *ordering and purchase* of all materials (as opposed to collection development, which involves *selecting* the materials to be purchased). Deals with vendors, licenses, contract negotiation, and budgets, and often collaborates with regional buying consortia to secure the best prices for the organization. Smaller public and academic libraries may combine the acquisitions and collection-development functions. Involves strong work-organization skills and attention to detail, as well as the ability to effectively negotiate and monitor vendor contracts and performance.

Bibliographer—creates subject-focused, usually annotated, lists of resources to be used for teaching, collection development, and scholarly research. Primarily in larger academic libraries. Best for those with strong research, analysis, and writing skills, a passion for a specific discipline or topic, and an interest in continuing to grow topic expertise.

Cataloger—creates the bibliographic records that allow us to find and retrieve specific items among the library's holdings. A bibliographic record will include a physical description of the item as well as noting its subject headings, classification number, and—depending on the nature of the collection—other information that will assist the user. Catalogers are in the forefront of the work being done with digitization and metadata issues, and are taking the lead on many virtual library access and retrieval issues. *Original* cataloging entails creating the entire record from scratch, while *copy* cataloging relies on cataloging that has already been created by national cataloging entity OCLC. Takes an extremely high level of attention to detail, an in-depth understanding of cataloging and classification structures, and an ability to apply them precisely. Often entails minimal people contact.

Circulation—manages all processes related to checking materials in and out of the library, and compiles statistics related to circulation data (for example, what resources are most popular based on their circulation numbers). Requires strong process orientation and attention to detail, high level of comfort with technology-based systems.

Collection development—relying on a wide range of reviewing and evaluation tools, identifies materials to purchase based on the nature of the collection and the library's constituency. For example, a public library collection would reflect a stronger consumer-interest focus, while a two-year college collection would have a less scholarly emphasis than would a research-level university supporting numerous doctoral programs. In academic libraries, collection development librarians may have a second master's degree in their subject area. Involves substantial interaction with peers and colleagues, ongoing monitoring of multiple and diverse review sources, and an ability to manage decision processes.

Document delivery and interlibrary loan (ILL)—obtains materials such as books, articles, reports, CDs, etc. that have been requested by patrons, students, or faculty and are unavailable in the library's existing collection. Most ILL and document delivery requests are processed through a collaborative online system, either regional or national, that transfers requests among participating libraries. The emergence of e-books, resource digitization, and full-text articles available online will have a substantial impact on how—and how much—document delivery and ILL is required in the future. Requires strong focus on following consistent (often technology-based) processes and attention to administrative detail; may involve some public contact, but minimal.

Preservation and conservation—maintains rare and archival materials through the management of environmental conditions (e.g., light, temperature, humidity), by controlling access to the materials, and by undertaking appropriate actions to repair damage and deterioration. Digitization is an increasingly important method for preserving delicate or deteriorating resources. Although some large public libraries with archival special collections are involved in preservation and conservation, this function is more usually found in special-collection archives of universities and cultural institutions. Although this is an increasingly technology-based function, it still often requires extreme patience and extraordinary attention to process details, as well as the ability to be painstakingly careful with physical objects.

Reserves—in academic libraries, maintains a separate collection of materials (including books, reports, articles, etc.) as stipulated by faculty to provide supplementary course materials for their students. *E-reserves*, or digitized full-text documents, are an increasingly popular solution for providing these resources online, with access through the library's website or portal. Online courses sometimes offer the option of embedding e-reserves directly into the online course delivery. Similar to document delivery/ILL work, the reserves function requires strong focus on following consistent (often technology-based) processes and attention to administrative detail. Generally involves interaction with both faculty and students.

Serials librarian—manages the subscriptions, receipt, check-in, shelving, binding, and sometimes contract negotiation for all of the library's periodicals (an especially important role for academic libraries), including digital subscriptions. Some shared activities with acquisitions and cataloging departments. Best for those with strong process orientation, ability to establish and/or manage administrative processes, and collaborate with other departments. Also requires ability to effectively negotiate and monitor vendor contracts and performance.

Systems librarian—responsible for the development and maintenance of the library's hardware, software, and networking capabilities. In most academic and many public libraries, integrated automation systems now coordinate the efforts of cataloging, circulation, serials management, acquisitions, e-reserves for academics, interlibrary loan, and the online catalog, so this is an increasingly critical role. Takes a strong combination of advanced technology skills, substantial cross-departmental collaboration, an ability to prioritize among many competing demands, and solid communication skills. Patience and an ability to remain calm are major pluses!

Visual resources librarian—depending on the type of library and its specific collections, organizes and maintains collections of digital images, film and/or video, photographs and slides, and similar types of visual resources. Position is found primarily in large academic, public, or special libraries with visual resource collections. May also be called "video" or "moving image" librarian. Job entails knowledge of video resources, their review sources, and their organizing and cataloging methodologies.

Webmaster—also known as the web manager, responsible for designing, assembling, and maintaining the library's website. This position is an increasingly collaborative one, and requires strong interpersonal communications and team-leadership skills to complement technology expertise. A critical role in public and academic libraries, and a component of many school librarians' jobs. In public and academic libraries, this job may require skills similar to those needed by a systems librarian: that is, a strong combination of advanced web-development skills, substantial cross-departmental collaboration, an ability to prioritize among many competing demands, and solid communication skills.

Administrative Services Roles and Activities

As noted above, administrative services include process organization, personnel management, budget setting, staff development, external liaison and communication, and leadership, among other functions.

These are standard functional areas within any organization. For example, the human resources department (or person) manages hiring and firing, personnel policies, staff legal issues, staff development, and benefits and compensation issues. The library dean or director puts together a budget, perhaps with the assistance of a business manager or finance director. Rarely are these positions one studies for in an MLIS program, except in the occasional management class. Instead, you may pick up these skill sets on the job, by taking a couple of marketing classes, or by developing a knack for putting together budgets.

All three of these areas—public, technical, and administrative services—offer opportunities to move into management positions, if that's a direction you'd like to go. Although each organization has a different hierarchy of terms, generally these positions include, in order of increasing responsibility (and salary) *coordinator, supervisor, manager, director* (at the department level), *head,* and *director* or *dean.* Larger organizations may also have *assistant, associate,* and *deputy* positions to further subdivide responsibilities. On the other hand, some job descriptions may say "Public Services Librarian," and indicate a position that is essentially a department head supervising six professionals. Consequently, if you're doing a job search, keep in mind that every library has its own unique terminology for management positions.

Multifunctional Positions

There are a number of roles within librarianship that are based on the ability to integrate several of the functions described above into a single position. Some of these are:

Archivist–responsible for managing the resources of a specialized collection of historical significance. The collection may include books, documents, letters, memorabilia, and other materials. The archivist may be responsible for processing the items, or may oversee the work of others (for example, catalogers or a digitization team). Archival collections may be found in public or academic libraries, as well as in many special libraries. Archivists often combine a history degree with their LIS skills, and also need to be adept at managing donor relations, i.e., have strong people skills, when needed.

Government documents librarian—oversees the library's collection of government documents, including hearing transcripts, reports, periodicals, statistical data, etc. Govdocs librarians have mastered both the unique Superintendent of Documents (SuDocs) classification system and an understanding of the legislative, judicial, and executive-branch processes that produce the documents in question. With the mandated migration of government documents to the Internet, this job increasingly involves aggregating and organizing online resources. Primarily found in larger academic libraries and those libraries (public and academic) designated as depository libraries. Entails strong organizational (and often cataloging) skills, plus the patience and/or passion necessary to stay current with the extraordinarily complex government information environment.

Map librarian—responsible for preserving and maintaining a collection made up primarily of maps and related cartographic materials. This type of collection can be found in academic institutions, some public libraries, and some special library collections. Maps included in such a collection are often thematic, that is, historic, scientific, demographic, etc. An obvious career choice for those with an innate love of maps who have also mastered the organizing principles of map cataloging and classification. Focus is generally on managing a specialized collection rather than on interacting with people, although in some situations (for example, working geology collections) this job involves substantial patron interaction.

Photo-archivist—responsible for preserving and maintaining an archive of thematically related photographs, for example, a history collection or a design-awards collection. Can be found in public or academic libraries with special collections, as well as in special libraries, wherever a collection of thematic photographs may be maintained. This job requires skills similar to those of a map librarian, substituting a passion for photography for that of cartography.

Rare books librarian—similar to archivists and photo-archivists, rare books librarians are responsible for maintaining a specialized collection of materials—in this case, rare books. Usually found in special libraries or in major academic institutions, whose rare book collections are often contributed by donors. Many of these books are now being digitized for preservation purposes and to make their contents available to a wider community of scholars. Combines a love and knowledge of rare books with a knowledge of publishing, printing, and book preservation. Similar to an archivist position, this role also occasionally demands strong people skills, as when managing donor relations.

Special collections librarian—a librarian who manages a specialized collection, which might include rare books, photographs, original manuscripts, etc. Often special collections are housed within a larger library, such as a major public or academic library, and they rarely circulate. A *special collection* differs from a *special library* in that the latter is an entire library established by its host organization (for example, a business or professional association) to meet the needs of that organization. As noted for map librarians and photo-archivists, special collections librarians generally must have solid knowledge of their collection's topic or focus area, as well as an understanding of how to organize and maintain it. The amount of people interaction is unique to each collection.

Is a Traditional Career Path For You?

Is it important to you to be associated with a public service or education mission? If so, then working in a public, school, or academic library might be a great option for you. Do you thrive in a structured workplace? Do you look forward to sharing professional camaraderie with other LIS professionals in your workplace? Would you feel "out of place" working in a nonlibrary setting? Then you may want to seriously explore one of the career paths open through public, school, or academic librarianship.

Resources

Multidisciplinary Coverage of Traditional Librarianship

Books

Bridges, Karl, ed. *Expectations of Librarians in the 21st Century.* Greenwood Press, 2003. 231 pp. ISBN 0313322945.
> More than fifty essays affirm that the core competencies of subject-area expertise, an understanding of key technologies, and strong interpersonal skills will continue to be the hallmarks of an outstanding librarian. The essays are highly personal statements of commitment to the core values of librarianship, and represent a good if somewhat eclectic starting point for those interested in the future of traditional librarianship.

Fourie, Denise K. and David R. Dowell. *Libraries in the Information Age: An Introduction and Career Exploration.* Libraries Unlimited, 2002. 303 pp. ISBN 1561086344.
> Structured as a textbook for an overview of all types of libraries, this book is especially strong in its coverage of traditional libraries and activities. The work leads off with a brief history of libraries, then explores types of library opportunities and the work common to all of them (e.g., library collections, materials processing, reference, etc.). A separate section covers job search information.

Reitz, Joan M. *Online Dictionary for Library and Information Science (ODLIS).* Libraries Unlimited, 2004. 800 pp. ISBN 1591580757.
> The best overall resource for checking out all the terms, phrases, and organizations found throughout the LIS profession. Reitz has provided clear, concise definitions for more than 4,000 entries that draw from publishing, printing, literature, and computer science as well as the diverse profession of librarianship. Should be a familiar and often-referred-to reference for all LIS students finding their way through the

confusing maze of LIS acronyms, issues, and opportunities. Can be purchased in its print iteration or accessed online at http://lu.com/odlis/ for free.

Roberto, Katia and Jessamyn West, eds. *Revolting Librarians Redux: Radical Librarians Speak Out.* McFarland, 2003. 229 pp. ISBN 0786416083. Taking a somewhat different stance than Bridges' contributors, the fifty-six contributors to *Revolting Librarians Redux* focus on alternative librarianship as it weaves through LIS education, daily practice in the country's libraries, and as social and political expression. An interesting and thought provoking read.

Rubin, Richard. *Foundations of Library and Information Science.* Neal-Schuman, 2004. 579 pp. ISBN 1555705189. Comprehensive overview of all aspects of the LIS universe. Not one of the more exciting reads, but thorough and authoritative, this text provides a solid grounding in the foundations underlying traditional librarianship.

Periodicals

American Libraries. American Library Association, 1907– . 11/yr. ISSN 0002–9769.
www.ala.org/
Sent to all ALA members, *American Libraries* provides an excellent overview of the current state of affairs for traditional libraries throughout the country. As the official organ of the organization, the magazine's content reflects a combination of ALA news and information and other contributed articles on topics of interest to librarians. Check the website for library-related news stories, a selected numbers of archived articles, and several archived columns, including Mary Pergander's excellent "Working Knowledge" career pieces. From the ALA website, select Products & Publications > Periodicals > American Libraries.

Library Journal. Reed Business Information, 1876– . 20/yr. ISSN 0363–0277.
www.libraryjournal.com
The most important resource for broad-based coverage of libraries, the library profession, and the industries that support it. *LJ* issues include news items, an events calendar, industry analyses, vendor overviews, features, profiles, and several special issues per year. Its book reviews are relied on by librarians for their objectivity and usefulness. The website is an extraordinarily content-rich resource with archived articles, salary surveys, a career resource center, and job postings all available for free. A key resource for all LIS professionals.

Articles and Columns

Lenzini, Rebecca T. "The Graying of the Library Profession: A Survey of Our Professional Association and Their Responses," *Searcher*, vol. 10, no. 7 (July/August 2002), pp. 88–97.
The article that launched a thousand discussions. Rebecca Lenzini, publisher of The Charleston Advisor and longtime leader in the library industry, surveys both the data and the profession's responses to see

what the demographic and retirement trends indicate and what they may mean to LIS professionals.

"Next Gen" column, *Library Journal*
www.libraryjournal.com
An occasional column written by various next-gen librarians that should be a must-read for all librarians, especially those in management and/or leadership positions. These writers represent the future of the profession, and their comments, questions, and insights provide an important window into potential new thinking. Select "New Librarians" from the Browse Topics drop-down menu to view past columns at the *Library Journal* website.

Associations

American Library Association (ALA)
www.ala.org
The most important player in the library profession. ALA's mission is to provide "leadership for the development, promotion, and improvement of library and information services and the profession of librarianship in order to enhance learning and ensure access to information for all." Representing public, academic, and school libraries, ALA is the only library organization that seeks to promote strong libraries of all types throughout society. The annual conference in June is huge, diverse, and often overwhelming for newcomers, but well worth attending at least once every several years for those who can afford to do so. Membership includes a subscription to the monthly *American Libraries* magazine. Discounted memberships for students.

American Society for Information Science and Technology (ASIST)
www.asis.org
With a primary mission of "leading the search for new and better theories, techniques, and technologies to improve access to information," the ASIST organization draws its membership from the computer science, linguistics, management, librarianship, engineering, law, medicine, chemistry, and education disciplines. Its website includes information about the society, its goals and programs; memberships (discounted for students); and many special-interest groups and chapters, including multiple student chapters. ASIST holds an annual conference (proceedings available) plus several special-topic gatherings. Substantially discounted student memberships.

Canadian Library Association (CLA)
www.cla.ca
CLA represents 57,000 library workers, vendors, public library board members, and LIS students in graduate or community college programs throughout Canada. The organization includes twenty-two special interest groups (e.g., action for literacy, entrepreneurship in librarianship, library and information services for older people) and numerous student chapters. Check the website for library career resources. CLA offers substantially discounted memberships for students.

New Members Round Table (NMRT)
www.ala.org/ala/nmrt/nmrt.htm
The focus of NMRT is to help those new to the profession find ways to engage and participate in association professional activities. Its goals

include structuring "formal opportunities for involvement and/or training for professional association committee experiences on the national, state, and local levels" and developing " ongoing programs for library school students that encourage professional involvement and networking." The NMRT electronic discussion list provides a way to connect with peers across the country.

Online Resources

The Entry Level Gap
www.libraryjournal.com/article/CA527965.html
Authors Rachel Holt and Adrienne L. Strock take a hard look at the decrease in the number of entry-level jobs open to new MLIS graduates. Based on their survey of 900 job advertisements from ten U.S. LIS job-posting sites, they found only 230 made the grade as full-time, permanent, professional-level positions, while only 99 would be open to those just entering the library world. This is a serious issue for the profession and for LIS students and graduates, and Holt and Strock have done an excellent job of documenting the problem and raising further questions.

How to Become a Librarian
www.libraryjournal.com/article/CA605244.html
Written by Rachel Singer Gordon, webmaster of the terrific Lisjobs.com website and author of *The NextGen Librarian's Survival Guide (Information Today, 2006)*, among other books, this white paper provides a brief but thorough overview of the profession. A fast read that tells you what you need to know to consider a career as an LIS professional, and where to go for further information. See also Singer Gordon's "Finding a Library Job" (www.libraryjournal.com/article/CA6250888.html) for similar treatment of the LIS job hunt.

NexGenLib-l: Networking with the Next Generation of Librarians
http://lists.topica.com/lists/nexgenlib-l/
Per the author, this electronic discussion list was created for "the next generation of librarians," primarily those under 30, though its members range in age from the early twenties into the thirties. Good complement to the NEWLIB-L list; check the website to subscribe.

NEWLIB-L
www.lahacal.org/newlib/
If you're a student or new to the profession, this discussion list is a great tool for connecting with others in the same boat. Its focus is on sharing experiences and exploring "ideas, issues, trends, and problems faced by librarians in the early stages of their careers." Check the website to subscribe.

Placements & Salaries Survey
www.libraryjournal.com
From *Library Journal*, this annual survey of MLIS graduate placements is posted every October. Access via Archives > [Year] > October 15th Issue. A very valuable overview of various "slices" of salary comparisons, e.g., by gender, geographic region, and type of library (public, school, college/university, special, government, etc.). A fascinating and extremely valuable resource for career exploration.

Public Librarianship

Books

Brumley, Rebecca. *Neal-Schuman Directory of Public Library Job Descriptions.* Neal-Schuman, 2005. 353 pp. ISBN 1555705235.
    If you're wondering what sorts of positions might be of interest within public libraries, this is the place to start. Brumley has gathered together more than 250 actual job descriptions from around the country; included for each are general summary of position, job responsibilities, education and skills required, and similar information. Although written for those responsible for writing job descriptions, this is also a great resource for those new to the profession and exploring job possibilities.

de la Peña McCook, Kathleen. *Introduction to Public Librarianship.* Neal-Schuman, 2004. 404 pp. ISBN 1555704751.
    Public libraries exist in a complex world of service mission, community expectations, government oversight, demographic diversity, and technological upheaval. McCook does an excellent job of helping students understand that complexity, but effectively makes the case that public libraries can nevertheless be well-managed resources of leadership and community impact.

Periodicals

Public Libraries. Public Library Association, 1961– . Bimonthly. ISSN 0163–5506.
    www.ala.org/ala/pla/plapubs/publiclibraries/publiclibraries.htm
    The official publication of PLA, *Public Libraries* covers industry news, association updates, and articles, columns, and feature stories of value to those managing the country's more than 9,000 public libraries. Recent articles (accessible to the public at the magazine's website) have included "Opposing the USA Patriot Act," "Branch Management," and "Increasing Technical Services Efficiency to Eliminate Cataloging Backlogs."

Associations

Canadian Association of Public Libraries (CAPL)
    www.cla.ca/divisions/capl/index.htm
    A division of the Canadian Library Association, CAPL is "committed to furthering public library service in Canada" through an exchange of information and ideas. Check the website for career information, public library resources, and the CAPL newsletter.

Public Library Association (PLA)
    www.pla.org
    Founded in 1944, PLA supports its more than 9,000 members through "a diverse program of communication, publication, advocacy, continuing education, and programming." Membership includes a subscription to the bimonthly *Public Libraries* magazine. PLA also publishes books and reports, offers educational symposiums as well as a biannual national conference, and supports various advocacy programs. Check out the PLA website for information about PLA committees and advocacy

groups, publications, and information resources about public librarianship. Student memberships available through primary ALA membership.

Urban Libraries Council (ULC)
www.urbanlibraries.org/
ULC membership comprises approximately 150 public libraries that are located in major U.S. metropolitan areas, and the vendors who support them. The organization's focus is on challenges and opportunities unique to urban libraries serving large and diverse populations, and on serving "as a forum for sharing best practices resulting from targeted research, education and forecasting." Although membership is at the organization level only, students especially will want to be aware of the innovative programs and research supported by ULC.

Online Resources

America's Libraries: Some Basic Facts and Figures
https://cs.ala.org/@yourlibrary/factsheet4.cfm
A broad collection of key statistics about all of America's libraries, including numbers of libraries by type, types of services provided, numbers of staff by type of library, information technology stats, total library expenditures with breakdowns by categories of spending and by type of library, and funding sources.

Public Library Listserv
http://sunsite.berkeley.edu/PubLib/
Founded in 1992, covers (among other topics): collection development, acquisitions, management and weeding, including traditional and new media; reference services; issues related to library facilities—security, new buildings, renovations; policy and guidance; trustee relationships; Internet access for staff and public; intellectual freedom; library administration; sundry library "how-tos" and queries for equipment; personnel issues; public library jobs; and related conferences. Check the website for instructions on how to subscribe.

School Librarianship

Books

Information Power: Building Partnerships for Learning. American Association of School Libraries and Association for Educational Communications and Technology, 1998. 224 pp. ISBN 0838934706.
The goal of *Information Power* is to help school library media specialists help students learn to be effective creators, researchers, evaluators, and users of information. It focuses on strategies and actions: guidelines, lesson plans, curriculum overviews, and programs. An extension of one of the most influential initiatives in the profession.

Woolls, Blanche. *The School Library Media Manager.* 3rd ed. Libraries Unlimited, 2004. 352 pp. ISBN 1591581826.
It may well be that Blanche Woolls knows more about school librarianship than anyone else in the country. This guide, written primarily for SLMC students but also of use to practitioners, covers all aspects of

school library media centers: history, management, facilities, personnel, budget, services, and issues such as filtering, federal mandates (e.g., No Child Left Behind), and eliciting faculty and administrative engagement. A key resource.

Woolls, Blanche and David V. Loertscher. *Whole School Library Handbook.* American Library Association, 2004. 448 pp. ISBN 0838908837.
Building on the successful model of ALA's *Whole Library Handbook* (ALA Editions, 1998), Woolls and Loertscher have produced a work that's basically "everything you wanted to know about school libraries but couldn't figure out who to ask." Articles, resources, tools, checklists, and more—an eclectic, engaging, and highly useful reference for anyone interested in school libraries.

Periodicals

Knowledge Quest. American Association of School Librarians, 1997– . 5/yr. ISSN 1094–9046.
www.ala.org/ala/aasl/aaslpubsandjournals/kqweb/kqweb.htm
The official journal of AASL, *Knowledge Quest* focuses on issues of interest to building-level media specialists, supervisors, library educators, and others involved in managing school library media centers. Check the website for excellent archived articles; students considering this career path should especially see Carol A. Brown's article, "Trends and Issues: What's Important for the 21st Century School Librarian?" Continues *School Library Media Quarterly.*

School Library Journal. Reed Business Information, 1961– . Monthly. ISSN 0362–8930.
www.schoollibraryjournal.com
Provides information, resources, and insight to librarians who work with kids and young adults, whether in schools or public libraries. Focus is on integrating "libraries into the school curriculum," becoming "leaders in the areas of technology, reading, and information literacy," and creating "high-quality collections for children and young adults." The website offers archives and a career center for subscribers only.

Teacher Librarian: The Journal for School Library Professionals. Rockland Press, 1998– . Bimonthly. ISSN 1481–1782.
www.teacherlibrarian.com/about_us/magazine.html
Previously known as *Emergency Librarian*, this publication explores topics of interest to school librarians who focus strongly on a teaching mission. Articles address such areas as collaboration, leadership, technology, and management. A useful collection of annotated links, articles, guides, and white papers can be accessed for free via the website.

Associations

American Association of School Librarians
www.ala.org/aasl/aaslindex.htm
The mission of the American Association of School Librarians is to advocate excellence, facilitate change, and develop leaders in the school library media field. AASL works to ensure that all members of the school

library media field collaborate to: provide leadership in the total education program; participate as active partners in the teaching/learning process; connect learners with ideas and information; and prepare students for life-long learning, informed decision making, a love of reading, and the use of information technologies. Student memberships available through primary ALA membership.

Canadian Association for School Libraries (CASL)
www.caslibraries.ca/
A division of the Canadian Library Association, CASL's mission is to provide a national voice for and promote excellence in school libraries, to provide members with professional growth opportunities, and to promote all forms of reading and information literacy. Publishes *School Libraries in Canada Online* (www.schoollibraries.ca).

Online Resources

AASL Recruitment to School Librarianship
www.ala.org/aasl/ recruitment
Information about careers as school library media specialists, including job outlook, state licensing, information about the job itself, and education requirements.

Information Power
www.ala.org/ala/aasl/aaslproftools/informationpower/
informationpower.htm
Information Power: Building Partnerships for Learning has been the major positioning publication, research project, and theme for AASL since its publication in 1998. This website contains a wealth of information about the initiative and its implementation, as well as information about the important role school library media specialists play in the learning dynamic (see "Role & Responsibilities of the School Library Media Specialist").

Job Outlook: A State-by-State Guide
http://slj.reviewsnews.com/index.asp?layout=article&articleid=
CA219977
This June 2002 overview by Nancy Everhart provides a good overview of the job prospects for librarians within all fifty states. For each, she's noted whether or not the state mandates certified school librarians for every school, provided the state's student:teacher ratio, and included a brief summary of the current status of its school libraries.

Academic Librarianship

Books

Budd, John M. *The Changing Academic Library: Operations, Culture, Environments.* Association of College & Research Libraries, 2005. 323 pp. ISBN 0838983189.
Budd, widely respected for his thought leadership within the profession, delivers an excellent overview of the challenges and opportunities facing academic librarians today. This book works equally well as a thorough introduction to the profession for students or as a good environmental scan for practitioners.

Periodicals

The Chronicle of Higher Education. Editorial Project for Education, 1966– .
Weekly. ISSN 0009–5982.
http://chronicle.com/
The leading publication for news, in-depth features, analysis, and job
information for higher education, including academic librarianship.
The *Chronicle* provides a useful overview of all aspects of higher
education—as an industry, a public good, and a profession. The website
offers some content for free (including a very extensive listing of posted
jobs—search on "librarians/library administration"), but you must be a
subscriber to access its large online archive of articles and career information. An extremely valuable resource for those interested in academic librarianship.

College & Research Libraries. Association of College and Research Li-
braries/American Library Association, 1939– . Bimonthly. ISSN 0010–
0870.
www.ala.org/ala/acrl/acrlpubs/crljournal/collegeresearch.htm
Articles of interest to those working in and/or managing college and research libraries. Topics covered include research studies, case studies,
new projects and initiatives (how undertaken, what results), and issues discussions. Articles are archived at the website, but are available
to ACRL members only. A refereed journal.

Journal of Academic Librarianship. Pergamon, 1975– . Bimonthly. ISSN
0099–1333.
http://authors.elsevier.com/JournalDetail.html?PubID=620207&
Precis=DESC
A highly regarded, referred journal, *JAL* provides academic librarians
a forum through which to share ideas, challenges, scenarios for the
future, and solutions for today. Much of the content is research-based,
which provides authority for the ideas discussed. An excellent and
useful, professional resource.

Associations

ACRL Distance Learning Section
http://caspian.switchinc.org/~distlearn/
With the exponential growth of online learning in higher education,
ACRL's Distance Learning Section is taking an increasingly important
role in identifying and promoting best practices in online librarianship.
This includes formulating and showcasing the *ACRL Guidelines for
Distance Learning Library Services,* which has become the standard
by which library services to off-campus students are measured.

Association of College & Research Libraries (ACRL)
www.ala.org/ala/acrl/aboutacrl/aboutacrl.htm
ACRL describes itself as "a professional association of academic
librarians and other interested individuals" dedicated to "enhancing
the ability of academic library and information professionals to serve
the information needs of the higher education community and to improve learning, teaching, and research." It membership (approximately
12,400 total) is primarily individuals, rather than institutions, and
those individuals represent many diverse communities (see Appendix

A for an overview of ACRL's sections, which reflect the range of its members). ACRL publishes *College & Research Libraries, College & Research Libraries News, Choice,* and a number of highly regarded monographs. At its website, see especially the "Career Opportunities from Across the Country" listings (ACRL > Publications > College & Research Libraries News > Career Opportunities) for descriptions of academic jobs throughout the country. A modest student membership discount is available.

Association of Research Libraries (ARL)
www.arl.org
The ARL mandate is to influence "the changing environment of scholarly communication and the public policies that affect research libraries and the communities they serve." The membership is made up of 123 institutions; there are no individual memberships. Its website however, has a rich collection of resources for everyone. See especially the sections on Diversity (www.arl.org/diversity), Career Resources (www.arl.org/careers/index.html), and the Leadership and Career Development Program (http://www.arl.org/diversity/lcdp/index.html), all resources and programs geared toward expanding the number of librarians from underrepresented racial and ethnic groups in academic librarianship.

Canadian Association of College and University Libraries (CACUL)
www.cla.ca/divisions/cacul/index.htm
CACUL "promotes professional development opportunities to its membership of almost 700 academic librarians," while also offering members "the opportunity to build community" through its electronic discussion list, and professional development workshops and conference programming. Check the website for professional development resources and CACUL publications, and the association's online discussion list.

Research Libraries Group (RLG)
www.rlg.org/
The more than 150 institutional members of RLG include universities, national libraries, archives, historical societies, museums, and similar institutions with substantial collections focused on research and learning. Founded in the mid-seventies by the New York Public Library and Columbia, Harvard, and Yale universities, it is now international in scope and membership, with a goal of ensuring access to research materials for scholars throughout the world.

Online Resources

Academic Library Newsletters in the United States
www.snhu.edu/Southern_New_Hampshire_University/Library/
Electronic_Resources/ALiNUS_Home.html
Links to more than 550 academic e-newsletters published by U.S.-based colleges and universities. Many of the newsletters are of strictly local interest, but others can be highly valuable. Search by newsletter title or university name. Links are unannotated, not surprising given the sheer number of newsletters included. An amazing resource from the Shapiro Library folks at Southern New Hampshire University.

Managing the 21st Century Academic Library: A Bibliography
www.lis.uiuc.edu/~b-sloan/future.htm
From the prolific Bernie Sloan, this bibliography points to mostly on-line resources that focus on managing today's academic library. Although it hasn't been updated since 2002, most of the links still work, and you can usually track down those that don't through an online database such as Library Literature. Bernie Sloan has authored and maintains a number of excellent online bibliographies, such as his "Library Support for Distance Learning" (http://people.lis.uiuc.edu/~b-sloan/libdist.htm) and "Bernie Sloan's Digital Reference Pages" (http://people.lis.uiuc.edu/~b-sloan/bernie.htm).

Notes

1. Bureau of Labor Statistics, *2004–2005 Occupational Outlook Handbook: Librarians*, U.S. Department of Labor. Accessed at www.bls.gov/oco/ocos068.htm on November 4, 2005.

2. American Library Association, "Facts about Libraries." Accessed at www.ala.org/ala/librariesandyou/libraryfacts/factsaboutli.htm on November 4, 2005.

3. Office for Research and Statistics, American Library Association, *2005 ALA Survey of Librarian Salaries*. Accessed at www.ala.org/ala/ors/reports/reports.htm on January 24, 2006.

4. Office for Research and Statistics, American Library Association, *Statistics about Libraries*. Accessed at www.ala.org/ala/ors/statsaboutlib/statisticsabout.htm on November 3, 2005.

5. "The SLJ Spending Survey," Marilyn L. Miller and Marilyn L. Shontz, School Library Journal, October 1, 2003. Accessed at www.schoollibraryjournal.com/article/CA326338.html on February 15, 2006.

6. Joan M. Reitz, *ODLIS—Online Dictionary for Library and Information Science*. Greenwood Village, CO: Libraries Unlimited, 2004. Accessed at http://lu.com/odlis/about.cfm on November 3, 2005.

7. National Center for Education Statistics, *Academic Libraries: 2000*. U.S. Department of Education, 2003; p. 68. Accessed at http://nces.ed.gov/pubs2004/2004317.PDF on November 1, 2005.

8. Ibid.

9. Office for Research and Statistics, American Library Association, *2005 ALA Survey of Librarian Salaries*.

4
The Nontraditional Path

What is an Information Professional?
An Information Professional ("IP") strategically uses information in his/her job to advance the mission of the organization. The IP accomplishes this through the development, deployment, and management of information resources and services. The IP harnesses technology as a critical tool to accomplish goals. IPs include, but are not limited to, librarians, knowledge managers, chief information officers, web developers, information brokers, and consultants.

What are Information Organizations?
Information organizations are defined as those entities that deliver information-based solutions to a given market. Some commonly used names for these organizations include libraries, information centers, competitive intelligence units, intranet departments, knowledge resource centers, content management organizations, and others.

—*Competencies for Information Professionals of the 21st Century*, rev. ed., June 2003, Special Libraries Association

As we've seen, traditional career paths can offer substantial rewards for those who pursue them. So, too, can nontraditional ones. Because there are so many different ways to approach nontraditional work, it can sometimes be challenging to figure out where to start. And because nontraditional opportunities are limited only by the imagination, the following should be considered only a sampling of possible paths.

For starters, there are a number of ways LIS professionals are reframing their skills in nontraditional ways. These include—

- Doing nontraditional things within a traditional library setting ("traditional," for purposes of this overview, being public, school, and academic)
- Doing traditional library roles but within an organization whose mission is not librarianship or education (usually a special library)
- Doing nontraditional things within traditional special libraries
- Doing these nontraditional activities embedded in operational units
- Doing library-focused activities outside of—but for—libraries and librarians
- Building on skills honed in a library-based job to bridge those skills into a new, nonlibrary role
- Creating your own job, either within a library or for a nonlibrary organization

Performing nontraditional activities within a traditional library setting. The most innovative public, school, and academic libraries offer excellent opportunities to create nontraditional career paths within their structures. This approach is based on taking an entrepreneurial approach to your career and looking for places to create unique contributions. For example, you might combine a subject expertise with a functional expertise to create your own professional niche.

What might this look like? In your job as a public librarian you might have developed a knack for creating highly effective outreach programs for specific underserved populations. Based on that ability, you might, in addition to creating those programs, decide to put your ideas into a best-practices idea bank that can be made accessible to public librarians throughout the region, if not nationally. You might eventually write articles or a book about unique outreach programs, and how to conceive, plan, and execute them, and then perhaps give workshops to other public librarians in how to do this. You will have created a new role based on your specialized skills, one that adds unique value to your public library employer while also establishing your expertise among other potential employers, clients, or constituencies.

Doing traditional library roles but within an organization whose mission is not librarianship or education. This has been the usual path for special librarians, where an individual or a team of librarians acquires or licenses, organizes, distributes, and maintains information resources that support the strategic goals of the organization. Special librarians' responsibilities generally fall within the categories of:

1. Identifying, aggregating, and managing internal information;
2. gathering, analyzing, synthesizing, and presenting external information; or
3. creating content, systems, and or services and products for internal and/or external use.

Depending on the size of the organization or its library, your specific job responsibilities might include one or all of these. Naturally, the characteristics of your job would also be influenced by what sort of special library you were in—generally, categorized by subject area or discipline covered (aerospace engineering, horticulture, pro rodeo), type of material in the collection (for example, industry standards, original manuscripts, photographs), or type of institution (e.g., corporation, trade association, cultural institution).

Although the centralized *corporate* resource—alternatively called the corporate library, the business or corporate information center, the knowledge center, and/or some other variation thereof—is losing popularity to a distributed or functional-team-based model, there are still many highly successful special libraries. (How many? According to numbers cited by ALA on its "Number of Libraries in the United States" web page, there are more than 9,500, not counting those found within public, academic, or armed forces or government agencies.)[1] Also, many organizations such as trade associations, nonprofits, and cultural institutions continue to employ librarians to support staff and membership inquiries as well as the information-gathering and distribution mandate of the organization.

The number of these types of alternative career paths open to LIS professionals is, in fact, only limited by your imagination. You might, for example, be a library director for a professional medical association; a children's librarian in a natural history museum; a librarian for an alternative magazine; director of a corporate business information center; a librarian for an industry research center; manager of a hospital consumer health information center; the librarian for a regional newspaper; director of library services for a botanic gardens; or information resources specialist for a Native American rights foundation.

Needless to say, special libraries might be located in almost any organization. Some of the most likely candidates are:

- Advertising agencies
- Architecture firms
- Art museums, institutes, and centers
- Consulting firms
- Corporations, medium to large, in all industries
- Correctional institutions (for example, prison libraries)
- Cultural institutions—museums, zoos, historical societies, presidential libraries
- Engineering firms
- Financial services, investment, market analyst, and venture capital firms
- Genealogy organizations
- Government agencies—federal, state, local
- Law firms
- Marketing and public relations (PR) agencies
- Medical libraries of all types including those in:
  - hospitals, university health centers, veterinary centers, and medical research facilities

- health/medical/life sciences companies such as those specializing in pharmaceuticals, bioengineering, or biomechanical devices
- professional associations supporting the medical and health sciences fields
- academic institutions focused on training health professionals such as doctors and nurses

- Military—on a base, as part of an operational unit, or with military academies
- Music libraries, including those for orchestras
- News organizations—print, broadcast
- Nonprofits
- Print media groups—magazine and book publishers
- Private libraries (often owned by individuals, families, clubs, corporations, or foundations)
- Professional and trade associations
- Recruiting (employment) firms
- Religious institutions (for example, churches and synagogues)
- Research institutes and think tanks
- Science and technology firms
- Corporate universities, supporting training and development initiatives
- Theater organizations
- Visual and art resources/film organizations

Doing nontraditional things within traditional special library roles.
Many special librarians find their opportunities to align with organizational strategy have increased as they've been asked to help build learning portals, take on records management, and set up centralized competitive intelligence monitoring systems through the library, among other activities. The focus here is increasingly on collaboration with key functional units within the organization, based on an ability to understand and support the group's strategic mission.

This sort of opportunity depends, however, on your willingness and ability to connect outside the library and get your broad range of strategically valuable skills "on people's radar." Department heads and key decision makers won't know what you can do unless you take the initiative to show them your capabilities.

The range of LIS activities and responsibilities possible within organizations is continually expanding. In addition to the more traditional corporate library work, some of the emerging roles include:

- Managing a physical library or information center, including the traditional activities of user needs assessment, collection development, acquisitions, serials management, electronic content licensing, user training, and document delivery
- Organizing and maintaining a corporate archive

- Designing and delivering training programs for Internet-based business research, whether face-to-face or online

- Leading or supporting creation of an enterprise-wide information architecture for organizing and providing access to enterprise information resources

- Creating and/or managing internal information resources enterprise-wide (may include knowledge databases, internal company communications, databases of employee expertise, customer presentations, client proposals, lab notes and/or engineering drawings, a best-practices/lessons-learned database, and technical reports, among other resources)

- Leading or assisting in process design to ensure that enterprise information resources are available at the point of need, i.e., at key decision points; includes helping other departments use enterprise information strategically

- Collaborating as the information specialist on other departments' projects and/or initiatives (such as new product development or market research)

- Managing external electronic content (may include identifying, evaluating, and licensing appropriate proprietary databases; creating and delivering face-to-face or online end-user training; working with the IT department to structure desktop access for users; participating in vendor training and user groups to stay current with product enhancements)

- Conducting primary and secondary research on individuals, companies, industries, competitive threats, potential opportunities, legislative and regulatory impacts, demographic trends, market share, and similar business drivers

- Creating customized content and/or information products such as executive information updates, internal and/or external newsletters, trend reports, ghost-written presentations/speeches/articles, meeting-prep briefings, executive-level current awareness alerts, issues backgrounders, and company blogs

- Providing synthesis and/or analysis of research findings to use in decision support, for example, trends analysis, scenario forecasting, SWOT analyses (strengths, weaknesses, opportunities, threats), data mining, market opportunity assessment, etc.

Another area of substantial opportunity for LIS professionals is the creation of internal and external online portals. Usually a sort of combination monster website and knowledge database collection, portals provide access to a wide variety of information geared toward supporting an organization's operations (internal) or its constituencies, clients, and/or customers (external). Regardless of whether focusing inward or outward, however, successful organization portals require similar types of work:

- Someone needs to design, test, and implement the portal's information architecture. A taxonomy must be developed, search functionality needs to be considered, metadata standards need to be established, databases need to be created and integrated, content needs to be mapped and managed. Throughout, processes and decisions need to be documented. Navigation tools and search capabilities need to be developed, tested, and refined.

- Someone needs to work with users to test functionality and usability issues, to identify knowledge needs and "nice-to-haves," to consider processes for integrating portal content into work flows and decision points. This assessment work takes place before and after the portal has been launched.

- And someone needs to take responsibility for content issues: what content goes in and why, what content is excluded (and why)? How will content be developed or acquired or licensed and by or from whom? How and by whom will content be maintained? Will archived blogs, electronic discussion lists, communities of practice be part of the portal? As part of thinking through content issues, governance policies and processes will also need to be developed regarding how content owners contribute to the portal.

Depending on their specific skills, LIS professionals are increasingly stepping into all of these roles.

Another area of opportunity for you as an LIS professional is compliance issues related to the Sarbanes–Oxley Act of 2002, which mandates financial reporting requirements for U.S.-based, publicly held businesses. Known variously as SOX, Sarbox, or just Sarbanes–Oxley, this law vaulted the normally low-key world of records management and retention into the front lines of corporate financial and legal procedures. Often many millions of dollars and possible prison terms ride on compliance with government regulations regarding documentation. Not surprisingly, substantial effort is now going into designing foolproof records management systems for storage and retrieval of critical financial documents.

Doing these nontraditional activities embedded in operational units. Although an increasing number of special libraries are falling prey to budget cuts, many smart companies are nevertheless holding on to their intellectual assets by embedding their information experts into functional departments.

These may include marketing (market research skills), business development (competitive intelligence and industry analysis skills), research and development departments (primary and secondary research), product development (patent searching, usability studies), information systems (web portal development, knowledge management systems, information architecture), training and development (online tutorials, best-practices research, best-in-class topic resources), communications/PR (speech-writing, white papers, statistics, quotes), and executive decision support (executive information services, environmental scanning, futures forecasting) among others.

Doing library-focused activities outside of—but for—the library community. Anyone who's worked in a school, public, or academic library for any length of time understands their environments and operations, which makes him or her an invaluable asset to organizations that market products or services to libraries. A quick check with the online *Librarian's Yellow Pages* (www.librariansyellowpages.com) identifies thousands of publications, products, and services under the headings of audio and video; automation; books and periodicals; CD-ROM/DVD-ROM and software; equipment, furnishings and supplies; services; children's, YA, and school librarians' resources; and law librarians' resources. All of these products and services are produced by vendors that employ individuals in product development, marketing, sales and product training, and management—preferably professionals with a working knowledge of the library market.

In addition, a number of consulting, outsourcing, and temporary employment organizations that work with libraries offer yet another career alternative that often provides a high level of scheduling flexibility.

A brief list of types of jobs that are library-focused but outside of libraries includes—

- Account rep/sales for library vendor
- Acquisitions editor for library/info science publisher
- Staffer for library-related association
- Staffer for library network or bibliographic utility, regional or national (for example, OCLC)
- Industry analyst for company tracking LIS/education market
- Consultant (marketing, systems, organizational development)
- Staffer for library employment, placement firm
- Faculty for LIS program
- Vendor trainer

Building on skills honed in a library-based job to bridge those skills into a new, nonlibrary functional role. Have you developed an expertise in project management, team-building, innovative marketing programs, content development, web design and implementation, community relations, or training? These are all skills that are readily portable into new organizations not necessarily associated with librarianship. A library director has the same skills necessary to run a nonprofit; a public library webmaster can be equally valuable for a start-up company; an instructional services librarian in an academic library can port these skills into another organization's training department.

This career option presents an interesting dilemma for a lot of LIS professionals. Many of us feel so much a part of the LIS community and its values that working in a field where we're no longer connected to it would feel, well, weird (at best). Others might be ready for just such a change.

Create your own. Identify a need on the part of a potential client or employer and apply your skill set to create a solution, resulting in a paying project or job. In her book *Thriving in 24/7* (Free Press, 2001), business consultant Sally Helgesen points out the importance of "thinking in terms of markets," that is, focusing on the project or workplace need rather than on "bosses, chains of command, lines of report, or tasks that must be completed." Using this approach allows you to create work that "involves a shift from doing work that has been assigned to selling work that you design and believe has value."

How do you go about creating your own work? Once you become familiar with an organization and its goals, processes, markets, issues, etc., start looking for unmet needs. (This assumes, of course, that you have already done such a great job in your current position that you're seen as a reliable, responsible, and capable professional.) Think creative, think strategic, and see if there's a role you can design that allows you to contribute to your organization in a new way. Write up your ideas in a proposal that focuses on benefits to the enterprise, ways your new responsibilities will align with strategic goals, and key aspects of the job you envision. Assume you'll be hit with questions about salary, title, handling current job or project responsibilities, and other "what abouts," and be prepared to answer them thoughtfully and with confidence.

Creating your own job is one of the most rewarding ways to grow your career. It lets you define work parameters that reflect your unique skills and abilities. Since the job you're describing hasn't been previously codified into anyone's HR manual, you often have much greater flexibility in terms of title and salary. And you get the challenge of taking on new work and making it your own, instead of following the path that countless others before you have laid down.

Building a Nontraditional Path

Here's an example of how some of these options might play out for someone who works in a public library doing reference and patron Internet training but also has a background in medicine. Some of these activities could be done full-time, some part-time, or as a sideline to your regular job.

- Become a corporate librarian or information specialist for bioengineering, veterinary medicine, pharmaceutical company

- Become a consumer-health specialist for a public library system, developing patron programs, online research guides, and a collection-development alerting service for all of the system's libraries, and/or create a service based on these components that can be offered to all public libraries nationwide

- Develop a research-oriented service for vets and/or doctors, creating information guides for their patients describing illnesses, treatments, and recommended resources (print and online) and/or create an alerting service for the vets and doctors on topics specific to their practices

- Become a librarian or information specialist for a medical/healthcare-oriented trade or professional association, and/or establish an "on-demand" research capability for the organization's membership, branded to the association

- Do research and analysis for a market research or investment firm specializing in the medical, healthcare, and/or consumer health industries

- Create and teach an online course on medical research for one of the online nursing or LIS programs

Obviously, not all of these ideas would be appropriate for every individual, but they illustrate ways to think about possibilities. Also, keep in mind that none of these necessarily requires a lifelong commitment, or a permanent change away from a traditional library career. Instead, they may simply be steps in developing a dynamic, diverse, and resilient career as an information professional. Defining myself as an information strategist today does not mean I can't choose to become certified as a school librarian five years from now. The goal is to design a career flexible enough that it can grow *with* you, rather than *keep* you from growing.

Workplace Environment

Nontraditional LIS work can be fun, challenging, and offer opportunities to engage in activities well beyond your comfort zone. Because you're surrounded by colleagues who rarely understand what information professionals do or know, you may be either underestimated or highly valued, depending on how good you are at positioning your skills strategically (more on that later).

Unlike in many traditional libraries, a career in a nontraditional setting may allow you more flexibility in terms of job definition and structure, hours scheduling, and career growth. With less rigidly structured job categories, nontraditional positions may allow you to take on new opportunities and higher-level responsibilities more quickly than if you were in a public, academic, or school library.

You may be with a nonprofit, you may be working for a commercial entity, but whether you're engaged in primary research, competitive intelligence, market analysis, knowledge management, or web-portal design, your goal will be to in some manner help the organization meet its strategic goals. Unless you're working for a nonprofit, the emphasis of all of your work will be on driving bottom-line revenues and profits plus future opportunities for your employer. For a nonprofit, your contribution may help expand membership, expand the visibility or impact of the organization, increase donations (or the number of donors), or directly support the mission of the organization with its constituency.

Although a nontraditional career path can offer stimulation and challenge, it can also be fraught with anxiety, for any number of reasons. First, special librarians are expected to have a very high level of professional knowledge about their topic area, because high-risk decisions (for example, medical decisions, corporate investments) may on occasion rest on their expertise. You'll need to not only know core LIS skills but also have a working knowledge of business basics, and also possess the ability to stay on top of existing and emerging knowledge and information resources in your organization's core discipline. Staying ahead of the knowledge curve can be exhilarating, exhausting, or both—often depending on how the week is going!

Corporate librarians face an additional challenge, as their libraries and information centers are being downsized or dismantled at an alarming rate. Job security simply doesn't exist, no matter how highly regarded the corporate library—or library director. However, offsetting the decline of corporate libraries is the emerging trend of "embedded" information professionals who become part of departmental teams such as marketing or product development or engineering. As part of such a team, your focus will be on accountability, speed, and active contribution. You'll be delivering just-in-time information, rather than collecting just-in-case resources. And you'll be evaluated on measurable outcomes and results, rather than on inputs and credentials.

Types of Work

The types of work—and job titles—involved in a nontraditional career are diverse and constantly growing, as creative information professionals come up with new, innovative ways to use their skill sets. But a selective list of some real-life positions and activities culled from job listings, colleagues, listserv postings, Michelle Mach's *Job Title Generator* (http://www.librarian-image.net/titles.pdf), and recruiting agencies includes the following items:

Abstract and/or annotation writer
Account representative (vendor)
Acquisitions editor (for information-industry publisher)
Archivist/curator
Association staffer for a library-related association
Associate director for information and technology
Bibliographer
Bibliographic database manager
Bibliographic instruction coordinator
Bibliographic utility staffer
Bioinformatics librarian
Business/industry analyst
Business information center director
Business information specialist
Business intelligence director
Cataloging/metadata librarian
Category architect
Chief information officer (CIO)
Chief knowledge officer (CKO)
Community website coordinator
Competitive intelligence
Consulting services (to libraries or organizations)
Consumer health librarian
Content developer
Content manager
Coordinator for assessment and continuous improvement
Coordinator, information services
Corporate information specialist
Corporate librarian
Corporate research librarian
Cybrarian
Current awareness manager
Curriculum materials librarian
Data services specialist
Database developer, editor, manager
Data mining
Designer—search and navigation tools
Developer of multimedia products

Development and community relations officer
Digital acquisitions coordinator
Digital archivist
Digital rights manager
Digitization specialist
Director of research services
Distance learning consultant
Distance librarian
Document manager
Economic intelligence specialist
Editor
Electronic content manager
Electronic products manager
Electronic resources cataloger
Electronic text and imaging center coordinator
Employment and placement services
Executive information services provider
Faculty member
Focus group leader
Genealogy librarian, genealogist
GIS specialist
Government information specialist
Grant writer, grants manager
Head, scholarly publishing office
Human resources librarian
Imaging coordinator
Indexer/abstractor
Information advisor
Information analyst
Information architect
Information project manager
Information research analyst
Information resources specialist
Information specialist
Information strategist
Instructional designer
Internet research specialist
Knowledge architect
Knowledge consultant
Knowledge manager

Knowledge network specialist
Learning resources team leader
Legal research specialist
Legislative analyst
Library personnel and consulting
  services (systems, website
  development, etc.)
Magazine librarian, director of
  research services
Management information systems
  (MIS) director
Manager, external content
Manager, electronic text and
  imaging center
Manager, library & learning
  technology groups
Market analyst
Market intelligence specialist
Market researcher
Medical indexer
Medical records manager
Metadata development specialist
Network administrator
Network services coordinator
Newspaper librarian
Regional or national network staffer
  (e.g., OCLC)
Online librarian
Online research specialist
Organizational development
  consultant for libraries
Patent searcher
Personal research assistant
Photoarchivist
Policy analyst

Preservation specialist
Primary research specialist
Private investigator
Product analyst
Product manager for information
  product
Prospect researcher
Public records specialist
Records manager
Regional library network
  manager
Research analyst
Research associate/manager/
  director
Research institute/think-tank
  librarian
Resource center manager
Risk management researcher
Sales associate for library or
  information product/service
  vendor
Senior information analyst
Software developer for information
  management product
State historical society librarian
Systems analyst
Taxonomist
Technical writer
Trainer (for example, for vendor
  products, or within an
  organization)
User interaction manager, software
  company
Virtual reference specialist
Web portal designer/manager

What these jobs entail varies from employer to employer (and often project to project). However, you can get a good sense of the breadth of each by running these specific titles through job posting sites, including those specific to the LIS profession as well as the general and nonprofit sites. The individual listings should provide descriptions that indicate the job's scope, responsibilities, and requisite skills. Many will also indicate where these roles are located within the various organizations.

Salary and Education

One of the advantages of a nontraditional career path is that just as job descriptions may be more flexible, so may be the salaries. *In general*, salaries for information professionals within nonlibrary organizations are higher—and more negotiable—than they would be for similar levels of responsibility within traditional libraries. In addition, there is often more room to negotiate nonsalary benefits, such as vacation time, flex-hours, professional development support and tuition reimbursement, etc.

According to the most recent SLA salary survey (2005), salaries for U.S.-based special librarians range from roughly $39,860 to $98,760, with an average salary of $65,482. For Canadian respondents, the salary range is $43,000 to $84,600, with an average of $63,083 Canadian.[2]

Although there will obviously be positions whose salaries are much lower—or higher—than the ranges indicated in the SLA survey, these numbers are a good indicator of what you might expect from nontraditional work.

In terms of education? Welcome to the world of lifelong learning. One of the greatest challenges—and delights—of a nontraditional career path is the ongoing need to expand and enrich your knowledge base. As noted, you'll need to have strong mastery of the basic LIS skills: depending on your position, this may include information research, organization, analysis, and presentation; content development and/or management; and/or system design and implementation.

You'll need to be familiar with basic business concepts, operations, and strategy in order to most effectively contribute to the goals of your organization, even if it's a nonprofit. And you'll need to understand the industry in which your organization exists, as well as its wealth of information resources. Needless to say, all of these are moving targets, so you'll want to have a strategy in place that enables you to keep up with the dynamic knowledge environment that defines information work.

For those following nontraditional career paths, the primary career resource is the Special Libraries Association (SLA), which provides professional development, networking, advocacy, and standards for its members. In recognition of the broad but varied expertise required by a nontraditional career, SLA created *Competencies for Information Professionals of the 21st Century* (rev. ed., June 2003), a document that identifies three types of competencies: professional, personal, and core competencies.

For professional competencies, SLA identified key abilities in four areas: managing information organizations, managing information resources, managing information services, and applying information tools and technologies. Among personal competencies, it noted items within a "set of attitudes, skills, and values." And among core competencies, SLA stipulated that information professionals make a commitment to—

- contributing to the knowledge base of the profession by sharing best practices and experiences, and continue to learn about information products, services, and management practices throughout the life of his/her career; and

- professional excellence and ethics, and to the values and principles of the profession.[3]

In addition to its detailed overview of key nontraditional LIS skills, *Competencies for Information Professionals of the 21st Century* also interprets those competencies in applied scenarios that demonstrate how each competency works in real life. You'll want to check these guidelines out—they provide a thoughtful and comprehensive overview of what today's (and tomorrow's) information professionals need to succeed. This document can be accessed at www.sla.org/content/learn/comp2003/index.cfm.

Exploring Nontraditional LIS Careers

As noted, nontraditional careers are basically limited only by your imagination, so when exploring the possible paths, you can be equally creative. As before, you'll want to combine two actions: gathering information and assessing your reaction to that information, as recorded in your career journal.

- To get a sense of job requirements for specific positions that might be of interest to you, go to several of the library employment sites and run specific job titles (for example, any of those listed under "Types of Work" in this chapter). What skills and education do they require? Do the activities they describe appeal to you? What types of organizations offer these sorts of nontraditional jobs? Which ones do your current career skills align with? Which ones do your passions and interests align with? Can you imagine yourself doing this type of work?

  Also try running these job titles through some of the non-LIS job sites such as Monster.com. Note your findings in your career journal, and start building "job profiles" or descriptions for specific job types that interest you.

- Join SLA (if you're a student, use your student discount!) so you can network with LIS professionals in nontraditional roles in your geographic region and learn more about the work they do. Set up information interviews, and ask questions that help define both the specifics of the jobs and their possible "goodness of fit" for you. (To get started, refer back to the interview questions suggested in the last chapter.)

- Once you've joined SLA, begin exploring the wealth of professional development resources on its website. With multiple communities of interest, career guides, and topic resources, this is an easy and effective way to check out paths that may engage you. Note any areas of particular interest, and consider joining the appropriate communities of interest to learn more.

- On an occasional basis, monitor the key LIS job sites to see (1) what new job titles people are using to describe nontraditional positions, and (2) what departments these jobs fall within.

- If you're a student, organize a "special librarians' day" seminar and have local special librarians and nontraditional LIS professionals come and talk about their work and careers. Be prepared with questions that elicit information of value to your career exploration, and record responses in your career journal. Be sure to send each speaker a thank-you note, and considering following up with those whose career choices and paths most interest you.

- Also if you're a student, interview several local nontraditional LIS professionals about their jobs and careers, with a focus on such questions as how they got their jobs, what skills they most rely on, what they wish they'd learned in grad school, what opportunities they see for LIS professionals, and perhaps other ways in which their organizations might use LIS skill sets. Then write up your findings for your student newsletter or listserv, as well as noting key points in your career journal.

- Now that you've gathered information, take some time to exercise your imagination. If a nontraditional path might be of interest, consider your "dream job," and all of its characteristics. Using the preference filters you worked through in Chapter 2, describe the specifics of both the work that you do and the environment in which you do it. Do you work with a small team or a large organization? Do you travel a lot? Is your work solitary or highly collaborative and engaged with others? Are you in a facilities-based library or working for a community organization or a corporate enterprise? What contribution are you making? Be as detailed and concrete as possible, so you can begin to build a profile of what your optimum nontraditional situation would be. Why? Because if you are considering this option, one of your biggest challenges will be to narrow down the choices to the ones that best fit you—so the more you know, the easier that will be.

Why You Might Love a Nontraditional Career Path

A nontraditional career path can be exciting, financially rewarding, full of exhilarating challenges, and ripe with opportunities to create, innovate, and chart new territory. To a much greater extent than with a traditional career path, you'll be in charge of your own agenda. You'll often be able to negotiate your salary, benefits, and work schedule, and you may end up expanding the borders of your existing position if not creating an entirely new job description. The opportunities are potentially huge, and based to a large degree on your smarts, creativity, and ability to create solutions with your skills.

On the other hand, a nontraditional career can also be chaotic, unpredictable, unreliable, and crazy-making. Impossible deadlines and last-minute crises can be a regular feature of some of these jobs. There is often the professional isolation of being the only LIS professional in the organization, there is essentially *no* job security and often no visible path for professional advancement, and there are frequently no seasoned info pros to mentor you up through the ranks. In order to have a successful nontraditional career, you'll need to take charge of your agenda, create your own opportunities, set your own priorities, and get used to continually demonstrating the value you deliver. You'll be out of your comfort zone on a regular basis.

Take, for example, the range of activities that make up the job of *Utne* magazine librarian Chris Dodge: he manages a collection of over 1,400 active periodicals; does reference and research to support editorial staff and freelance writers; participates in weekly editorial team meetings, writes the bimonthly "Street Librarian" column; creates bibliographies; connects the editorial team with publications, articles, information; and fosters connections with the community, especially alternative independent presses and librarians who collect their works. In his spare time, Dodge is a passionate voice for the activist librarian movement.

Or consider the work of Cindy Hill, Manager of the Sun Microsystems library and past-president of the Special Libraries Association. She had originally pursued her MLIS in order to become an elementary school librarian after beginning in the profession as a library assistant in her local public library. Asked about her current position as the head of a high-tech, international company's corporate library, Hill said:

> *Why do I continue having this strong emotion about my choice of profession? The number one reason is that it's all about collaboration and working with people. I enjoy finding and developing relationships with our external partners (content providers and others), internal partners (clients, IT, teams and business units with which we can share best practices and knowledge), and the library team so that we can provide the best resources and services to our clients.*

Comparing school and corporate librarianship, Hill pointed out that although "at first I didn't realize that there are many similarities between the two environments," she later found that "both groups are ones with which long-term relationships can be formed. In the school environment you're continually with the same students, teachers and parents, usually for several years. In the corporate world, you're also with a group of people for many years, providing a similar opportunity."

Not all jobs have quite this diversity of opportunity and collaboration, of course, but many of them come close. Might this be a path for you? Possibly—if you thrive on change and challenge, are comfortable being in charge of your own outcomes, don't mind working outside of the library community, like to learn new things, and are okay moving *very fast* when the circumstances demand. It can be a great option for individuals who do better with projects than with routine work, or those who feel constrained by the more structured career paths of traditional librarianship.

Resources

Books

Bates, Mary Ellen and Reva Basch. *Super Searchers Do Business.* Cyberage Books, 1999. 207 pp. ISBN 0910965331.

The *Super Searchers* books all follow the same format: industry experts are interviewed about the work they do, how they do it (approaches, processes, and tools), and what tips and advice they'd give others trying to develop skills in the specific skill area. Resources cited within the profiles are then compiled at the end of the book for a consolidated "hit-list" of best-in-class topic sources. Although the online resources may become outdated fairly quickly, the "how-to" information from successful practitioners remains quite valuable. Other useful titles in this series include . . . *Go to the Source, . . . on Wall Street, . . . on Competitive Intelligence, . . . Cover the World,* and . . . *on Health & Medicine,* among many others. Check the publisher's site (http://books.infotoday.com/books/index.shtml) for a full listing. Especially valuable for LIS professionals who want to expand their business and industry research skills.

Goleman, Daniel. *Business: The Ultimate Resource.* Perseus, 2004. 2,208 pp. ISBN 0738202428.

There is so much information packed into this monster reference book that the phrase "MBA in a box" springs to mind. For those of us working in business environments but lacking its background and language, this work provides a brief but useful overview of nearly every business operations and management topic imaginable. Topic contributors are recognizable leaders in their field, and their articles are supplemented by a 5,000-entry dictionary, a 3,000-entry resources section, and industry overviews and numerous biographies. A key resource for quickly developing an understanding of how the business world operates. See also its companion title, *The Best Business Books Ever: The 100 Most Influential Business Books You'll Never Have Time to Read* (Perseus, 2003), which will quickly bring you up to speed on the most quoted and respected business works.

Mount, Ellis and Renee Massoud. *Special Libraries and Information Centers: An Introductory Text.* 4th ed. Special Libraries Association, 1999. 334 pp. ISBN 0871115018.

With a goal of "serving as an introduction to the nature and operation of special libraries and information centers," this textbook leads off with an overview of both and then groups the remaining chapters under the broad areas of management, user services, technical services, collections, library facilities and equipment, and professional activities and networks. An appendix profiles ten special-library practitioners and three info pros in alternative positions. Although in need of an update, this is still an excellent resource for understanding special librarianship.

Scott, David Meerman. *Cashing in With Content: How Innovative Marketers Use Digital Information to Turn Browsers Into Buyers.* Information Today, 2005. 256 pp. ISBN 0910965714.

Scott surveys the best practices of twenty organizations—both for-profit and nonprofit—who have learned how to use online content to drive the strategic goals of the organization. These might include creating a revenue stream through online sales by offering reference materials and user support content at the website, providing compelling narratives that increase online donations for community organizations, or offering online proprietary information and analysis to members only as a means of incenting people to join an organization. Almost all of the roles discussed in Scott's book are ones that LIS professionals could easily step into.

Periodicals

Information Outlook. Special Libraries Association, 1997– . Monthly. ISSN 1091–0808.

Formerly titled *Special Libraries* (1910–1996), SLA's official publication provides a forum for showcasing best practices, discussing emerging issues, and supporting information professionals across the diverse range of job responsibilities reflected in the SLA membership.

In addition to the more general approach of *Information Outlook*, almost all of the associations described below provide publications (print or online) that address their specific practice areas.

Articles

"Alternative Careers" issue, *InfoCareerTrends*, March 2005
http://www.lisjobs.com/newsletter/archives.htm
A collection of articles written by alternative-career practitioners. See also the September 2003 issue ("Branching Out") and the November 2002 issue ("Specialization").

Wallace, Linda K. "Places an MLS Can Take You," *American Libraries*, vol. 32, no. 3 (March 2002), pp. 44–48.
Profiles eleven individuals who have taken their MLIS degrees in unique directions, with a description of the type of work they do and how they landed their positions. Can be accessed online at www.ala.org/ala/hrdr/careersinlibraries/al_mls.pdf.

Associations

American Association of Law Libraries (AALL)
www.aallnet.org
AALL represents more than 5,000 professionals working in "law firms; law schools; corporate legal departments; courts; and local, state and federal government agencies." Check the website for information about AALL; its caucuses, chapters, and special interest sections; AALL online professional development offerings; and its "Competencies of Law Librarianship" statement, especially valuable for students considering this career path. Steeply discounted student memberships available.

American Society of Indexers (ASI)
www.asindexing.org
Founded in 1968, ASI promotes excellence in indexing, abstracting, and database-building. The ASI website offers a directory listing of indexers, links to resources of interest to indexers, articles and position papers about indexing, and information about ASI's special interest groups, which offer an interesting range of specializations (business, psychology/sociology, sports/fitness, culinary, web, gardening/environmental, among others). No student membership discount, although a slight discount is offered to new members.

American Theological Library Association (ATLA)
www.atla.com
ATLA's more than 1,000 members—individual, institutional, and affiliate—draw from all avenues of theological and religious study, regardless of denomination. It supports an extremely active publishing mandate, which includes the highly regarded ATLA Religion database and related products. Hosts an annual conference and supports professional development seminars. Steeply discounted student memberships.

Art Libraries Society of North America (ARLIS / NA)
www.arlisna.org
ARLIS/NA describes itself as "a dynamic organization of over 1,000 individuals devoted to fostering excellence in art librarianship and visual resources curatorship for the advancement of visual arts." It hosts an annual conference, supports an electronic forum that includes job postings (ARLIS-L), and publishes a semiannual print publication (*Art*

Documentation), among other activities. Divisions (academic, art & design school, museum, visual resources), sections (architecture, cataloging, reference & information services), and roundtables (book arts, decorative arts, gay & lesbian interests, management, new art, public librarians, serials, space planners, women and art) let members connect with special interests. Check the website for publications (fee-based). Substantial student membership discount.

Association for Information and Image Management (AIIM)
www.aiim.org
AIIM now subtitles itself "the ECM Association," so it can clearly position itself in the Enterprise Content Management space, which it defines as the "technologies used to capture, manage, store, preserve, and deliver content and documents related to organization processes." The association publishes a number of resources, offers topic-focused electronic discussion groups, and professional development resources. Don't miss the really cool poster (www.aiim.org/poster/puzzleposter.html), which lays out the ECM landscape (with definitions). An indication of how much this discipline has changed it that AIIM was originally founded in 1943 as the National Microfilm Association. No student membership discount.

Association of Moving Image Archivists (AMIA)
www.amianet.org
A fairly young organization (established 1991), AMIA represents more than 750 members "concerned with the acquisition, preservation, exhibition and use of moving image materials." The organization supports education and publication initiatives, hosts an annual conference, establishes and disseminates standards, and fosters collaboration throughout the world. Check the website for a wealth of publicly available information about best practices as well as an overview of the state of education for moving image archivists. Steeply discounted student memberships.

Association of Prospect Researchers for Advancement (APRA)
www.aprahome.org
Per APRA, "advancement researchers are the development officers on the front line of data management, uniquely positioned—and qualified—to gather, interpret, analyze, and disseminate the information critical to securing support for nonprofit organizations." APRA's more than 2,100 members can take advantage of its educational programs, networking opportunities, publications, and career resources. For the latter, see especially the Career Resources section of the APRA website, which describes requisite skill sets, summarizes results of a member-characteristics survey, and has a job postings directory. No student discount for memberships.

Association of Records Managers and Administrators (ARMA)
www.arma.org
ARMA has evolved from a not-too-visible group of highly capable records-management types into one of the most important and respected organizations on the front lines of the compliance (Sarbanes–Oxley) issue. Records managers have always been experts in how to organize, maintain, and provide access to all sorts of organization records. But they're also specialists in critical issues like records retention, legal and regulatory compliance, disaster recovery, electronic storage,

and corporate digitization initiatives. ARMA should hold special interest for LIS students and professionals interested in the intersection of technology, business, records, and legal issues. The ARMA website primarily features information about the organization, but exploring the resources on the site will also turn up useful overviews of many records-related topics. Steeply discounted student memberships.

Business Reference and Services Section (BRASS)
www.ala.org/ala/rusa/rusaourassoc/rusasections/brass/brass.htm
One of the largest, most active, and most influential special interest groups, BRASS membership includes "reference librarians, business information specialists, and others engaged in providing business reference and information services." Check the content-rich website for the section's "Core Competencies for Business Reference" and the annotated collection of topically organized "Best of the Business Web Sites." You can elect to join BRASS as part of your ALA membership.

Canadian Association of Special Libraries and Information Services (CASLIS)
www.cla.ca/caslis/index.htm
The diverse membership of CASLIS includes special libraries personnel, information specialists, documentalists, vendors, and others involved in delivering special library services throughout the country. A division of the Canadian Library Association.

Church and Synagogue Library Association (CSLA)
http://wa-net.com/~csla
CSLA has an exceptionally strong mission of information dissemination in service of its members' needs. To this end, it offers CSLA members training sessions, publications, a peer community, an annual conference focused on continuing professional education and networking, a monthly publication, and a series of topical guides in areas such as selecting and cataloging materials, reference services, and handling archival materials. There is no student discount, but individual annual memberships are a very modest $35.00.

Major Orchestra Librarians Association (MOLA)
www.mola-inc.org
Established in 1873, MOLA has as its primary focus improving communication among orchestra librarians, with a secondary focus of "assisting librarians in providing better service to their orchestras, presenting a unified voice in publisher relations, and providing support and information to the administrations of performing arts organizations." Its annual conference offers education and networking opportunities, a quarterly newsletter highlights issues of common interest, and an electronic discussion list keeps members in touch. If this is a potential career choice for you, be sure to read "The Orchestra Librarian: A Career Introduction," listed under Resources > Publications (be patient; it's slow to load). Member dues are based on the budget size and type of orchestra, but apprentice memberships for students who are accepted into the organization are a quite reasonable $20 per year.

Medical Library Association (MLA)
www.mlanet.org
Over 100 years old, MLA has more than 4,700 individual and institutional members based in the health sciences information field. Focus areas include education of health information professionals; health

information research; and promoting universal access to health sciences information, national and international. The MLA website includes information about the organization, a solid collection of career information resources, and descriptions of and links to the association's two dozen sections (e.g., cancer librarians, dental section, hospital libraries, and medical informatics). Steeply discounted student memberships.

Music Library Association (MLA)
www.musiclibraryassoc.org
Music librarians can be found in "large research libraries such as the Library of Congress or the New York Public Library; in the music section or branch library in universities, colleges, and conservatories; in public libraries; in radio and television station libraries; with music publishers and dealers; with musical societies and foundations; and with bands and orchestras." The MLA represents librarians from all of these arenas, with a focus on music librarianship, its materials, and its careers. For those interested in music librarianship as a possible career path, check out "Music Librarianship—Is It For You?" on the website. Steeply discounted student memberships.

National Association of Government Archives and Records Administrators (NAGARA)
www.nagara.org
The association is dedicated to the improvement of federal, state, and local government records and information management. NAGARA supports this mission through an annual conference; quarterly publications that address trends and issues at the national, state, and local levels; numerous govdocs initiatives, and various continuing education opportunities. The website primarily describes NAGARA and its activities, but has also a brief but useful collection of association links under the Related Organizations section. No discounted memberships for students.

National Association of Media and Technology Centers (NAMTC)
www.namtc.org
NAMTC members include regional, K-12, and higher education media/tech centers, plus the vendors who work with them. The organization's focus is to promote leadership through "networking, advocacy, and support activities that will enhance the equitable access to media, technology, and information services to educational communities." Check out the website for information and resources related to motion/digital media and copyright, as well as a glossary of two dozen acronyms.

Society for Competitive Intelligence Professionals (SCIP)
www.scip.org
Competitive intelligence (CI) is an important component of business research across all industries and businesses. SCIP membership comprises both independents and CI specialists who work for businesses, so there is a broad range of experience and knowledge to share within the group. Check the website under CI Resources for salary information, white papers, articles, career information, and several overviews of the CI process. Steeply discounted student membership fees for full-time students only.

Society of American Archivists (SAA)
    www.archivists.org
    With over 4,000 members, SAA is an extremely active organization
    in terms of member education, publications, development of policies
    and standards, and taking a leadership role in the emerging electronic
    records environment. Check the SAA website for a list of the society's
    sections and roundtables, career information, and numerous informa-
    tion resources related to archives work. Substantial discount for stu-
    dent members.

Theatre Library Association (TLA)
    http://tla.library.unt.edu
    Since 1937, TLA has supported librarians, curators, and archivists
    working with collections in the areas of theater, dance, performance
    studies, popular entertainment, motion pictures, and broadcasting. It
    achieves its mission of "development and promotion of professional li-
    brary expertise and standards" through annual conferences and other
    meetings, publications, book awards, an electronic discussion group,
    and affiliation with related organizations. The TLA website focuses pri-
    marily on information about the organization, but it also has an exten-
    sive unannotated listing of theater-related resources. There is a modest
    student membership discount, but the dues are already exceptionally
    inexpensive.

Online Resources

Alternative Careers Workshop
    http://studentorg.cua.edu/asis/march98.htm
    Five presentations given by panelists at a workshop sponsored jointly
    by ASIS, AGLISS, and SLA. The panelists, all of whom were using
    their MLS degrees in alternative ways, discussed the type of work they
    do, how they ended up doing it, the benefits and drawbacks of their
    career choices, and the job prospects for MLS graduates in their areas
    of practice.

Best of the Lists
    www.montague.com/review/buslibbest.html
    Hosted by the The Montague Institute, a company that consults on
    "knowledge base consulting," this list aggregates posts from multiple
    electronic discussion lists under broad topics of interest to information
    professionals. These include managing information, organizing infor-
    mation, product reviews, and tips and techniques (competitive intelli-
    gence, current awareness, importing S.I.C. codes into a database, etc.).
    The site also provides a "where to find it" section with articles (gener-
    ally from BUSLIB-L) on finding things like analyst studies, case stud-
    ies, and intranet standards.

*Choosing Law Librarianship: Thoughts for People Contemplating a Career
    Move*
    www.llrx.com/features/librarian.htm
    Written by law librarian Mary Whisner in 1999, this excellent article
    will still resonate today for those contemplating a career in law librar-
    ianship. Whisner addresses all the key issues—pay, characteristics of
    the work, and the importance of both law and library degrees to career
    success.

Competencies for Information Professionals of the 21st Century
www.sla.org/content/learn/comp2003/index.cfm
Revised in June 2003, this document represents the best thinking among leading special librarians as to what skills, abilities, and attitudes best define today's (and tomorrow's) successful and effective special librarian. It groups these within the frameworks of professional competencies, personal competencies, and core competencies, and for each defines what each competency entails and how it demonstrates itself in practical application through "applied scenarios." Competencies include managing information organizations, managing information resources, and managing information services, among others. A must-read for anyone in the special library world, and an insightful guide for students considering this career path.

Education & Careers
www.aallnet.org/services
Excellent, content-rich collection of articles and overviews of a career in legal librarianship, from the American Association of Law Libraries.

IU SLIS Job Successes
www.slis.indiana.edu/careers/view_jobsuccess.php
Interesting listing of jobs that MLIS grads have taken, most of which are nontraditional. A great place for all students to research possible alternative career paths, even though it focuses solely on the experiences of graduates from Indiana University's School of Library and Information Science.

SLA Career Center
http://sla.jobcontrolcenter.com
A content-rich site that includes job listings, a spot to post resumes, access to virtual advisors, articles and resources, and data from the most recent salary survey. Some of the content is members-only, but there is sufficient freely available material to make the Career Center a useful visit for nonmembers as well.

Special Libraries Management Handbook: The Basics
www.libsci.sc.edu/bob/class/clis724/SpecialLibrariesHandbook/INDEX.htm
This is a fascinating collaborative project authored by the students in a Special Libraries and Information Centers course at the University of South Carolina College of Library and Information Science. The handbook consists of contributed "chapters" written by the students over a five-year period (1999–2004) on such topics as "communicating with upper level management," "instruction issues in special libraries," "online vendor selection," and "starting a special library from scratch." The range of topics covered is quite diverse, and although this isn't an "authoritative" source, it is so well executed that it is quite useful.

Notes

1. "ALA Library Fact Sheet 1—Number of Libraries in the United States." American Library Association. 2005. Accessed at www.ala.org/ala/alalibrary/libraryfactsheet/alalibraryfactsheet1.htm on November 3, 2005.

2. "2005 SLA Salary Survey." Special Libraries Association, 2005. Accessed at www.sla.org/content/resources/research/salarysurveys/salsur2005/index.cfm on November 3, 2005.

3. "Competencies for Information Professionals of the 21st Century." Rev. ed. Special Libraries Association, 2003, p. 4. Accessed at www.sla.org/content/learn/comp2003/index.cfm on November 3, 2005.

5
The Independent Path

... librarians are applying their information management and research skills to ... database development, reference tool development, information systems, publishing, Internet coordination, marketing, web content management and design, and training of database users. Entrepreneurial librarians ... start their own consulting practices, acting as freelance librarians or information brokers and providing services to other libraries, businesses, or government agencies.
—Occupational Outlook Handbook, 2005

So far, we've considered traditional librarianship and the broad range of jobs within school, public, and academic libraries, as well as the incredible diversity of nontraditional LIS career possibilities. In addition, almost any aspect of information work can be done as an independent.

This path can be as simple as doing the work you've previously done as an employee, but doing it instead as a newly minted contractor. Or it can mean starting a new product or service business—alone or with colleagues—based on expertise you've gained along the way as an LIS professional.

In addition, there are many different approaches to working as an independent. You might work with a single client, for example, being a contract substitute librarian for one library district. Or you might become a "solo," a one-person shop offering your services, for example, as a freelance indexer to publishers around the country.

On the other hand, you might want to build a business that includes several employees, thereby extending your company's ability to handle multiple clients and projects simultaneously. Or you might decide you'd rather not take on the management and overhead of employees, so as an alternative you decide instead to join a loose network of information pros who come together on a project basis, participating based on the expertise needed on specific projects.

Alternatively, you might prefer to sign up with a "temp" agency that specializes in information work. This strategy lets someone else worry about the marketing, management and client relationships, while you simply show up and do the work (performing at the highest level of excellence, of course!).

The bottom line is, all the choices are completely up to you: what work you do, how you do it, what markets or clients you go after (as well as, occasionally, what clients you fire), what you charge, how you grow/expand your business (if this is a goal for you). These are but some of the major choices you'll make as an independent.

What Work Would You Do?

Consider all the things that traditional librarians do, from cataloging to reference to indexing to bibliographic instruction to research. All of these can be—and have been—done on a contract basis, either for traditional libraries or special libraries. (Remember, in an era of downsizing, outsourcing key activities to competent LIS contractors is one of the best ways for organizations to continue to get the necessary work done.)

Then consider those activities described for the nontraditional path— these are all candidates for freelance or contract work as well. The emphasis on strategic management of knowledge assets means businesses increasingly need people who know meta-tagging, know how to build taxonomies, know how to research international market opportunities, know how to research and write white papers, know how to do competitive intelligence, know how to analyze and summarize key information. A lot of this work is done on a project basis by outside contractors ... such as you.

Or, think about doing these same sorts of activities within a broader context. For example, your expertise in marketing libraries might turn into a consulting business developing marketing plans for nonprofits and cultural institutions. Years you spent designing and implementing your academic library's web portal could translate into a business developing websites for alumni associations or career colleges. A successful track record as a bibliographic instruction librarian might launch you on an independent path as a corporate or association trainer or an online teacher or a freelance creator of online tutorials for businesses.

Other examples might include freelance cataloging; creating and maintaining research guides and online tutorials for virtual libraries; developing web portals and online communities for clients; launching an information brokerage or freelance research company; providing current awareness services for start-ups in emerging industries; being a consulting editor for one of the library-focused publishing companies; or doing freelance prospect (i.e., donor) research for a nonprofit.

Independents have pursued careers as freelance booktalkers and/or storytellers, manuscript evaluators and consulting acquisitions editors, adjunct faculty (classroom-based or online), library building consultants, organizational development consultants, writers (books, articles, and online content), workshop and seminar presenters, and grant writers. Some of my colleagues have set up and maintained technical libraries for local tech firms, cataloged personal libraries for wealthy clients, specialized in market research or patent searching, taken on systems and networking projects, built reputations as freelance legal researchers, provided research training to specialized groups, done trend analysis for marketing companies, written position papers for nonprofits, worked as freelance genealogists, edited manuscripts for LIS publishers, put together research guides for virtual libraries, done contract cataloging—all based on skills they've developed as LIS professionals.

Regardless of what service you offer, you may want to keep in mind the differing perceptions of the terms freelancer, contractor, and consultant. Generally, in the business world someone who does freelance work is assumed to be doing an occasional activity whose performance standards have been assigned and are monitored by project supervisors. A contractor is someone who may be involved in more complex, higher-level activities that may also involve a long-term project or assignment. A consultant generally comes in at a strategy level, identifying the parameters of a problem and recommending its solution. Sometimes the consultant also implements the solution, although often this is completed either by internal staff or by contractors.

How Would You Work?

Depending on which of the many paths you might choose, your workplace environment can vary wildly. For example, if you worked for clients you'd probably have a working environment that combined either an out-of-home office or home-office space with time spent in your clients' offices. (Some of the best known independent info pros who've chosen the solo option have worked successfully from offices in their homes for years.)

If you'd rather build a business that includes employees, you'd probably find it easiest to lease office space that would accommodate your team (in fact, many residential zoning laws forbid operating such a business from home). If part of a collaborative network, you might all choose to work from your homes or might instead decide to share space and an administrative staffer. And if you were temping, your working environment would change with each new assignment. Some of this work might be virtual, some on-site.

As you think about an independent option, think also about the preferred working environments and arrangements you explored in Chapter 2. If you had the choice (which you would), would you prefer to work from a home office or share office space with other independents? Would you prefer to work regular, consistent 9–5 hours Monday through Friday? Or would you rather take Wednesdays off for skiing, yoga, or golf—and then work several evenings a week to round out your forty hours?

Given the option, would you prefer to work for national clients, which would probably entail a substantial amount of business travel, or for local organizations, which would keep you closer to home on weekends, but possibly also limit the number and size of potential clients?

Would you prefer to work solo or as part of a loose network of colleagues with complementary skills where you could hand off work to each other? Or perhaps as part of a more tightly integrated, collaborative team that could take on larger opportunities and projects as a group? Or perhaps you might choose to contract with an agency that placed you on temporary projects (and also relieved you of any marketing responsibilities)?

Would you plan to work a full-time schedule, or work part-time? Would you be willing to work 24/7 to meet last-minute client deadlines, or instead work only on those projects and activities not likely to interfere with other personal commitments?

These are among the choices you would have as an independent to shape the structure and flow of your worklife.

What Market Would You Target?

Will you focus on the library market, or on clients outside the library world? Specialize in nonprofits, or work only with the telecommunications or healthcare or education industries? Will you specialize in working with government agencies, and develop an expertise in navigating the red tape necessary to secure large and lucrative government contracts? Will your product or service be applicable across a broad range of organizations, or will you be targeting a small niche market?

The answers to these questions will determine how large or small your market segment might be, with corresponding benefits to each choice. A broad-based target market means you'll have lots of potential customers, but reaching them will drive your marketing costs proportionately higher. You may also have greater competition going after a large target market, and it may be more difficult to differentiate your service among those being offered by others. Also, the more competitors in the marketplace, the likelier that your potential clients will expect you to compete with lower prices.

A niche market, on the other hand, offers the benefits of a more tightly focused (and thus less expensive) marketing effort, an easier opportunity to build your brand visibility and reputation, and probably less competition with correspondingly less pressure to lower prices. However, a niche market has one very important drawback. That is, if your product or service is tied to the health and well-being of a particular market segment, and that segment suffers a downturn, so will your business. This is also one of the benefits of targeting a national market rather than a local one. If your focus is on local clients, and your regional economy goes into recession, you have no other markets to turn to.

If your preference is to target a niche market, whether regional, industry-specific, or a particular type of organization, it's still possible to protect against downturns. By keeping an eye out for how your product or service can bridge to new markets and taking initial steps now to create those bridges in terms of market knowledge and contacts, you'll be well prepared should the need arise.

What Would You Charge?

Again, many variables: do your prices need to respond to a competitive environment? Are you working in a geographic location where fees are generally higher or lower than the national average? Will you charge nonprofits less than you charge for-profits? Will you base your fees on what you need to earn to cover your monthly overhead, or on what the market will bear, or on an hourly charge basis that includes your invisible costs such as training/professional development, association memberships, marketing time, etc., plus a reasonable profit?

"How do I price my services" is an ongoing topic among independents, as we struggle to find a formula that is logical, defensible to clients, and applicable in every situation. Oh that it were possible! Instead, we usually end up developing guidelines that shape our pricing approaches to various types of projects.

One of the biggest questions is whether to price by the hour or by the project. Generally speaking, services marketers recommend that you price by the project (after having established internally the hourly rate that you need to cover). The challenge for novices—okay, for experienced independents as well—is to correctly estimate how many hours a given project is likely to take. When you're first starting out, you'll pretty much be guessing. But the more often you've done a certain type of work, the more familiar you'll become with the process and time involved. This will make projects more predictable, and your time estimates much more reliable.

One way to solve this dilemma for those new to contract work is to do a small, representative piece of the project, and see how long it takes. For example, if your project entails processing a corporate archive, try looking at a small but representative set of materials to get a sense of how long it would take to process this selection and what sorts of issues might arise. This then allows you to extrapolate to the entire project and more realistically estimate the time involved. If, for example, one box of documents took you 3 hours to process, and there are fifty boxes, you can estimate that the project may take you 150 hours. Add a 10 percent "unforeseen disasters" margin, to bring you to 165 hours. If you charged \$50/hr., your estimate for the job would be \$8,250 plus approved expenses; at \$100/hr., you'd be in the range of \$16,500.00 (before adding in a profit margin).

Of course, when you get into the project you'll undoubtedly encounter all sorts of challenges that didn't surface in the first run-through, and you'll wish that you'd bid more. But every time you do another project, you'll have a better sense of what to look for—and what contingencies to plan for in your estimate.

Another common approach for business researchers is a "do not exceed" budget, which can range from \$500 to \$2,500, depending on the client's request. The purpose of this type of budget is to allow the researcher to explore a given topic and appropriate resources to see how much information exists and how readily available it is. At the end of, say, a \$500 expenditure of time and database costs, the researcher gets back to the client with his or her findings. This is usually either the information sought, or an assessment of what information is available and next steps (and associated costs) in obtaining that information.

Although there are no perfect answers for pricing that will apply in all situations, the best coverage of pricing issues can be found in Bates' *Building & Running a Successful Research Business*, Chapter 13, "Setting Rates and Fees," as well as in Alan Weiss's *Value-Based Fees: How to Charge—and Get—What You're Worth* (both described in Resources below).

How Would You Get Clients?

This is the really challenging one. Most of us feel fairly confident that we can do the work a client asks of us—once we have that client. But actually *getting* that client is a whole different matter.

Services marketing is, to quote a recent book title, "selling the invisible." As is the case for all independents regardless of profession, assume marketing efforts will generally take up a substantial amount of your work week (at least 40 percent), especially when you're just starting out. And assume you'll be trying all sorts of things to get your message out, establish your brand, and increase your visibility within your target market.

What kinds of things might that include? You'll network mercilessly, attending business luncheons, speaking at professional group meetings, presenting at conferences, and volunteering in the community or with organizations relevant to your market. Some independents find cold-calling effective, while others avoid it at all costs.

An informative, polished, and professional-looking website is imperative, as are business cards and perhaps minimal print collateral (for example, a trifold 8 1/2 × 11 brochure). You may want to consider a quarterly e-newsletter with content relevant to your target audience as a way of staying in their consciousness. Another option is to find pro bono work that allows you to demonstrate your skills to your target audience (and connect with their key issues) in a way that showcases your value to potential clients before you're ready to ask them for paying projects.

Paying close attention to how you "package" your deliverables (for example, the reports you create for your clients) is another way you touch your market. Your goal always is to add value, to reinforce the proposition that you are highly competent, and your contribution to your client's goals of great value. The key here is to focus not simply on delivering data, but on building relationships. The more work that comes to you through existing clients, the less time you'll need to invest in developing new ones.

As with pricing questions, there is no right marketing strategy that fits every circumstance. You'll simply try them all to see what works most effectively for your particular service and market. But the key point is that marketing is a huge commitment for any independent, and if you don't think you'd be able or willing to undertake it, then an independent option probably isn't for you.

How Would You Create and Maintain Your Support Community?

One of the downsides of being an independent can be that generally you're working on your own *a lot*. Although some people thrive on this solitude, others find it can quickly lead to feelings of isolation and loneliness. It's easy to feel—and be—out of the loop of tips and trends and water-cooler conversations, where so much informal knowledge is shared. The trick is to create your *own* water cooler space.

True, they may be virtual, but online communities and electronic discussion groups offer an extremely effective way to reach out and connect with someone ... or lots of someones. Joining one of these online forums, whether public or private, offers you the opportunity to build connections with peers, benefit from the knowledge of others doing work similar to yours, and share your expertise with an appreciative community.

Another alternative is to become active in a local chapter of a key professional organization, which will engage you in regular meetings and group projects. (Volunteering to do the newsletter immediately makes you the most well-connected person in the organization!) Or organize an informal group of colleagues in your area that gets together weekly or monthly to swap war stories, raise questions or problems, and brainstorm solutions. Schedule regular lunches with local colleagues, or consider taking or

And Don't Forget to Think About . . .

Those were the really big questions that all start-ups face, but certainly not the only ones. If the independent path is an option you'd like to explore, then it's time to start researching the next set of questions, and noting your answers in your career journal. They will form the underpinning of your business and operations plans, so think through carefully your answers to the following questions:

- What management structure will your business have?
- How will you describe your product/service to others in fifty words or less? Make sure you've got a great "elevator speech" that clearly identifies your value proposition.
- Who/what is your competition, and how will you compete against them?
- How will you get your first project, and then convert that project into an ongoing client?
- How will you pay your bills if you don't land any clients for twelve months?
- How will you stay connected to others in your profession regionally and nationally?
- How will you establish and maintain your brand?
- How will you obtain payment from a nonpaying client?
- How will you handle technology crises?
- How will you continue to expand your knowledge base? This includes your knowledge as a business owner whose goal is to expand your business and earn a profit; as a service provider with specialized topic knowledge and knowledge of information resources; as a marketer who needs to understand both who else might need your skills and how to connect with them; and as a business manager who needs to master key performance tools.
- How will you handle vacations and illness?
- How will you handle too many projects?
- How will you fund your start-up costs?
- How will you handle family and friends' disruptions and expectations while you are working?
- What contracts do you need, and how will you deal with a client's contract that has unacceptable terms?
- What will your project proposals include, and how will they be formatted?

The good news is that there are several excellent books available to help you work through each of these issues. The reality-check news is that until you've thought all of these through and are confident that you've addressed each one, you're probably not ready to launch.

teaching a class in your area of interest to build new relationships with those who share your passion.

If you're a student, another way to create and maintain your future support community is to take a leadership role among your fellow students now, so that you can continue to connect as alumni—and colleagues—after graduation.

Although it takes more time and effort to be part of an active community when you work alone, with a little creativity it *can* be done. Doing so will not only help you feel less socially and emotionally isolated, it will also allow you to stay current with the best thinking going on in your field.

So You Want To Start a Research Business

One of the most popular independent options of interest to students is that of information broker. This is no surprise—many of us went into the LIS profession because we loved research. We thrive on the hunt for information, and the process of research is a delightful challenge that has kept many of us looking for answers well beyond when a sane person would have done the sensible thing and gone to bed. If you're one of those "I'm not gonna quit til I find the answer!" types, does this mean you were born for a career as an information broker? Maybe yes, maybe no.

As Mary Ellen Bates points out in her excellent *Building & Running a Successful Research Business: A Guide for the Independent Information Professional* (Cyberage Books/Information Today, 2003), being a successful information broker means you are both good at research *and* good at being an entrepreneur. Among the skills she identifies as critical to this type of work:

- Subject expertise in your practice area, or, if intending to be a research generalist, the ability to master new topics quickly (think of this as the ability to "learn on the fly," and at the point of need)

- An understanding of how to effectively package information to best meet the needs of your client

- Research skills, to include phone interviewing, mastery of commercial databases as well as print and Internet-based resources, and an ability to navigate government resources

- Time and workflow management skills (to keep your head above water when all those projects land on the same day, with the same deadline)

- Business skills (negotiating, marketing, selling, cash flow management, and often most importantly, the ability to insist on being paid as agreed)

- Business operations knowledge (basically, how businesses work, and what it takes to be profitable)

Like other types of independent work, being a successful information broker depends not only on knowing how to find, package, and present information, but also on how good you are at running and growing a business.

Income and Education

There is a *much* greater range of incomes for independents than for those who take either traditional or nontraditional LIS jobs. The reason is the high number of variables, including—

- What type of product/service you offer
- How much your clients value and will pay for your product/service
- The type of market you target (for example, high-tech Fortune 500 companies vs. nonprofits)
- The size of your potential market
- How frequently your clients request/purchase your product/service
- Where your client base is located (as with traditional/nontraditional salaries, generally clients in large urban areas are willing to pay higher rates than are those in small rural areas)
- How much work you're able to land
- How many years you've been working to build your client base
- How much time you spend marketing
- How effectively you market
- How many hours you're willing to work
- How effectively you manage your time
- How effectively you manage your accounts receivables—in other words, are you willing to insist that you get paid in a timely manner?

Within those—and other—variables, the income can range from zero to six figures annually. The key thing to remember, however, is that *you* are the one who controls most of these variables. The choices you make will determine *all* of your outcomes, including your income—which theoretically is what you're shooting for when you decide to become an independent.

Although many independents note that it's wise to assume *at least* two years before you'll be bringing in enough money to support yourself on your income, it may take longer than this—or less time, if you launch with a high-volume, existing client. Also, keep in mind that although you may be billing $50 (or $150) an hour, you are also covering a multitude of expenses that previously were your employer's responsibility. A good rule of thumb is to figure that between taxes and business expenses, your net "take home" pay will be just a bit more than half of the amount you bill out.

Job prospects are potentially huge—outsourcing, contingent/contract workers, and individuals brought on board on a project basis are trends that are growing exponentially. But again, *how* huge independent "job prospects" are depends on how effectively you market your service; how many clients need your services right now, and how rapidly you can profitably expand that market, among other factors. It's all part of the basic independents' mantra: while your opportunities are only limited by your imagination, the outcomes are all up to you.

In terms of education, as an independent you'll need three kinds of knowledge: the specialized expertise for which you charge your fees; the

Exploring the Independent Career Path

Becoming an independent is such a big step, it's a good idea to try it out before making a life-changing, long-term commitment. Try one or all of the following activities to "get your toes wet," recording your responses in your career journal. Did you enjoy the work? Were you engaged in the process and happy with the outcome? Would you be willing to learn more about it, and to do so on an ongoing basis? Would you feel comfortable marketing that type of product/service to others?

1. Try interning with a local information broker or one you can work with online.

2. Create web content on a voluntary basis for a local nonprofit whose mission you support.

3. Subcontract on a "moonlighting" basis for a contract cataloger.

4. Research your potential market—including players, trends, issues, and a SWOT (strengths, weaknesses, opportunities, threats) analysis—and write up your findings as a trial client project.

5. Sign up to do book reviews for *American Reference Books Annual*, *FreePint*, *Library Journal*, or *Reference Books Bulletin*, or write articles for other publications to build knowledge of information sources and develop your writing skills and process.

6. For the local public library, create an online tutorial that helps seniors find great resources for their grandkids.

7. Volunteer to do the kind of work you think you might want to do professionally so you can start to learn more about the skills involved, understand the time it takes to do this type of work, and begin building a portfolio of project experience and credentials in your possible practice.

8. Find or create opportunities to try out your dream work via your existing job, even if it means working extra hours for no pay.

9. Do a marketing plan, and test it. To pull together a marketing plan, you'll need to determine, at a minimum, who will purchase your service and why. You'll need to segment your market, so that instead of broadly targeting, for example, special libraries or business start-ups, you'll narrow your pitch to just that slice of the market that has a compelling need for your service. This could mean targeting corporate librarians who've recently had to downsize staff or business start-ups in the biotechnology industry.

    Once you've segmented your market and discussed your proposed service with several potential clients, you'll have a better sense of 1) what marketing message will resonate; 2) who and where within given organizations decision makers are (this is your target focus); and 3) probable pricing assumptions. You'll also have a better sense of whether or not you'll be able to market day in and day out.

Although this is a very brief overview of doing some rudimentary market research, the point is to help you understand how important marketing activities—and market knowledge—are to your success. Can you easily approach people and talk about your service? Are you comfortable coming up with a strategy for marketing your service? Are you willing to network, network, network? For most independents, marketing is the really tough part. But it is also the make-or-break component: if you can't market yourself, then it will be extremely difficult to succeed as an independent.

Additionally, if you're a student, consider . . .

- joining the Association of Independent Information Professionals (AIIP), taking advantage of its steeply discounted student memberships. Besides giving you the opportunity to access its wealth of online professional resources, this will allow you to sign up for AIIP's discussion list, which provides an incredibly valuable compendium of insider tips, savvy advice, and best-practice suggestions worth many times the price of membership.

- interviewing independent information professionals in your area and then writing up your findings for the student newsletter; check the publicly available AIIP membership directory (www.aiip. org/AboutAIIP/directory_home.asp) to find independents who live in your area.

- taking every research class you can, and if possible, getting hands-on experience with the big three: Dialog, LexisNexis, and Factiva.

- taking at least one business class for one of the electives in your LIS program—consider marketing, management, project management, business communications, or organizational behavior.

If your test runs tells you that although you love the work, the marketing would drive you nuts, then you're probably better off considering either subcontracting to another independent or doing freelance work in addition to your regular employment. At the very least this will allow you to continue to build a portfolio of projects and assignments without jeopardizing your professional standing (or your mortgage), and it may also provide an opportunity to start building visibility and a client base before you take the independent leap, should you eventually decide to do so.

requisite business acumen to start, manage, and grow a business; and an understanding of effective marketing practices. It's critically important that you do not assume that having the first kind of knowledge will give you a pass on having the other two. So take a class or two in entrepreneurship through your local chamber of commerce or community college. Read marketing books, join the Association of Independent Information Professionals (AIIP) and peruse its listserv archives for invaluable marketing tips and techniques. Brainstorm with other independents, research "services marketing," and attend conference presentations on doing business as an independent.

Once you're confident in your entrepreneurship and marketing skills, your challenge will be to stay ahead of the curve in your area of expertise as well as with emerging trends for your market. You may want to consider expanding your area of expertise to a related field—for example, you may want to extend your basic business research practice by also adding a specialization in competitive intelligence, and you'll need to grow that skill base. Or you may want to build on your basic cataloging and classification skills with an expertise in taxonomy building. Both of these new skill bases will require you to learn new disciplines—and to find the fastest, most cost-effective way to do so.

Also, you'll need to stay abreast of advances in your office technologies, including communication tools, search engines, and digital presentation software. Unlike when you are employed, you'll be doing all of this on your own time, so you'll need to develop a time- and cost-effective approach for mastering your ongoing learning curve.

The reality is, some people find working as an independent to be an ideal fit with their personalities, while others find that despite their initial assumptions, it's the fastest route to personal and professional misery.

In fact, most successful entrepreneurs share several key characteristics. After going through your self-assessment process, you should be able to determine how many of these fit your profile and preferences. For example, entrepreneurs generally have—

- A strong willingness to take (informed) risks, and still be able to sleep at night (usually)
- An expectation that their efforts control their outcomes
- A willingness to take the initiative
- Strong self discipline
- Effective time-management skills
- An ability to quickly master new knowledge
- A willingness to work *very* long hours when necessary
- A willingness to take on all aspects of the business, from business strategy to marketing to client relationships to clerical work

Ideally, independent information pros should also have—

- An ability to deal with irregular income
- A strong professional network of colleagues with a variety of skills and contacts
- A willingness to travel for business
- A desire to stay ahead of the curve regarding emerging trends, technologies, products, and potential market opportunities
- A comfort level with change, accompanied by a willingness to try new things
- A willingness to put their personal lives on hold if project/client deadlines intervene
- An ability to juggle multiple projects without losing control of them

Bottom line: launching as an independent is a risk that entails tremendous hard work for an uncertain payoff. But it can also be incredibly rewarding, a wonderful way to live the life you want to live, and the best way to maximize the financial return on your professional skills. You're always dealing with something new (although this carries with it its own level of anxiety), you never have to ask permission for a day off (although you'll find yourself frequently working weekends, at least in the beginning), and you'll rarely get bored. And given today's employment climate, this career choice may turn out to be the best route to lifetime employment.

Getting Started As an Independent

If, after exploring all the questions we've raised, you still feel like this is the career path for you (or one you'd like to at least consider), there are a number of ways to move forward—some slow and steady, others a leap off the cliff. Consider one or more of the following approaches:

- **Building an initial client base through volunteering.** This will bring you projects you can point to, clients who can attest to your skill and professionalism, and an expanding network of connections in the community. It can also let you hone your expertise in a "safe environment" where the expectations aren't quite so high as they would be with, say, a $25,000 project at stake.

- **Doing your independent work as an after-hours sideline in addition to your day job.** Has someone gotten wind of your special expertise and asked you to take on a project in your spare time? If you can devote the time to it and there is no conflict of interest with your current employer, this allows you to build your expertise, client base, and portfolio with very little associated risk. You may want to encourage this by letting everyone in your community of friends and colleagues know that you're available to take on small projects (that can be done during nonbusiness hours) in your area of expertise.

- **Interning with an independent practitioner.** Find someone who's doing what you want to do, and see if it would be possible to work with them for a specified time period, doing activities that will let you hone your skills while benefiting the practitioner's business. Agree up front that no clients of the organization with whom you're interning will ever be approached by you.

- **Working as a subcontractor for another independent.** Although this approach doesn't push you to start developing your marketing muscles, it's nevertheless a good way to start building up a portfolio of projects. Also, you may learn marketing strategies by observing how the independent you're working with markets his or her business.

- **Talking your employer into outsourcing your present job—to you.** One of the most popular ways of getting started as an independent is to turn your employer into your first client. This makes sense because they know the caliber of work you do, know they can rely on you to perform, and know you understand the organization and its priorities.

- **Jumping into the deep end.** If you feel you've done your homework, understand your market, have completed all the business start-up planning and "administrivia," and are ready to launch your service, then consider putting everything else aside and go for it. Although this is a much less risky approach if your household has a second income to rely on, for some people "taking the leap" is the only way to go.

Why You Might Love Being an Independent

If you love the freedom and independence only available to someone who's self-employed, and you're able to deal with the financial uncertainty of no steady paycheck, then you might thrive on the life of an LIS independent. For whom is this career choice most comfortable?

Given the marketing requirements, unless you're a subcontractor or working for a temp agency, this path is best for outgoing people comfortable with risk-taking, multitasking, and constant change. You need to be willing to seek out and extend yourself in professional/social situations, respond quickly to multiple client needs and deadlines, and deal with the day-to-day administrivia that is a part of every business.

But if you have a reasonably high level of self confidence, are comfortable taking the initiative, and don't mind the challenge of a nonstop learning curve, then the rewards of an independent career are likely to far outweigh its challenges for you. You have the freedom to work on projects that interest you, and to set your own professional agenda. You may work way too many hours, but it will be *your* decision to do so, and you will reap the rewards of your efforts.

In fact, this is one of the key considerations of an independent path. You're in charge, you can do whatever you want—as long as you understand that you and you alone are entirely responsible for your business's well-being. Its reputation depends on how well you perform every day both as a specialist in whatever it is you offer to clients *and* as a business owner/manager.

If you thrive on that kind of challenge, then you just might find an independent career to be a perfect fit.

Resources

Books

Bates, Mary Ellen. *Building & Running a Successful Research Business: A Guide for the Independent Information Professional.* Cyberage Books/Information Today, 2003. 472 pp. ISBN 0910965625.
Don't even consider becoming an information broker without reading this book first. Those who have heard Bates speak at LIS conferences will recognize her voice here: smart, funny, realistic, and supportive. Bates walks readers through the entire range of issues related to starting, running, and growing the business, plus takes you through a "day in the life" scenario that provides a realistic view of what this career choice really looks like. She makes it clear that if you're thinking about this line of work, you'll need to master both your core marketable skills *and* the competencies necessary to be an entrepreneur—and then provides the insights necessary to do so. A key resource for both students and practitioners.

Bond, William J. *Going Solo: Developing a Home-Based Consulting Business from the Ground Up.* McGraw-Hill, 1997. 272 pp. ISBN 0070066426.
An introductory overview of the practicalities and logistics of starting a consulting business from a home office. "Consulting" in this case can apply equally well to any of the many types of information services LIS independents offer, so although the information isn't tailored to your specific situation, it nevertheless provides a useful overview of the business side of your information practice.

Edwards, Sarah and Paul Edwards. *The Practical Dreamer's Handbook: Finding the Time, Money, and Energy to Live Your Dreams.* Putnam/Tarcher, 2000. 304 pp. ISBN 1585421251.
Sarah and Paul Edwards are prolific authors of excellent books on working independently. They are always enthusiastic, optimistic, and supportive, but also quite practical. This book has more of a new-age feel to it than most of their others (*Secrets of Self-Employment, Getting Business to Come to You, Finding Your Perfect Work*, etc., all published by Tarcher), but is nevertheless a useful and engaging resource for organizing your thoughts regarding working as an independent.

Mason, Florence and Christopher S. A. Dobson. *Information Brokering: A How-to-Do-It Manual.* Neal-Schuman, 1998. 144 pp. ISBN 1555703429.
Mason and Dobson, two former librarians turned information brokers, provide an overview of info brokering as a career/business choice, the practicalities of running a small business, and their recommended ways to market your business and find clients. Although the book is somewhat out of date, the authors nevertheless provide sound advice for those considering this path.

Neidorf, Robin. *Teach Beyond Your Reach: An Instructor's Guide to Developing and Running Successful Distance Learning Classes, Workshops, Training Sessions and More.* CyberAge Books, 2006. 248 pp. ISBN 0910965730.
Online teaching and training is an emerging area of opportunity for independents who have specialized knowledge to share. The challenge is figuring out how to create an online curriculum and delivery format that best supports the learning process. Neidorf, an experienced online teacher and a member of AIIP, shares best practices and examples, surveys the tools of the trade, and covers such key issues as instructional design, adult learning styles, and student–teacher interaction, among others. A key resource for those contemplating online teaching.

Pink, Daniel. *Free Agent Nation: The Future of Working for Yourself.* Warner Business Books, 2002. 384 pp. ISBN 0446678791.
Daniel Pink started the "free agent nation" discussion when he published an article in the December 1997/January 1998 issue of *Fast Company* magazine. This book is a further exploration of the economic trend toward free-agency—that is, working as an independent—with an overview of what it means, how it works, and why it represents the future workforce. Pink is an unabashed champion of this career choice so tends to gloss over some of its more difficult aspects, but the book is nevertheless an interesting and motivating read if you're considering free agency.

Sabroski, Suzanne. *Super Searchers Make It On Their Own: Top Independent Information Professionals Share Their Secrets for Starting and Running a Research Business.* Cyberage Books/Information Today, 2002. 336 pp. ISBN 0910965595.

One of the titles in the popular "Super Searchers" series, *Make It On Their Own* is a collection of interviews with eleven independent information professionals. The individuals profiled represent different industries and areas of expertise, and among them touch on such issues as client relations, starting up, day-to-day business realities, balancing personal and professional responsibilities, time management, and similarly useful topics. At the end of each profile is a hit list of "Super Searcher Power Tips," and the book concludes with a listing of the more than 200 resources mentioned throughout the text. Like sitting down with a group of really successful mentors and listening to them share war stories, best practices, and their most useful tips.

Sheth, Jagdish and Andrew Sobel. *Clients for Life: How Great Professionals Develop Breakthrough Relationships.* Simon & Schuster, 2000. 288 pp. ISBN 0684870290.

If one of the biggest challenges in becoming an independent is getting clients (and it is), then one of the best responses is to make sure that every client you *do* land stays landed. Sheth and Sobel focus on how to build client relationships that benefit both your client's best interests and your bottom line. *Clients for Life* is based on the assumption that your business is a proactive rather than reactive one; in other words, you actively seek to understand and contribute to the client's goals rather than waiting for the client to call you with a question. It's a position that takes time and effort, but wouldn't you rather be doing that than cold-calling?

Sinetar, Marsha. *To Build the Life You Want, Create the Work You Love: The Spiritual Dimension of Entrepreneuring.* St. Martin's, 1995. 210 pp. ISBN 0312141416.

Sinetar gained attention in the late eighties for her popular *Do What You Love, the Money Will Follow* (Dell, 1989). In *Build the Life You Want*, she focuses on the spiritual aspects of an independent path and the various ways in which our careers (and their transition points) may lead us to it. Affirms that it's possible to be an entrepreneur without abandoning your personal values.

Varian, Hal R. and Carl Shapiro. *Information Rules.* Harvard Business School Press, 1999. 352 pp. ISBN 087584863X.

Varian is Dean of U.C. Berkeley's School of Information Management and Systems, and Shapiro Professor of Business Strategy at Berkeley's business school. This book represents an interesting melding of those two vantage points, and should be required reading for those who develop and market information products and services for the technology driven network economy. Although the authors focus on major corporations in their examples, their ideas about pricing, customer lock-in, and product versioning (among others) have value to even the smallest enterprise.

Weiss, Alan. *Million Dollar Consulting: The Professional's Guide to Growing a Practice.* McGraw-Hill, 2002. 292 pp. ISBN 007138703X.

Weiss's books are legendary among independents for their practical, hands-on advice and counsel. *Million Dollar Consulting* is useful even for those who would be happy billing out substantially less than that, as it addresses so many questions that independents of all sizes deal with every day. Topics include landing clients, pricing, growing the business, building sustainable client relationships, and many other strategic topics. Other equally valuable books by Weiss include *How to Establish a Unique Brand in the Consulting Profession* (Pfeiffer, 2001) *Value-Based Fees* (Pfeiffer, 2002), and *Getting Started in Consulting*, 2nd ed. (Wiley, 2004).

Periodicals

Connections. Association of Independent Information Professionals, 1986– . Quarterly. ISSN 1524–9468.
www.aiip.org
Connections is available to AIIP members only, but the current issue can be read by going to the AIIP website and selecting About > Newsletter. This will give you a good sense of current issues of interest to the membership.

Fast Company. Fast Co., Inc., 1995– . Monthly. ISSN 1085–9241.
www.fastcompany.com
Imagine hanging out with a friend who is smart, funny, hip, and knows all the coolest people. Okay, so sometimes she's a little bit *out there*, but she still comes up with enough interesting ideas to keep you hooked on those Saturday brunches ... that's *Fast Company*. It covers cutting-edge business trends and ideas, showcases the insights of thought-leaders, and almost always has something useful for career strategists. More engaging than intellectual, *Fast Company* is a great resource if your career focus is on the business world.

Information Outlook. Special Libraries Association, 1997– . Monthly. ISSN 1091–0808.
www.sla.org/content/Shop/Information/index.cfm
Although members of SLA receive this publication as part of their membership benefits, it has sufficient value to non-SLA members as well that it is worth considering a subscription. There is substantial overlap between special librarians and independents in the resources they use, the knowledge and expertise they share, and often as clients and service providers for each other. *Information Outlook* is, consequently, not only a good tool for independents in their day-to-day practice, but also a good resource for staying abreast of potential clients and their issues.

Online. Information Today, 1977– . Bimonthly. ISSN 0146–5422.
www.infotoday.com/online
Online has been covering the information industry, including its products, services, issues, and opportunities, for more than twenty-five years, during which time the definition of "online" has gone through several transformations. The publication continues, however, to focus on topics critical to information professionals and the work they do. Scope of coverage includes "articles, product reviews, case studies, evaluation, and informed opinion about selecting, using, and managing electronic information products, plus industry and professional information about online database systems, CD-ROM, and the Internet." The website provides title access to past issues, some of which are available for free, others for a fee. See also Online Insider (www. onlineinsider.net), a blog by editor and industry guru Marydee Ojala.

Searcher: The Magazine for Database Professionals. Information Today, 1993– . 9/yr. ISSN 1070–4795.

www.infotoday.com/searcher

The complement to *Online, Searcher's* content is geared toward those who do professional-level database research. Coverage includes "online news, searching tips and techniques, reviews of searchaid software and database documentation," interviews with industry thought-leaders, and editorials. The website provides title access to past issues, some of which are available for free, others for a fee. A must-read for business researchers.

Articles

Longo, Brunella. "How a Librarian Can Live Nine Lives in a Knowledge-Based Economy," *Computers in Libraries*, vol. 21, no. 10 (November/December 2001), pp. 40–43.

A fascinating look at how one information professional's career has transitioned through time to respond to market changes and emerging opportunities. See especially the author's concluding bibliography, which is indicative of the very broad range of knowledge necessary to continually expand career horizons.

Kangiser, Angela. "After the Research: Information Professionals' Secrets for Delivering Results," *Online*, vol. 27, no. 1, (January/February 2003), pp. 26–32.

A useful overview of creating "value-added deliverables" that reports on the best practices of numerous info pros. An excellent complement to the earlier Kassel article on the same topic (see below).

Kassel, Amelia. "Value-Added Deliverables: Rungs on the Info Pro's Ladder to Success," *Searcher*, vol. 10, no. 10 (November/December 2002), pp. 42–53.

"Adding value" is a critical step in moving from a data-delivery role into a more strategic (and higher-paying) role as an information professional. A large part of that process is packaging—how you present the research you have gathered, what you add to it (e.g., rankings, synthesis, evaluation, etc.) that moves it from raw data to actionable information. This is a classic article on what to do, how to do it, and key resources that make adding value easier and faster.

Associations

Association of Independent Information Professionals (AIIP)

www.aiip.org

The key resource for anyone considering a career as an independent information pro. AIIP is a very active, knowledge-rich organization whose members are legendary for their willingness to share best-practices, business tips, product recommendations, and any other type of information that will help fellow members succeed. Membership in the organization brings access to the AIIP electronic discussion list, perhaps the most valuable learning tool available for independents, and a community of colleagues who will cheer your every success. Check the website for career information, publications, and information about the organization and its events. Steeply discounted student memberships.

Independent Librarians' Exchange (ILEX)
    www.ala.org/Template.cfm?Section=indecons
    A section of ALA's Association of Specialized and Cooperative Library
    Agencies (ASCLA), ILEX provides programs, publications, and net-
    working for librarians and other information professionals working
    outside of traditional libraries. If you're an ALA member and would
    like to connect with fellow independents (or those interested in this
    career path), this is the place to do it.

Society for Competitive Intelligence Professionals (SCIP)
    www.scip.org
    Competitive intelligence (CI) is an important component of business
    research across all industries and businesses. Many IIPs include com-
    petitive intelligence as part of their service offering; some specialize
    only in CI. SCIP membership comprises both independents and CI spe-
    cialists who work for businesses, so there is a broad range of experience
    and knowledge to share within the group. Check the website under CI
    Resources for salary information, white papers, articles, career infor-
    mation, and several overviews of the CI process. Steeply discounted
    student membership fees, but for full-time students only.

Online Resources

Be Your Own Boss
    www.sla.org/chapter/ctor/resources/career/settingshop.htm
    Created by Ulla de Stricker and Ron Davis from SLA's Toronto chap-
    ter, *Be Your Own Boss* is an online questionnaire that will help you
    determine whether the independent info pro career path is for you.

The Independent Info Pro Business (a.k.a. "Information Brokering")
    www.batesinfo.com/info-brokering.html
    Links to a number of resources Mary Ellen Bates has compiled on life
    as an information broker. At the website see also her archived "tips
    of the month," which provide an ongoing "heads-up" about new search
    tools, research tips, and emerging issues of interest to IIPs. Bates is one
    of the leaders in the independent information professional (IIP) world.

The Independent Information Professional
    www.aiip.org/Resources/IIPWhitePaper.html
    An overview of the various types of independent information profes-
    sional careers, including those involving general business and industry,
    legal research, the healthcare industries, public records, banking and
    finance, government and public policy, and science and technology. An
    excellent starting point if you'd like to get an overall sense of what IIPs
    actually do.

Information Broker FAQ
    www.marketingbase.com/faqs.html
    A quick overview of the market for info brokers, skills and attitudes
    needed, typical services offered, working as a part-time info broker, etc.
    Useful and practical information for those considering the profession,
    from highly respected industry broker and mentor Amelia Kassel.

Resources
    www.aiip.org/Resources/

In addition to The Independent Information Professional white paper noted above, this section of the AIIP website also offers "Getting Started as an Independent Information Professional," a bibliography of resources on Info-Entrepreneurship, and a listing of courses relevant to information brokering offered by various schools.

Sologig

www.sologig.com

From Careerbuilder.com, this site was launched in 2002 to "bring together talented freelancers, consultants and independent professionals (Soloists) with the most qualified employers from across the United States." You post your professional profile, they post their projects, and you both get to search for a match. See the resource center for useful "how to succeed as a solo" articles.

Starting a Business: Advice from the Trenches

www.alistapart.com/articles/startingabusiness

Written for website designers, this resource nevertheless has applicability for anyone who's contemplating launching as an independent. The author's overview is practical and down to earth, and includes both advice and resources.

Steps in Starting Your Own Business

www.rileyguide.com/steps.html

A useful collection of resources (business plans, tutorials, advice, government agencies, etc.) under the headings of "Steps in Starting Up," "Finding Help," "Funding for Your Business," "A Little Legalese," and "Setting Up the Office." From the Riley Guide people.

Training

Information Broker Mentor Program

www.marketingbase.com/mentor.html

A highly regarded program run by Amelia Kassel. For over twenty years, Kassel has successfully specialized in industry, company, and competitive and market intelligence research through her company, MarketingBase. Her mentoring program covers the basics you'll need to get started in the profession, then coaches you through the start-up crazies, helps you navigate and master the major online databases critical to business research, walks you through marketing strategies targeted to specific market opportunities, and generally helps you launch your career ideas into a business reality.

6
Creating Your Professional Portfolio

The people who get on in this world are the people who get up and look for the circumstances they want, and, if they can't find them, make them.
—George Bernard Shaw

You've explored your unique interests, aptitudes, and preferences. You've looked at traditional, nontraditional, and independent career options that build on your LIS professional skills. Now it's time to consider how those skills match up with the career opportunities you might want to pursue. To do that, you'll need to rethink, reframe, and rephrase how you interpret (and present) those skills.

In the library profession, we generally think of our skills in terms that connect with readily understood and categorized positions: reference, readers' advisory, cataloging, circulation, network administration, archives, and collection development, among others.

These positions are essentially "predefined" for us. For example, we expect that a good reference librarian knows how to answer questions asked by patrons, students, faculty, and employees. He or she knows how to interview the patron to clearly understand the question, knows the range of information resources that are appropriate to the task, and is able to use them effectively and successfully to deliver the correct answer. Top-notch reference librarians are usually also adept at—

- teaching others how to find and use appropriate information resources

- preparing print and online tutorials and guides on specific subjects

- creating and presenting workshops and seminars on information topics of value to specific audiences

- continually monitoring multiple sources to learn about (and how to use) new information resources

- evaluating competing information products and services and recommending which to use, license, or purchase

- evaluating print and online resources for authority, credibility, and usefulness

- creating a supportive, welcoming dynamic to diffuse the library "intimidation factor" for patrons

- creating online content for the library's web portal with a focus on special communities of users

- tracking down information that might seem impossible to find to others

- listening for the nuances within a patron's question that indicate a different direction—or answer—may be warranted

- maintaining a positive attitude toward patrons despite the occasional challenges of dealing with the public, students, co-workers, and bosses

All of these attributes are taken for granted as part of the job description for "reference librarian." However, any one of these could also be a key skill in other types of jobs, including those in nonlibrary environments. It all depends on how you frame them.

Each of the activities noted for reference librarians above involves a skill that has value across a broad range of organizations and opportunities. A good reference librarian has a dynamite combination of information and people skills, as do most individuals in the library profession. However, your ability to both understand *and frame* those skills effectively will determine how easily you move from one professional opportunity to another as you move through your career.

Reframing your skills is a process that asks you to *identify and understand your skills in a broader context*. In addition, you need to—

- **reconsider the language you use to describe your skills.** You must describe what you can do in terms that resonate with your audience, which means you need to understand *their* needs and describe in *their* language.

- **rethink and repurpose what you can do with your skills.** What roles, responsibilities, and opportunities would your skills prepare you for if there were no libraries?

- **develop confidence in your skills—and your contribution**. Because most traditional LIS jobs are predefined, or very specific regarding what activities and responsibilities they entail, we rarely have to push much beyond our "competence zone." Reframing your skills has as its goal, however, getting you into *new* opportunities—where you'll need confidence in both your skills and your ability to navigate unknown territory.

Understanding Your Skills

What do information skills look like? For starters, most MLIS graduates have at least a baseline level of expertise in the four core areas of:

- finding and/or acquiring information
- organizing and/or managing information
- working with the public
- managing organizations

But take those core skill areas and consider them a bit more closely, with an eye toward describing them to a nonlibrarian. What might they look like? For starters:

Finding and/or acquiring information. These are research skills, which entail being able to understand and refine a question; identify, evaluate, and use appropriate resources among the zillions that exist; analyze and synthesize the information discovered; and if appropriate, present well-written, articulate, focused summaries and recommendations. Research skills may be broad-based or centered on an advanced subject expertise you may have developed.

In addition, those doing acquisitions have also developed skills in purchasing, license negotiating, and vendor relations. Many special librarians have experience in negotiating enterprise content purchases. Information professionals involved in collection development are skilled in the ability to understand, evaluate, and choose among the various types and formats of available resources, and are also comfortable working with teams of colleagues to develop collection strategies.

Organizing and/or managing information. Yesterday's reasonably predictable job of "cataloger" has now expanded into an extremely diverse role that ranges from traditional materials cataloging to creating taxonomies for digital products, to understanding the critical role of metadata in digitization initiatives. But the core skill underlying all of these roles is the ability to create and/or apply standardized systems that organize—and allow for the efficient retrieval of—information.

Great catalogers and other "information organizers" are extraordinarily attentive to detail, adept at creating conceptual relationships, and attuned to how users locate and retrieve information. Additionally, their understanding of cataloging and classification systems often comes with a high level of technology and systems expertise.

Working with the public. Depending on where they work, LIS professionals deal with many "publics"—patrons, students, faculty, co-workers, clients, to name a few. Traditional public services work may include working the reference desk (in person or online), offering readers' advisory, doing bibliographic instruction, delivering outreach programs, running children's story hours, organizing corporate end-user training sessions, or proctoring exams for local online learning students.

Given this broad range of activities, info pros working in public services areas must possess strong communication skills, an ability to deal effectively with many different types of personalities, and an ability to "think on their feet" in response to an ongoing barrage of questions and information demands.

Managing organizations. Library directors and deans, school librarians, and heads of organization information centers are all responsible for managing enterprises, regardless of size. They establish organizational goals and priorities, set performance expectations, allocate resources, create budgets, deal with personnel issues, manage external relationships (with bosses, boards, and donors, among others), and respond to an exciting variety of crises, craziness, and (on a good day) opportunities.

Effective LIS managers must have solid leadership capabilities, an ability to both motivate people and hold them accountable, and a willingness to shift focus in response to shifting circumstances. They understand each functional area that reports to them; so, for example, even if they don't know how to catalog a book, they understand the process, the skills required, and the issues involved.

All of the skills and abilities described for these four key areas are vital to the traditional work that LIS professionals do within the library field. But for those who want to broaden their options within traditional LIS career paths, they can all also be valuable to other roles within the profession. And for individuals who would like to explore career options outside of traditional library environments, these skills can be effectively "repurposed" for broader application.

In fact, these capabilities can be valuable to government agencies, nonprofits, business start-ups, large corporations, professional associations, and myriad other employers—or clients. The key is to understand how to frame or describe not the *titles* of the jobs you've held, but rather the *value* of what you can do.

Describing Your Skills

How would you describe your skills to nonlibrarians, no jargon allowed?

You can find information—credible, reliable, actionable information—fast and often cheap. You know what makes for good online content, and can often create it yourself. You can teach, and design and deliver both online and face-to-face training. You expertly organize large collections of things so that others can find and use items in the collections, and are great at customer service and coaching. You work effectively in team-based and collaborative environments, usually possess excellent communication skills, and demonstrate a strong sense of community service, regardless of the specific community. Some LIS professionals possess extraordinary analytical skills, while others excel at creating highly innovative outreach programs. All of these skills are demonstrated in the jobs you do.

In order to translate these terrific LIS skills and experience into broader opportunities, however, it's necessary to *describe* them in language that resonates with the individuals who provide those opportunities. That means—

- using business terminology to describe LIS activities (for example, "created user-friendly, actionable guides to best-in-class topic resources" instead of "created pathfinders")

- focusing on the value and benefits we bring rather than the titles we've had (consider "led the development and launch of the first program to support adult learners in the community," rather than "director of adult services"); and

- emphasizing outcomes and results rather than activities and roles (for example, "developed collaborative programs with several local nonprofits that resulted in a 20% increase in our program participation" rather than "ran outreach programs").

For example, someone who's worked as a systems librarian in an academic library might emphasize his or her history of leading collaborative teams that created technology solutions; project management skills that resulted in a new system implementation on time and under budget; review and evaluation of five vendor proposals that resulted in negotiated cost savings of 15 percent to the organization; creation and leadership of a campus-wide integrated teaching technologies group that monitors and introduces advances in teaching technologies.

Leadership, team building. Project management, budget and resource oversight. Vendor evaluation, contract negotiation and licensing, cost reductions. Taking initiative, leading collaborative projects, focusing on emerging opportunities. Phrasing skill descriptions in terms of results, accomplishments, and value added allows them to resonate with *any* employer, not just the traditional library human resources person (who would, by the way, also find them exemplary).

It's also an effective way for you to recast how *you* think about your capabilities. One of the things many of us do is downplay the value of what "comes naturally" to us. If you're a whiz on the Internet, but you figure this is just part of your job and you're good at it, chances are you're not going to think of this as a particularly valuable or noteworthy skill. But the reality is, a whiz on the Internet can bring exceptional value as a business researcher, competitive intelligence specialist, donor prospect evaluator, or any number of strategic roles.

So get into the habit of acknowledging what you're good at, with a focus on what your skills have accomplished. Don't be shy about this; you *do* bring value, and it's up to you to highlight it in language that's meaningful in the nonlibrary world. Still shy about this? Recruit a friendly colleague who understands what you do and will happily describe to you your greatest assets. And when you think about or describe those assets, understand that they contribute value to many types of organizations, both within and outside of traditional librarianship.

Repurposing Your Skills

Information skills (often library skills in disguise) are in demand. But to connect your information skills with the range of potential opportunities, you need to rethink the application of those skills and get comfortable "repurposing" them.

For instance, a research capability would enable you to also excel at these value-added activities:

- Investigating people, issues, organizations, and industry trends
- Undertaking primary as well as secondary research
- Designing research projects
- Creating and delivering an executive information service

- Providing data analysis, synthesis, and evaluations/recommendations
- Researching and assessing donor prospects
- Creating presentation content
- Providing market forecast and trend information and tracking
- Preparing an assessment of market opportunity
- Providing current awareness / alerting services
- Creating newsletter content
- Writing abstracts and summaries of key business publications
- Creating customized web content
- Preparing company, market, and/or competitive profiles
- Undertaking patent research
- Researching and analyzing sales prospects
- Developing initial information components for scenario planning
- Providing core knowledge for SWOT (strengths/weaknesses/opportunities/threats) analyses
- Writing internal and/or external topic briefings or white papers
- Working with the information technology team to provide technology assessment

Or consider the ability to organize and manage information and information systems. Increasingly critical to the success of organizations, this may go way beyond the "knowledge management" descriptor. For example, an information professional with expertise in this area might appropriately highlight his or her ability to:

- Analyze and map business processes
- Design systems and supporting processes for supporting internal knowledge transfer
- Oversee the development and application of topic-specific taxonomies
- Evaluate and choose among vendor-provided storage, access, and retrieval options
- Align technology analysis/implementation with organizational strategic goals
- Develop training materials and provide system training to users
- Implement best-practice project management tools and processes
- Monitor emerging technologies and issues related to business intelligence management
- Collaborate with other departments to develop an integrated, enterprise-wide intranet
- Plan, implement, and document a system-wide information architecture

- Develop databases to support operations, such as customer relationship management or Sarbanes–Oxley compliance
- Lead project teams
- Create the infrastructure of internal or external communities of practice
- Organize and undertake an employee skills inventory

Or perhaps you've spent your career in public services. Your ability to navigate an information interview, your strong verbal and written communication skills, your ability to work supportively and effectively with all sorts of personalities, and your familiarity with teaching end-users the intricacies of various information resources mean your skills would easily port to these related opportunities:

- Customer service management
- Product development
- Market research
- Focus group management
- Vendor representative
- Sales
- Training and development
- Teaching
- Instructional design
- Online teaching
- Outreach/program development for organizations other than libraries
- Online Q&A librarian, providing answers to customers and clients
- Running an information and referral program for a government agency

Strong research and writing skills transfer easily into policy analysis; a systems network background can bridge to developing corporate intranets. Reference and user services translate into product development and customer service roles for information product vendors, while working with donors and friends' groups would be equally effective for a multitude of nonprofits.

Library managers have the most easily repurposed skill set, because effective managers are critical to the successful running of all organizations. So a library manager who can demonstrate a successful track record of leadership, staff development, budgeting, community relationships (regardless of what that community may be), crisis management, and the host of other challenges that come with day-to-day management can easily transfer these skills into other organizations, whether from one type of library to another, or from a library environment into a business, nonprofit, or government agency.

The key concept here is *transferable skills*. These are skills that bring value to many environments, rather than being specific to a given organization. Although you may have learned and practiced them in the context of traditional library work, they can be applied to new and/or nontraditional types of library work or to new nonlibrary work opportunities. As noted above, these can include technology skills, an ability to work with customers/the public, management expertise, communication skills, and overall information research and/or management abilities, among many others.

The easiest way to explore repurposing your skills is to start reading job descriptions, both library-focused and nonlibrary, for industries or organizations that interest you. Check out the wording they use to describe various positions, and line up your skills against their specifications. Adapt their language to describe your capabilities. That way, potential employers who don't understand what a Library Specialist Grade IV is capable of will still have a chance to understand the value you bring.

Developing Confidence in Your Skills

Figure out what your most magnificent qualities are and make them indispensable to the people you want to work with.
—Linda Bloodworth-Thomason

An important part of reframing your skills—and your career options—is having the confidence to take them into new arenas. How can you convince potential employers that you're as valuable as you say you are if *you're* not convinced? Traditionally, the LIS "acculturation process" has rarely included assertiveness training, self-esteem strengthening, confidence-building, or risk-taking among its professional development priorities.

So it's up to us to make sure our confidence factor is where it needs to be. This means understanding and celebrating the value of your knowledge. It means respecting your skills, and expecting that others should as well. It means knowing that what you deliver adds value to projects, and organizations, and communities. It means that you express confidence and assurance in your conversations, and model a professional demeanor that calmly says "I understand that I am/will be an asset to any organization I work with."

Now, since this isn't usually part of the MLIS training in grad school, sometimes you have to start out just *faking* that confidence level. But you can also practice it the way you'd rehearse an upcoming speech or presentation. Imagine yourself in a leadership position in a team meeting, or speaking with the mayor, or briefing the company CEO, or addressing the donor meeting, and practice speaking and presenting your ideas from a position of strength rather than a position of hesitancy (which is perceived as weakness, which then automatically diffuses your credibility). The first few times you attempt this, it may feel awkward, but keep working on it. Practice on the person checking your groceries, in your next job interview, with colleagues willing to role-play with you. If you want your professionalism to be taken seriously, you have to do it first.

One way to begin building your confidence factor is to reconsider your work history, with an eye toward noting your history of growth, accomplishments, and contribution. In other words, reframe your career from the "portfolio" perspective.

Putting Together Your Portfolio

Think of your career portfolio as an inventory of projects, achievements, contributions, innovations, initiatives, and other cool things you've done along the way. They don't necessarily have to be library-related, but you want to focus on activities that demonstrate a growing capability to assume responsibility, analyze information and use it effectively to make strategic decisions, and identify and implement solutions to problems/challenges. Look back over your career history: when did you demonstrate leadership, great communication, team management skills, and knowledge growth? (By the way, grad school is a great place to start building all these portfolio elements!)

Once you start thinking through how to reframe your career history along these lines, you begin to understand how LIS skills can transfer— and be valuable—inside and outside traditional library environments. Approaching your career from this perspective moves you from "this is what I know" to "this is what I can *do* with what I know," which then moves you to "and this is why I'm such an incredible asset." Recasting your career into a portfolio-based approach also gives you an extremely valuable tool with which to shape your career and its opportunities.

The physical expression of your portfolio can be anything that works for you—from your career journal to an outline of key themes and activities to a graphic or visual map of work you've done, projects you've worked on, skills you've mastered, and the connections among them. The point is to use a method that helps you identify the connections and themes central to your worklife.

Creating a portfolio-approach resume. Time to take out your career journal and get ready to start taking notes, because translating your portfolio into a written document entails rethinking both the information you provide and the way in which you organize it. A portfolio-approach resume differs from a standard one by focusing on skills mastered and applied, outcomes achieved, and solutions initiated rather than on titles held. A quick overview of the differences between the two would be:

Standard Resume	Portfolio Resume
Job parameters	Accomplishments
Activities/tasks	Outcomes/results
Position	Projects

Essentially, a portfolio-approach resume documents demonstrations of competence.

Designing Your Portfolio

As you mine your career experiences for portfolio entries, you'll want to focus on transferable skills. They will be of two kinds: discipline-specific skills such as reference or serials management or cataloging, and professional cross-disciplinary ones such as leadership or project management. Any potential employer will immediately understand the value of your cross-disciplinary skills. However, as was noted previously, you'll want to

Reviewing Your History

To begin to "translate" your career history into a professional portfolio, consider what activities you've engaged in that match the descriptions below, and fill them in (either on this page or in your career journal).

Took responsibility for _____

Led the creation of _____

Assembled and managed team that _____

Organized and executed _____

Wrote the _____

Changed the _____

Designed the _____

Assessed and evaluated _____

Spoke on behalf of _____

Researched and recommended _____

Created program to enhance _____

Initiated community outreach program _____

... that resulted in ...

... cost savings of _____

... increased donations in the amount of _____

... expanded visibility for _____

... new opportunities for _____

... higher patron usage levels for _____

... greater attendance at _____

... this new program _____

The idea is to demonstrate an ability to contribute to an organization's goals and the professional effectiveness to do so successfully, whether those organizations are libraries or other types of enterprises. And be sure to note in your journal if there are other achievements not included here, whether part of professional or volunteer activities.

describe your library-specific skills with a broader context, so resume reviewers will immediately understand their applicability to nonlibrary enterprises.

Putting together a written document that represents your professional portfolio will help you work through the four key areas of reframing your skills—identifying and understanding your skills in a broader context, shifting the language you use to describe your skills, rethinking and repurposing what you can do with your skills, and developing confidence in your skills and contribution. The overall goal is to demonstrate both to yourself and others the breadth and depth of your skills—and your value.

As an example of the difference between the traditional and portfolio approaches, consider the following job-history descriptions, one a traditional chronological rendering of jobs and job descriptions, the other a portfolio approach that focuses on achievements.

Traditional Resume Job History Overview

2001-Current Director, Corporate Information Services

> *Responsible for managing corporate information resources (print and electronic) performing research as requested, negotiating vendor contracts, and assisting with company website as needed.*

1997–2001 Assistant Director, Knowledge Center

> *Assisted director in overall management and maintenance of company library, responsible for collection development for engineering department.*

1987–1994 Information Specialist, Community Nonprofit

> *Did research projects, answered questions for staff and public, maintained resource library.*

Portfolio Resume Job History Overview

Key Accomplishments

> Developed the first information collection on microenterprise opportunities in community, which helped increase the number of microenterprise start-ups by 20 percent per year from 1988 through 1994.
>
> Created company-wide knowledge-sharing initiative among staff engineers that led to the organization's first online community of practice; based on the success of this COP, the engineering department won its first-ever "company innovators" award.
>
> Led the creation and launch of a company-wide business intelligence portal that enabled product design, customer service, and marketing teams to elicit and receive feedback from key customers; the resulting "feedback loop" was so successful that it has now been integrated into all product development initiatives.

Engagement Experience

Information strategy. *Have worked with nonprofits and corporations to help them determine how to align internal and external information resources with their strategic goals. Sample strategic goals have included increased visibility in the marketplace, higher membership numbers, greater consumer interest, positioning as a thought-leader or industry authority, and/or new revenue streams.*

Content development. *Have developed successful print, presentation, and online content to drive organization's strategic goals. Content has included articles, white papers, speeches, knowledge guides, online tutorials, online reference tools (timelines, glossaries, industry overviews, etc.), resource directories, and communities of interest, among others.*

Research. *Have conducted primary and secondary research for nonprofit and corporate employers, especially in the areas of education, business, competitive intelligence, trends forecasting, and information services.*

As you can see, the portfolio approach clearly tells prospective employers what you're capable of, and in what ways you'll be a valuable contributor to their organization.

Growing Your Portfolio

What if your career so far hasn't offered you much of an opportunity to demonstrate competency, or participate in any interesting projects, or come up with any cool solutions? Then it's time to get started, using one of the many ways to "bulk up" your portfolio. Keep in mind that you're also bulking up your experience and expertise, and the confidence that goes with that, as you add bullet points to your portfolio.

The first place to check for portfolio fodder is your current job. Volunteer for projects just getting started, where your skills can contribute. As you do so, keep in mind your timeframe. In her article for *Info Career Trends*, Sally Gibson makes the wise point that you should "volunteer for short-term projects if you do not plan to stay in your current situation for very long. This way, you will have the opportunity to see a project through from beginning to end."[1]

See if there are any work-flow issues that could benefit from new, more streamlined processes—and design them. Decide to become the local expert on some aspect of your job (or an area of professional interest) and then share what you learn with your colleagues and/or professional community. Seek out opportunities to collaborate with peers from other departments to develop interdepartmental initiatives where useful. Ask your supervisor what he or she feels would enhance the success of the department (or its efficiency, or morale, or visibility, etc.), then lead a brainstorming session with like-minded colleagues to identify (and then implement) solutions.

Let others know you're looking for professional growth opportunities, and be willing to say yes even though it may mean more work for no increase in pay. Okay, *usually* it means more work for no pay increase, but keep in mind that you're basically investing in your career, in the same way you would be if taking a class to increase your skills. Essentially, you're building a career base from which to launch multiple professional opportunities.

If your workplace doesn't lend itself to portfolio-building, look next to your professional associations (including graduate student groups). Once again, volunteering is key. Taking on the organization newsletter can demonstrate your ability to write and edit, to lead team projects, to work with print or online layout and design software, to meet deadlines, and to coordinate group efforts. Becoming program chair demonstrates an ability to manage multiple, ongoing projects with constantly shifting personnel and logistics challenges, an ability to deal calmly and effectively (on a good day) with last-minute crises, and an ability to envision, organize, and execute programming ideas that align with the goals of the organization.

If you're looking for an opportunity to demonstrate your leadership capabilities, run for executive office. As president-elect, you'll have an opportunity to suggest—and then follow up on—new initiatives, processes, or opportunities. Or consider becoming the group's webmaster, where you may be creating valuable new online content to support a membership drive, or reorganizing the site to create a best-in-class knowledge portal, or implementing technology fixes that enable new interactive site capabilities. Or create a new role—chief learning officer—and develop a professional development agenda for which you identify and organize access to key information resources for association members.

The opportunities to contribute are endless, and can be at the local, state, regional, national, or international level, depending on your interests. But it's up to you to take the initiative to make a difference, and create "portfolio-worthy" outcomes.

On the other hand, if LIS-related professional organizations aren't your passion, consider volunteering for something that *does* matter to you, and again going for maximum impact from the skills you contribute. Create a web presence for your local League of Women Voters, do donor research for the American Red Cross, help your town's synagogue (or church or temple or mosque) create a theology library, develop information resources for the local women's microenterprise lending group.

Do an information guide for new pet owners for the local Humane Society, teach a class on Internet research at the senior center down the street. Research and write a position paper for your favorite political candidate. Solicit donations for a career-resource library at the local teen center, or volunteer to spend one day a month teaching high-school seniors how to find financial aid resources. Use your LIS skills to contribute to a cause you believe in, whether by doing research, organizing existing information, creating an information collection, helping create a web presence, or some other professional-level activity. This will allow you to start using your skills to build a better world while also strengthening those skills.

If you're an LIS student, consider these options for growing your portfolio entries:

- Join or start a student chapter of a national organization and volunteer for a position that lets you demonstrate or broaden an existing skill.

- Whenever possible, consider your class projects and assignments to be "trial runs" of professional-level projects and imagine how you would package and present the information within a nonlibrary environment.

- If possible, structure your internships, practicums, and/or capstone projects so that they are project-based, and enable you to either demonstrate or broaden a key competency.

Most importantly, keep in mind that what's important in the long run is not what courses you've gotten A's in, but how many ways you can strategically apply the knowledge you've gained.

As you go about building your portfolio, look for ways to demonstrate key professional strengths, including the ability and willingness to—

- take initiative

- create innovative solutions

- make effective, well-reasoned decisions

- locate, analyze, and draw actionable conclusions from information

- effectively use print and verbal communication skills to achieve goals

- monitor and make the best use of financial resources

- participate in place-based and virtual teams

- collaborate across departmental boundaries
- organize and execute projects on your own
- lead and/or manage teams, projects, or initiatives
- learn as needed—in other words, yes, you have an existing capability, but you can also grow quickly with new opportunities
- invest yourself for the benefit of others

As you can, start shaping your job to focus on projects, opportunities to demonstrate initiative, participation, and contribution. As you do this, consider how best to describe those projects and accomplishments in the language that reflects the values of potential employers, whether libraries, the corporate world, nonprofits, or others.

Look for ways to broadbase your skills. For example, if you did bibliographic instruction or user education, how would you describe those activities in ways that have value to the nonlibrary world? As noted earlier, one of the best ways to get a sense of this is to read nonlibrary job descriptions in related areas (e.g., training), and see what words and phrases are used to describe various functions. Another great way to do this, and always lots of fun, is to sit down with colleagues over a cup of coffee or glass of wine for some serious descriptive brainstorming. . . .

Benefits of a Portfolio Approach

Taking a portfolio approach to your career delivers a number of benefits.

For those of us who have had, shall we say, somewhat *eclectic* careers, it's a way of bringing together what might seem like disparate, disconnected pieces of jobs and activities into a cohesive whole. I've worked in many jobs for many employers in a number of different industries; yet from a portfolio approach, what counts is the projects I've worked on in each of those jobs. Have they demonstrated an increasingly strategic role? Have they showcased an ability to take initiative, manage complex projects, bridge professional communities, expand my knowledge to meet the needs of the opportunity? This type of professional growth may not jump out at a potential employer or client from a traditional resume—and in fact, you may not have noticed it yourself if you've been thinking of your career as simply a series of job titles. A portfolio approach gives you a different perspective.

Another benefit is that by reframing your career this way, you're more likely to see themes or connections that might not have been otherwise clear to you. Considering the things that have been rewarding to you, what do the projects you've worked on or the various types of work you've done have in common? Were they all focused, for example, on designing processes? On being a change agent in peoples' lives? On developing information content? This can be an important part of your self-assessment exploration, because it will help you highlight threads of continuity you may want to develop in more depth.

Putting together your professional portfolio will also help you identify areas where you might bulk up your skills, education, or experience to fill in gaps—or further develop potential areas of opportunity. Based on this examination, for example, you might decide a lateral move that doesn't provide more money or a higher-level title is still worth going after because it offers oversight of a terrific project or will help you learn valuable new skills.

A portfolio approach can help you expand your career by bridging into new areas rather than by recareering. What's the difference? *Recareering* is when you pretty much walk away from the professional base and expertise you've built over the years and begin an entirely new career from scratch (translation: you're the lowest one on the totem pole). *Bridging*, on the other hand, allows you to extend the reach of your existing career by using the skills and competencies demonstrated in one arena—or type of library, or professional discipline—to another. By focusing on building up and out from the base you've already assembled, you avoid having to start paying all those dues all over again. Your portfolio can help you identify those transferable skills and eventually document them to a future employer.

Lastly, taking the time to pull together a portfolio-type overview of your career will help you understand more clearly where you are today and where you want to be headed. By understanding the overall shape and direction of your career so far, you'll be in a better position to assess what future investments of time, effort, and intellect will get you to where you want to go.

The Art and Science of Landing the Job

Cover letters, portfolio resumes, interviewing skills—how effectively you present yourself to a potential employer often depends on your ability to master these key tools. Happily, there are some terrific resources to support that mastery. Consider:

Resume Writing and Interviewing Techniques That Work! Robert Newlen, Neal-Schuman, 2006. One of the publisher's familiar "How-To-Do-It-Manuals for Librarians" titles, this work is useful for both jobs in traditional library fields and those outside them. Updating Newlen's earlier *Writing Resumes That Work* (1998), this guide provides an excellent framework for shaping and then presenting your achievements.

Although the focus of Sarah L. Nesbeitt and Rachel Singer Gordon's *The Information Professional's Guide to Career Development Online* (Information Today, 2002) isn't writing cover letters, assembling portfolio resumes, or acing the interview, all of these are well-covered in the book's chapters on electronic resumes, library job hunting online, and researching employment situations.

Woven throughout the archived issues and articles of Rachel Singer Gordon's *Info Career Trends* newsletter (www.lisjobs.com/newsletter/index.htm) are many practical insights on job interviewing, resumes, and the process of applying for jobs. See especially "Library Interviews: Improving Your Odds" by Karen Evans in the September 2004 issue, and the articles in the January 2001 issue, whose theme is "The Library Job Hunt."

For practical advice from outside the LIS community, consider the information-rich "Career Advice" section of careerbuilder.com (www.careerbuilder.com)—see especially the articles under "Cover Letters & Resumes" and "Getting Hired." Also check out the tips at Monster (www.monster.com) in their "Career Advice" section under the headings of "Interview Center," "Resume Center," and "Job Search Basics."

For insider tips on acing information interviews, see "Informational Interviewing: The Neglected Job Search Tool" (http://interview.monster.com/articles/informational/#). Informational interviewing is a key strategy for those exploring career options, and Monster contributing writer Carol Martin describes ten steps necessary to make the most of your interview. Another useful resource from the content-rich Monster.com career and job site.

If you're a student, consider asking your faculty and/or student advisers to help you set up a mock-interview day, where local practitioners help students practice and refine their interview skills through simulated interview situations. It provides a priceless opportunity to become familiar with the types of questions you'll be fielding (as well as asking) in a safe environment where the goal is to coach you to success.

Resources

Books

Bridges, William. *Creating You & Co.: Learn to Think Like the CEO of Your Own Career.* Perseus Books Group, 1998. 208 pp. ISBN 0738200328.
The follow-up to *Jobshift* (see below), *Creating You & Co* has a stronger focus on the actions you can take to ensure your ongoing ability to engage with meaningful work (and get paid), whether as an employee or an independent. Bridges calls his book a "do-it-yourself career development program," and his focus on identifying and making the most of your unique professional assets echoes the portfolio professional theme. The tactical complement to *Jobshift*.

Bridges, William. *Jobshift: How to Prosper in a Workplace Without Jobs.* Addison-Wesley, 1994. 272 pp. ISBN 0201489333.
A more conceptual than actionable overview of what the world of work will look like as it transitions from jobs to projects and portfolios. Bridges builds an "Americanized" and popularized response to the key idea presented by British management consultant Charles Handy in *Age of Unreason* (see below), i.e., that the stable workplace is devolving into an environment of discontinuous change and highly impermanent working relationships. A bit dated, but conceptually useful.

Hakim, Cliff. *We Are All Self-Employed: The New Social Contract for Working in a Changed World.* Berrett-Koehler, 2003. 250 pp. ISBN 1881052796.
A thoughtful exploration of the importance of moving from an employed to a self-employed mindset, and the implications for your career and life of making that transition. See especially the chart on pages 8 and 9 that compares the differences between the two in terms of attitudes and applications, regardless of whether you're drawing a paycheck.

Handy, Charles. *The Age of Unreason.* New ed. Harvard Business School Press, 1998. 288 pp. ISBN 08758443018.
The book that predicted the de-jobbing of the workplace as a social and economic phenomenon. Handy, a British organizational management

expert, argued that the historical workplace of stable jobs and lifelong employment was going to be replaced by a working environment characterized by constant, random, and discontinuous change. He predicted the emergence of a new class of workers called "portfolio professionals" whose work would be project-based, networked, and decentralized. A fascinating work upon whose ideas many others have built.

Reinhold, Barbara Bailey. *Free to Succeed: Designing the Life You Want in the New Free Agent Economy*. Plume, 2001. 258 pp. ISBN 0452282519. *Free to Succeed* is hardcore "how-to": lots of checklists, charts, statistics, and exercises—to be expected of an author who's also a professional career coach. But much of her advice is both thought-provoking and actionable, even though its focus is not specific to the LIS profession. A useful resource for brainstorming ideas and possibilities.

Articles

Grealy, Deborah S. and Barbara A. Greenman. "Special Librarians Set New Standard for Academe," *Information Outlook*, vol. 2, no. 8 (August 1998), pp. 17–22.
Grealy and Greenman take a look at SLA's core competencies from the vantage point of academic librarians, and explain how they can easily transfer into the academic environment. An interesting take on the transferability and adaptability of core professional skills.

"Promotion" issue, *Info Career Trends*, July 2002
www.lisjobs.com/newsletter/archives.htm
A collection of articles written by practitioners on the topic of professional visibility, creating a "successful dossier," and other recommended approaches for advancing your career.

Weathers-Parry, Patte. "The Librarian's Portfolio," *Info Career Trends*, January 2001. Accessed at www.lisjobs.com/newsletter/archives/jan01pparry.htm on June 25, 2005.
Weathers-Parry does a great job of combining her insights as a former career trainer with her LIS credentials and expertise to present a practical guide to assembling an effective professional portfolio for LIS careers. She explains what a portfolio is, why it's useful from a career standpoint, and how to go about putting one together.

Zipperer, Lorri. "Librarians in Evolving Corporate Roles," *Information Outlook*, Special Libraries Association, vol. 2, no. 6 (June 1998), pp. 27–30. Although written several years ago, this article nevertheless provides an interesting and well-thought-out overview of the ways in which special librarians can repurpose their LIS skills to play new roles within the corporate environment.

Online Resources

Internet Librarianship: Traditional Roles in a New Environment
www.ifla.org/IV/ifla66/papers/005–120e.htm
This paper was authored and presented by Kate Sharp, University of Bristol (UK), at the sixty-sixth IFLA Council and General Conference in August 2000. It's an interesting and thought-provoking tour through

the various new roles open to LIS professionals in the "age of the Internet." An excellent example of transferring LIS skill sets to new career opportunities.

Transferable Job Skills

www.quintcareers.com/transferable_skills.html

Part of the Quintessential Careers site presented by QuintCareers, this resource brings together five practical articles on identifying and showcasing in-demand transferable skills. Three of the articles deal with shaping cover letters so that they most effectively highlight your transferable skills, while the two others speak to their strategic value to your career and provide a detailed list of transferable skills organized by category (communication, research and planning, human relations, organization/management/leadership, and work survival). Not specific to LIS careers, but nevertheless applicable.

Note

1. Sally Gibson, "Personal Interests and Organizational Needs: A Balancing Act," *Info Career Trends*, 6(3) (May 2005). Accessed at www.lisjobs.com/newsletter/archives/may05sgibson.htm on October 27, 2005.

7
Growing Your Career

As we've seen, reframing your professional experiences through a portfolio lens lets you showcase the patterns and major accomplishments of your career to date. It can help you identify areas of interest that you might want to pursue further, or directions in which you might want to extend your professional "reach" (for example, bridging your reference skills into doing a column on business information resources for the local business journal).

This reframing process will also, however, help highlight gaps in your knowledge base, areas where you may want to actively reframe how the world perceives those skills and what they can do, and/or a need to more actively build your professional support community. What do you need to learn, how do you need to position your skills, and with whom do you need to build relationships in order to grow your career? These three elements will help build the underlying foundation of your resilient career.

The Learning Edge

In a world that is constantly changing, there is no one subject or set of subjects that will serve you for the foreseeable future, let alone for the rest of your life. The most important skill to acquire now is learning how to learn.

—John Naisbitt

One of the most powerful ways of opening up new career opportunities is through continually expanding what you know, and what you are able to do. It's often critical to being promoted by your current employer, it provides a competitive advantage when you are applying for a new job, and it's frequently the key to bridging existing skills into a new professional arena.

135

In some areas, such as academic librarianship or highly technical special librarianship jobs, a second master's degree in addition to the MLIS is often part of the job description, or at least highly preferred in job applicants. In addition, many LIS pros who've been in the workforce for a while consider graduate degrees in related fields such as knowledge management, technical communications, instructional design, or geographic information systems (GIS) as a way of opening up new job opportunities. Many LIS professionals in the corporate environment find that having an MBA gives them an extra element of credibility in conversations with senior executives.

But even if your career aspirations don't depend on another degree, you should still assume ongoing learning will be a pretty regular part of your career plans. In the words of Grace Anne DeCandido to MLIS graduates at SUNY Albany, "You have your degree, but you make your education every day. One of the great joys of being a librarian is that it is the last refuge of the renaissance person—everything you have ever read or learned or picked up is likely to come in handy."[1]

When thinking about your own career, the questions to ask involve what sorts of skills and knowledge add value to your professional "asset base," what options exist for expanding your professional expertise, how you personally learn most easily and effectively, and what steps you can take to ensure your knowledge stays up to date—if not ahead of the curve.

What Do You Need to Learn?

Two terms that are familiar to planners in all organizations are *gap analysis* and *SWOT analysis*. A gap analysis is an assessment of existing resources versus resources needed to achieve a stated goal, and identification of the gap between the two. From a career perspective, this means you would list your current skill set and knowledge base, identify the skills and knowledge necessary for potential jobs you'd be interested in (think job posting sites), and determine what skills fall into the gap. This becomes the basis for your learning agenda.

In a SWOT analysis, you identify strengths, weaknesses, opportunities, and threats. In terms of your career, your strengths and weaknesses would be based on which of your skills you have confidence in and which could use some work (or are nonexistent). Your opportunities and threats would focus on what career paths might be open to you based on your existing or future skills, and what paths might be closed to you if your knowledge doesn't keep pace with information and technology advances.

Either one of these approaches will help you develop your personal learning agenda, a set of learning goals that will map out what things you want to learn more about in the coming months/years, and how you will go about learning them.

What types of skills or expertise will add value to your professional portfolio? These will differ for everyone, since your aspirations will probably be quite different from those of your friends. However, it may help to think about them in the general categories of—

- discipline-specific professional skills and areas of expertise
- general professional skills
- business skills common to all organizations, including nonprofits, government agencies, and libraries

- personal competencies, what SLA describes as those "attitudes, skills and values that enable practitioners to work effectively and contribute positively to their organizations, clients and profession."[2]

Discipline-specific professional skills and areas of expertise. This area focuses on the core skills associated with LIS professionals. This might include reference and/or research; organizing information; putting together technology-based information systems; developing knowledge collections; creating web content; providing bibliographic instruction, etc. But it may also include advanced subject expertise in a specific discipline, say Japanese history or chemical engineering or law. Skills in web portal or intranet design and implementation, competitive intelligence, taxonomy-building, and information architecture would also be considered "discipline-specific" areas of expertise.

What makes for a basic skill set here? Several individuals and organizations have weighed in on this question. In "The Newly Minted MLS: What Do We Need to Know Today," information broker Mary Ellen Bates was asked what skills she'd like to see in every library school graduate. Among other skills, she listed—

- Basic librarian skills
- A basic proficiency in the traditional online services
- Basic Internet skills, "all the way from searching the Net to building Web sites"
- A solid grasp of the information landscape and when to use which information source
- "Value-added librarians," comfortable with multiple roles such as "researcher, counselor, planner, manager, assessor, team member, problem-solver, and computer printer repairman"
- Teaching (not just training) skills
- Strong "people skills"[3]

For those either working in the corporate world or hoping to do so, SLA's *Core Competencies for Information Professionals in the 21st Century* identifies four types of discipline-specific competencies: managing information organizations, managing information resources, managing information services, and applying information tools and technologies. Although few of us are proficient in all four of these areas, most LIS professionals targeting the corporate environment should check out SLA's examples of competency in each of these areas for a personal "gap analysis."

General professional skills. These competencies support your ability to perform your job responsibilities effectively, regardless of what they are. These skills can be honed in graduate school as well as on the job—yes, there really *is* a payoff to all those group projects! Some of the most important (and useful) professional skills include—

- Communication skills: verbal, written (including print and online), and listening
- Teaching/training/coaching skills, which include not only subject knowledge but also an understanding of how to help others learn

- Presentation skills, which encompass the ability to create effective Powerpoint slides, to speak confidently and persuasively to groups large and small, and to speak to the media on behalf of your organization when appropriate

- Time management, which includes a clear understanding of the limitations imposed by a 24-hour day

- Leadership skills, including the ability to inspire, motivate, set priorities, model accountability, and practice self-leadership in your own life

Business skills. Based on an understanding of how organizations (not just businesses) operate, these skills are often critical to professional advancement. However, there is rarely sufficient time to cover them in any depth in most MLIS programs, which leaves most of us scrambling to pick up this knowledge "on the fly." These skills may include:

- An ability to analyze and synthesize information, *and* the ability to draw from it and effectively present your conclusions to senior executives

- Solid business acumen; an understanding of your organization's strategic goals, the arena within which it operates (be that social services or bioengineering), and your proactive role in helping to implement key strategies

- An ability to analyze and improve business processes, both in your department and throughout the organization

- An understanding of the product (or program) development lifecycle, with an emphasis on key information components of the process and how your skills support them

- Strong project management skills, with an ability to effectively manage the key resources of time, personnel, and money against stated objectives and deadlines

- Familiarity with basic strategic planning approaches (understanding that each organization usually has its own unique variation of these processes), and an ability to plan for your department as well as an ability to contribute to enterprise-wide planning activities

- An ability to manage staff fairly, consistently, and with an understanding of current performance-improvement practices

- An ability to manage vendor relations, including developing RFPs (requests for proposals), evaluating proposal responses, and negotiating contracts

Personal Competencies. Deb Grealy and Barbara A. Greenman applied these same concepts to academic librarians (and other LIS professionals) in their article "Special Librarians Set New Standard for Academe," an exploration of how SLA's core competencies statement applies equally well to academic librarians. They pointed out that the competencies could be "categorized broadly under five general headings: Vision, Service, Networks, Professional Growth, and Political Acumen." In addition, noted the authors, "many of SLA's competencies embody vision-related attributes. These include a positive response to change, a recognition of needs for specialized clientele, a "big picture" orientation, and a proficiency for prioritizing and planning with a time/energy focus."[4]

What Are Your Learning Options?

Once you've identified *what* you need to learn, you next need to determine *how* you're going to learn. The good news here: we live in the age of the free-agent learner. That means regardless of your circumstances, there are multiple ways to expand your skill set. It will be up to you to determine which options are best for you at any given time.

There are a number of questions to think about before you look at which choices work best for you. For example, do you prefer a formal learning experience (i.e., interacting with an instructor in a face-to-face or online classroom, either with fellow students or independently)? Or perhaps an informal experience, such as working with a mentor or learning community, reading a book, taking an online tutorial? Does online learning work best for your hectic schedule, or does the learning dynamic of face-to-face classroom interaction suit you better?

Is getting official credit for your learning important for your career, or would a noncredit option work just as well for you? (Often this choice is related to employee tuition reimbursement.) Is it important that your education be delivered within the context of an MLIS program (perhaps through a continuing ed course), or is it useful to take courses outside the profession? For example, sometimes for purposes of building a portfolio, it makes more sense to take courses outside the library profession to demonstrate your interest in and ability to bridge multiple disciplines. (It's also a great way to start building a broader professional network.)

Once you've thought through those options, you'll want to next consider how and where: on the job, from the LIS profession, from your own professional community, from an MLIS program (as either an enrolled student or as an occasional, self-directed learner), or from other sources.

Learning on the job. Learning on the job can include on-site training programs, project work, professional development funds, and tuition reimbursement.

Workplace training is a great option when available: you don't have to pay for it, it leaves your nights and weekends free, and you can immediately put into practice what you've learned. Also, it's often focused on in-demand *transferable skills*, so that you can be boosting your value to the organization and bulking up your portfolio at the same time. Many organizations have a dedicated training budget for all employees, and it just makes sense to make sure you take advantage of every dollar available to you.

Your workplace is also a great place to learn by doing. Work projects give you an opportunity to develop new skills by working with experienced pros, and you'll get immediate and ongoing feedback on whether your skills are up to the task. As you create your learning agenda, think about opportunities to volunteer for new initiatives within your organization based on what new knowledge or skill development they'll offer.

Professional development funds are dollars made available for conference attendance, job-related workshops, seminars, and preconferences, as well as job-related courses or classes. This can be an important benefit when you're building a portfolio, so be sure you're taking maximum advantage of your employer's support and consider it one of the items you might include in salary negotiations.

Tuition reimbursement is money paid either directly to you (the student-employee) or an accredited education institution for undergraduate or graduate for-credit courses. You usually need to demonstrate some relationship between your job responsibilities and the course/degree program you want to pursue, but many organizations are fairly flexible here. Also, it's not necessary to take only graduate-level courses; if a local community college has a dynamic course in portal design, there's no reason not to take it. Your tuition reimbursement amount may be tied to your class grade, and you'll most likely be attending class during evenings or weekends (even with online learning), but you'll have an opportunity to broaden your skills with only an investment of time, rather than money.

In the words of Priscilla K. Shontz in *Jump Start Your Career*, "Make sure you leave smarter than you started."

Learning from the LIS profession. It's often noted that one of the really great things about this profession is peoples' willingness to share knowledge. That means you're part of one of the world's biggest learning communities.

Find successful local practitioners who have done what you're interested in doing, take them to lunch, and ask them what the key skills are in their position—and how they learned theirs. Even if they can't take the time for lunch or coffee, most will at least be able to respond with an e-mail answer, albeit a brief one (and possibly a few weeks down the road).

Enlist one of the most valuable and easily accessed learning tools of the professional community by signing up for the best blogs, electronic discussion groups, and RSS feeds in your areas of interest. Get a sense of who's most knowledgeable, most innovative, most credible on a given topic, and track their thinking.

Sign up for online and regional courses, workshops, and one-day seminars through professional associations like the Special Libraries Association, the Public Library Association, or the Medical Library Association (and their regional chapters). Check out classes offered by your local library council, state library, or regional bibliographic utility, or look into regionally delivered vendor training. Consider joining a local users' group focusing on a new skill you want to develop, or start one yourself. Check into attending preconferences at state and national association conferences and conventions if their focus aligns with your learning objectives.

Even if you can't attend their preconferences, conferences themselves offer a wealth of learning opportunities. A survey of their presentation topics will provide an excellent overview of emerging and hot issues throughout the profession or in the specific focus area of the conference (for example, Internet Librarian). Session presentations usually emphasize best-practices, current thinking, effective solutions, systems, and processes—in general, actionable information.

In addition to helping you identify thought leaders in a given discipline (whose writings and presentations you can then track), conferences may also connect you with experts willing to answer e-mail questions from you at a later date. Also, exhibitors and vendors are there to share information with conference attendees (well, actually they're there to sell things, but the easiest way to do that is to share information), and often offer free user meetings, product training classes, and demonstrations.

Keep in mind that, in general, all LIS and LIS-related associations have strong education and professional development mandates as part of their missions. Therefore, be sure to check the websites of any associations in your area of interest to see what sorts of education programs they offer, many of which may be available to you online.

Learning from your own professional community. Don't forget that your network of professional colleagues is an incredibly valuable, informal, and readily available source of knowledge and expertise. As we go through our careers, we build relationships with fellow students, co-workers, association colleagues, people we meet as fellow panelists at professional conferences, and myriad other connecting points. This community of colleagues is not only one of the most rewarding aspects of having a long career, it also offers a rich source of advice, counsel, and insight.

LIS professionals are legendary for their willingness to share information with each other, and learning from friends is one of the fastest, most enjoyable ways to expand your knowledge base. The only caveat: be ready to be a resource for others when your knowledge needs to be tapped.

Learning in grad school. Being in grad school is a terrific opportunity to learn—but it's up to you to set your own learning agenda in order to most effectively position yourself for maximum career opportunity. Every course you take provides two learning paths that should go forward side by side: the structured learning identified in the course syllabus, and the self-directed learning you identify for yourself.

For example, in a business research class, your learning agenda might include researching the telecommunications industry, trends in corporate information centers, or social entrepreneurship if these are areas of interest for you. In an information ethics class, you may decide to perfect your presentation or group leadership skills. In a knowledge management class, you may choose to research bioinformatics for your class project with an eye toward expanding your sci/tech expertise. Or for your paper in your Information Access and Retrieval course, you may decide to interview several thought leaders to understand not only current practice but also future trends. You may decide to do a practicum or internship in a related field—say, publishing—in order to broaden your understanding of how this industry works. Approach every course assignment asking "what do I want to learn with this?," rather than "what do I have to do to get an A on this?" Align every paper, project, and class activity with your personal career agenda whenever possible, and you will be both learning the core LIS knowledge and positioning yourself for your postgraduate career.

The key is to establish and follow your own learning goals along with your professor's, so that you are learning both the core knowledge as framed by the profession as well as the general professional skills and personal competencies that will help you create the career you desire.

Learning after grad school. In the old days (okay, several years ago), in order to take advantage of MLIS courses, it was necessary to show up on campus. Today, we can often choose between the options of campus-based or online learning. We have the option of completing a course, a certificate, or a graduate degree. Few of these options are inexpensive, but they can be an effective and reliable way to expand a key skill area. Alternatively, they can offer an excellent way to bridge into new career opportunities. A certificate in competitive intelligence might be used to land a job with a corporate business development group, a course in bioinformatics to position you for a health sciences information center.

To keep costs down if employer tuition reimbursement isn't available and credit isn't an issue, consider that most MLIS programs will allow you to audit courses (for no credit) at a reduced fee.

Learning from other sources. Community colleges. Non-LIS graduate programs. Free universities. Training CDs. Books. Web tutorials. Private training companies not affiliated with the LIS world. The IT guru down the hall. Your kids, who knew more about the digital surround by the sixth grade than the rest of us will ever catch up with. A mentor who will coach you through your learning path.

There are many, many ways to expand your knowledge and skills, depending on what criteria you need to meet. If you are able to focus on the learning itself and don't need a credential or credit to document it, then consider the least expensive options first, including informal learning.

Mapping Your Learning Agenda

Whether you're a student or an LIS professional, it's important that *you* be in charge of your learning agenda. It's one of your strongest tools for maximum career flexibility and ongoing career growth. And the best way to organize and follow through on that agenda is by creating a personal education map.

An overview of what you need to learn to continue to move toward your career goals, this infinitely changeable document should reflect the "knowledge feed" coming in through your information monitoring and outside reading. Your goal will be to identify key skills that will complement, enrich, or extend your core professional competencies in response to emerging opportunities. But for starters, and to organize your thinking, take out your career journal and start working through the questions shown in "Your Career Map", being sure to note your responses in your journal.

Make a commitment to the critical role of education in your career, and put yourself in charge. Your ability to keep learning in the coming decades will determine your ability to keep working, participating, and contributing. As you work through your learning agenda, remember to incorporate opportunities to try out various learning styles until you find the ones that work best for you. Try to be conscious of your learning process, and how to set up the circumstances and environment that work best for you. Music or silence? Two hours every weeknight or eight hours on Saturday? Lunch hours at the library or Thursdays with your student group? Practice coaching yourself through that awkward beginning stage where you feel like you'll never figure things out. Pay attention to how your positive or negative attitudes about learning new material impact your learning effectiveness.

Shaping Perceptions

As you expand your knowledge base, the next challenge to growing your career is to take charge of how you—and your skills—are viewed in the world.

How many times have we heard that perception is everything? Consider, then, this comment from a review of Louis Rosenfeld and Peter

Your Education Map

Consider the four skill areas—discipline-specific, general professional skills, business skills, and personal competencies. Then in your career journal create a four-column table that focuses on the key questions: what do I need to learn, how will I learn it, when will I learn it, and how will I practice it? Your table might look something like this:

Need to Learn?	How?	When?	Practice?
How to give more effective presentations	Read three best books on speaking and presenting, take a Powerpoint class through Web Junction, ask colleagues to critique my presentation style	One book every two weeks starting next week; Powerpoint class one week after books completed, colleague critique after every presentation, then review notes on the weekend	Find opportunity to give one presentation every other month to different types of audiences, e.g., colleagues, patrons/customers, community members
Grant-writing	Take grant-writing class at local community college	This fall	Volunteer to write grant proposals for local humane society and other community groups

Your "How" options are nearly endless. Will you attend a workshop or read a book? Join an association or sign up for an online class? Consider your job, your grad school classes—how can they be adapted to support your learning agenda? What projects will you volunteer for in order to practice a key career skill? You're responsible for your own professional growth, so put yourself in charge of your learning agenda for every new project, class, opportunity.

Explore the least expensive learning options in your community, investigate online learning programs and courses, and find out what your employer's tuition reimbursement, professional development, and workforce training policies are.

Also, if you are considering a major commitment such as a second master's degree, assume each class will take roughly twelve to twenty hours per week of study time, and do a "test run" for a month to see whether or not you can actually carve out that amount of time without a total derailment of your work and personal lives. What will you be giving up, and is that acceptable? Equally important, will this level of commitment be sustainable over the coming months and years?

Some ideas for broadening your career skill set if you're a student? Think about...

... taking classes either within or outside your LIS program that ramp up your communications skills. These include your ability to write clearly, concisely, and authoritatively; your ability to create and deliver effective presentations; and your ability to understand and respond to gender and multicultural communications issues in the workplace.

... using grad school to learn how to think about the processes and skills you're using. For example, use your cataloging class to explore the broader process of organizing information, your reference class to consider the dynamic of interpersonal information exchange, team projects to think about group dynamics, motivation, etc. Consider *why* as well as *how*, build a knowledge base of abstract understanding that will position you to apply knowledge and understand patterns in new situations.

... using those classes that require substantial amounts of studying to try out the various methods of mastering new information, with the aim of discovering the approaches that are most effective for you.

Your goal here will be to focus your learning efforts in a way that most effectively supports your career goals, with the understanding that as those goals change, the learning agenda supporting them will as well.

Morville's best-selling classic, *Information Architecture for the World Wide Web* (O'Reilly, 1998), in *The Denver Business Journal*, August 21–27, 1998:

> *With many fine thinkers in the field, the publisher's choice of two librarians for its authoritative book on the subject is a curious one. Nonetheless, the leading publisher on Internet topics provides a useful primer.*

Or consider this moment from my days heading up a business that had created and was marketing a virtual library for online students. I was being interviewed by the business writer for a major city newspaper for an article about the company and the product, and the writer asked me how we had created the library. When I proudly explained that we had been working with over 100 academic reference librarians and subject specialists from throughout the country, he looked at me in stunned surprise and said "Librarians? Librarians have been creating this? I thought librarians just basically got the books down off the shelf for you and then put them back. Do they really know enough to do this?"

Mindful that whatever spiffy (if gratifying) zinger I came back with was likely to see its way into print, I tried to calmly point out to him the multifaceted and intellectually complex world librarians and other information pros navigated on a daily basis. He was amazed and clearly a bit skeptical (although later one of our most outstanding grad students went to work for his organization, so I have no doubt he now understands just what an asset her skills are). This man was well-educated, a journalist immersed in the world of information, someone we might hope would "get it." No such luck.

The reality is, a devoted minority of the community—whether that is the public, school, academic, or corporate community—think we're terrific, invaluable, worth every penny invested. The rest of the world has opinions that fall on a continuum ranging from "nice to have and worth the investment when we have enough money" to "I don't know, what do they do?" to "we can't afford this, and everything's on the web anyway, so why would we need it?"

The profession as a whole continues to grapple with the issue of public perceptions, looking for ways to market its resources and services to its constituencies in ways that demonstrate value. Sometimes it works, other times budget cuts override best intentions. What this means to you from a career perspective, however, is that it's going to be up to you to define how you want the world to perceive you. If your target audience (i.e., potential employers and/or clients) has a preconceived, constricting notion of who and what librarians are—and are capable of—it's going to be up to you to change those perceptions.

The way you do this is by creating you own personal brand. In the marketing world, a brand is the collective characteristics that the market attributes to a given product or service. Think of Ben and Jerry's, Apple, Nike, Target, Estee Lauder. Whether or not we use their products, we associate specific brand characteristics with each.

Those brand characteristics are communicated through language, actions, visuals, and advertising. Library branding guru Chris Olson describes these as "brand touchpoints," defining them as "all of the physical, communication, and human interactions" that our audiences or constituencies have with us. Explaining how SLA manages its branding initiatives for its various markets, she further elaborates:

> *The concept of a brand touchpoint is key to understanding and managing the brand experience and its impact on memories and perceptions. . . . Touchpoints can include websites, newsletters, phone conversations with staff members, conferences, press releases, division initiatives, advertisements, networking introductions, sponsorships, awards, publications, announcements, mentoring chats, presentations, chapter meetings, referrals, seminars, exhibit displays, promotion items, interviews, communities – to name a few. Each touchpoint offers us the opportunity to establish and build our brand into a positive experience and memory.*[5]

Creating your personal brand will entail many of the same types of touchpoints. You communicate your brand every day through:

- your language—is it hesitant or confident, friendly or cold, arrogant or supportive, professional or careless? If you want to be known as someone who's energetic and takes initiative, passive or hesitant language will undermine that perception.

- your dress—does your clothing reinforce the way you want your potential employer or client to think of you? This differs radically from constituency to constituency, but it helps to look like the person you want to connect with, which may either be the employer *or* the employer's constituency (for example, students, if you're an academic librarian).

- your contributions—do the projects you work on/volunteer for demonstrate the professional characteristics you want to be known for? For example, your brand may include a commitment to community service, or a passion for outdoor sports, or innovative thinking.

- your public communications—if you blog, post to electronic discussion lists, have a website, write articles, contribute to newsletters, or give presentations, you are creating the public's perceptions of your brand by the topics on which you focus, the language and writing style you use, the values you espouse, and the issues you champion.

- if you're a student, your grad-school participation—are you known for bringing energy and intellectual engagement to the class, or do you make it clear you're uninterested; do you find ways to support your student colleagues, or avoid unnecessary contact; do you organize dynamic student programs or let others do all the work?

How you present yourself to your professional world will signify to others what to expect of you and how to treat you. Are you sending a consistent message that says "I expect to be treated as someone with substantial value to contribute?"

Robin Fisher Roffer, author of *Make a Name for Yourself* (Broadway, 2002), suggests the "holy trinity" of a great brand are consistency, clarity, and authenticity. (And who would argue with a branding expert who cites as one of her examples the librarian at CNN who "refers to herself as the 'Information Goddess of popular culture'?")

But Roffer makes an important point,which is that branding is not representing yourself to be something you're not. It's simply making sure that the world has an opportunity to see all the terrific things you *are*. Are you creative, enthusiastic, reliable, a "go-to" person? Do you want to be known as a change agent, a social activist, a decisive leader? Do you want potential employers and/or clients to think of you as a smart and savvy strategist who can also execute effectively? Whatever you are at your authentic core, this is what you want to make visible to your professional environment.

Think of branding as simply taking the initiative to shape others' perceptions of your skills and abilities before they form opinions based on faulty assumptions that will limit your ability to contribute. It's an opportunity to showcase your strengths.

Your Community of Colleagues

Lastly, as you continue to build your professional knowledge and position it within your environment, you'll also want to focus on the breadth and depth of your professional community. There are many good reasons to go to work every day, not the least of which is being able to buy groceries. But the longer your career, the more likely you'll find that the real reward of professional work is not money, but relationships—the community of colleagues who share your values, your stories, your concerns and commitments.

Through a stroke of good fortune, this same community of colleagues is also your strongest ally when it comes to creating your resilient career.

Building Your Professional Community

Nearly every day brings an opportunity to build the relationships that woven together make up your lifelong professional community. The key thing is to approach this not so much as an investment in your career success but rather as one of the richest rewards of life: being in a position to support others. The key question is—what can I do to help?

Consider the following "short-list" of ways you might be able to help a colleague:

Passing along information about a job opening

Sharing your expertise to help someone do his or her job better

Brainstorming ideas with a colleague needing to develop new solutions

Providing introductions and connections among colleagues

Recommending someone for a job

Bringing someone in on a committee

Publicly applauding someone's efforts or accomplishments

Pinch-hitting for someone on a professional commitment

Sharing information of value you've come across

Contributing your expertise to a colleague's social cause

Mentoring younger (or older!) colleagues

Publicly sharing credit with everyone who has contributed to a successful effort

Now you try. Take out your career journal and think back through your career so far. Note in what ways people have helped you in your career, and whether or not you have been able to return the favor. Now think about ways you can imagine helping others, based on what you know or who you know. This reciprocity is the heart of building a professional community that allows you to contribute to the success of others. It's also what allows them to participate in yours.

We're not talking "rolodex networking" here—we're talking the trust that begins to build when you have an opportunity to say "how can I help?" to a co-worker, or a fellow committee-member, or a classmate. About the lifelong friendships that evolve out of shared professional challenges and efforts. About the goodwill that grows from your willingness to share knowledge, expertise, and credit for accomplishments.

When you seek to build a professional community by asking "how can I help you" rather than "how can you help me," you create relationships whose foundation is giving rather than taking. The goodwill and trust that builds from this is not only invaluable and intrinsically rewarding at the deepest human levels, it also becomes extraordinarily helpful when you need to expand career options. The people you know also know lots of other people—and if you've been a caring and responsive colleague, they'll probably be willing to help connect you with names, job opportunities, or potential projects.

Your community of colleagues can not only give you good career advice, they can also tell you when you're entirely off base. They can be your brain-trust on emerging trends and issues in an area of professional interest, giving you the confidence that comes from knowing you don't have to know everything. Why? Because your diverse family of colleagues not only pretty much *does* know everything, they're also willing to share. (Because, of course, *you* have been willing to share in the past....)

Building your professional community is as much an investment in your resilient career as continually expanding your knowledge base and shaping how the world perceives you as a professional. Although all three will require your willingness to invest time and effort to grow and sustain them, all are also likely to open up unforeseen pathways of opportunity.

Resources

Books

Bruner, Robert F. *The Portable MBA*. 4th ed. Wiley, 2002. 384 pp. ISBN 0471222844.
The fourth edition of the book that launched the series, *Portable MBA* is included here as an example of a type of resource—the topical introduction or overview. For individuals trying to quickly come up to speed on a given subject, books like *The Portable MBA* (if well done) offer a great solution for quick "top-level" understanding. You won't have an in-depth knowledge of the topic, but you should be able to understand most of the jargon, key points, and issues under discussion— think "just-in-time" learning. Other *Portable* titles include *Finance and Accounting, Strategy, Management, Entrepreneurship, Marketing, Economics*, and *Project Management*. Quality varies among titles.

Ellis, David B. *Becoming a Master Student*. 10th ed. Houghton Mifflin, 2002. 400 pp. ISBN 0618206787.
This book is designed as a very practical "how-to" guide for students trying to understand how to most effectively study and learn. It is primarily skill-focused with some treatment of psychological and emotional issues. For a completely different viewpoint, check out Guy Claxton's books—*Hare Brain, Tortoise Mind: How Intelligence Increases When You Think Less* (Harper Perennial, 2000) and *Wise-Up: The Challenge of Lifelong Learning* (Bloomsbury USA, 2000)—which embrace a less rational, more intuitive approach to learning.

Gardner, Howard. *Frames of Mind: The Theory of Multiple Intelligences*. 10th ed. Basic Books, 1993. 440 pp. ISBN 0465025102.
The classic work on the seven types of intelligence: bodily-kinesthetic, linguistic, logical-mathematical, musical, personal, and spatial. Will help you understand how you learn most effectively, and enable you to tailor your studying and learning processes appropriately.

Goleman, Daniel P. *Emotional Intelligence: Why It Can Matter More than IQ*. Bantam Books, 1997. 268 pp. IBSN 0553375067.
Goleman defines emotional intelligence as those characteristics such as self-awareness or empathy that enable us to be successful in both our personal and work lives. Although some are born with these characteristics, others can develop them and so greatly improve their social competence—and effectiveness in all areas of their lives. An

exceptionally engaging and valuable book, as is Goleman's *Primal Leadership: Learning to Lead with Emotional Intelligence* (Harvard Business School Press, 2004).

Helgesen, Sally. *The Female Advantage: Women's Ways of Leadership.* Doubleday, 1995. 302 pp. ISBN 0385419112.
The Female Advantage was one of the first books to document that not only did men and women have different styles of leadership, but that the female approach could be highly effective. An important resource for women who aspire to LIS leadership roles, especially since there is relatively little training in this area in most MLIS programs.

Nelson, Bob, Peter Economy, and Ken Blanchard. *Managing for Dummies.* 2nd ed. For Dummies, 2003. 384 pp. ISBN 0764517716.
This title is representative of others in the... *for Dummies* series: basic information, clearly written for those needing a primer on a given topic. These types of books can be an excellent starting point for those trying to understand the key points of a skill area, and who don't need an in-depth treatment. The series, which is expanding rapidly, includes computer and IT, basic business, and "soft" or people skills titles. Quality varies among titles.

Roffer, Robin Fisher. *Make a Name for Yourself: Eight Steps Every Woman Needs to Create a Personal Brand Strategy for Success.* Broadway, 2002. 224 pp. ISBN 0767904923.
Roffer describes herself as a "brand strategist," and although some of her strategies seem a bit, shall we say, *out there* for most of us, her underlying concepts make good sense: the world has a way of perceiving us, whether we shape those perceptions or by default let someone else do it for us. Her eight steps apply equally well to men and women, whether in traditional, nontraditional, or independent career paths.

Periodicals

The many LIS-related periodicals provide an excellent way to stay current with the profession and also to learn more about emerging ideas, issues, and technologies. We have noted the major publications, such as *Library Journal, Information Outlook*, and *American Libraries*, and almost all of the associations (and their larger special interest groups) also have topical magazines or newsletters whose focus is knowledge transfer.

There is also an increasing number of special-interest online publications; among the most frequently quoted are:

D-Lib Magazine
www.dlib.org
Focuses on "digital library research and development, including but not limited to new technologies, applications, and contextual social and economic issues." A place for thought leaders among the digital library community to share knowledge. Free archives at the website.

First Monday
www.firstmonday.org
Hosted by the University of Chicago's library staff, *First Monday* is an open-access, peer-reviewed journal devoted to the study of the Internet and its related issues and impacts. Its advisory board—and contributors—represent the thought leaders in this area. A challenging, and important, publication on a key topic for all LIS professionals.

LIBRES

http://libres.curtin.edu.au

A scholarly, refereed electronic journal with an international scope. *Libres* presents "new research in Library and Information Science," and is published by the Department of Media and Information, Curtin University of Technology in Perth, Western Australia. The journal sections include Research and Applications (e.g., "Types of Information Needs among Cancer Patients: A Systematic Review"), Essays and Opinions ("Profile of Australian Library Technician Students") and sections devoted to reviews, news from other journals, news and announcements, and conferences and meetings.

Articles

"Continuing Education" issue, *Info Career Trends*, May 2004

www.lisjobs.com/newsletter/archives.htm

A collection of articles exploring various approaches to continually expanding one's knowledge base.

"Education," LIScareer.com

www.liscareer.com/education.htm

A collection of articles from online and print publications that address both what we may need to learn and options for obtaining that education. In addition, Education includes links to related websites and print resources.

Wallace, Marie. "Climbing the Learning Ladder," LLRX.com

www.llrx.com/columns/guide69.htm

An excellent, user-friendly overview of individual learning approaches and how to most effectively derive value from your continuing education efforts. One of a series of online columns on career issues from Wallace.

Associations

In addition to the academic programs available to the profession, all of the major LIS associations offer professional development options. These may include online short courses, satellite-delivered seminars, tutorials offered at the website, preconference workshops, certification training, and other learning opportunities. Check the associations' websites for specific offerings, as well as whether or not they are available to members only.

Online Resources

About.com

www.about.com

With content generally written by knowledgeable amateurs, there are several About.com sites that may be of interest to those expanding their knowledge base. See About > Education > Adult/Continuing Education for information about how adults learn, financial aid for adults, and articles such as "Baby Boomers in College." See the Business page for information about business practices, industries, small businesses, and general business knowledge. Or check out the Computing and Technology page for both basic and advanced information about this constantly changing field. The About.com information varies in breadth, depth, and reliability, but can often provide just the clean overview of a topic you need in a pinch.

Continuing Education Clearinghouse
    www.ala.org/cetemplate.cfm?section=ceclearinghouse&template=/
    cfapps/contedu/searchmain.cfm
    A database of CE offerings from ALA and ALA-affiliated units. Use
    the "Advanced Search" feature to search by region, audience (e.g.,
    academic, public), level (e.g., beginning, advanced), subject (e.g.,
    administration and management, library in society, preservation of
    library materials).

Continuing Professional Development
    www.lis.uiuc.edu/clips/2002_10.html
    Assembled in 2002 by Marianne Steadley and hosted by the Uni-
    versity of Illinois, Urbana-Champaign, LIS program, this is a use-
    ful compendium of information about and resources for continuing
    professional development for LIS professionals. Among the topics
    Steadley covers are current awareness; research, publication, and ser-
    vice; networking; mentoring; and interactive continuing professional
    development.

*Directory of Institutions Offering ALA-Accredited Master's Programs in Li-
    brary and Information Studies*
    www.ala.org/Template.cfm?Section=lisdirb
    A searchable listing of and links to the fifty-six accredited LIS pro-
    grams. You have the option to limit your search by these criteria: face-
    to-face courses at other locations; primarily face-to-face with select on-
    line courses offered; primarily online with some face-to-face courses
    required; satellite or other broadcast methods; or 100 percent online
    program.

Learning Styles
    www.ldpride.net/learningstyles.MI.htm
    Although this site is hosted by a commercial group, it nevertheless of-
    fers a number of tests for assessing your personal learning styles. A
    useful starting point for learning more about how you learn most effec-
    tively.

Learning Styles Home Page
    http://web.indstate.edu/ctl/styles/ls1.html
    From Indiana State University's Center for Teaching and Learning,
    this resource is organized into three sections: models (or types) of learn-
    ing styles, articles about learning styles, and an inventory of learning
    styles approaches, some with links to further information. For those
    who want to explore learning styles from an academic standpoint.

Learning Times
    www.learningtimes.com
    Learning Times is an online community of education and LIS profes-
    sionals interested in exploring issues, ideas, and their implications. It
    hosts online conferences and webcasts, discussions, and debates (syn-
    chronous and asynchronous); supports member networking and com-
    munities of practice; and sponsors best-practice case studies. Member-
    ship is free.

Library Journals, Newsletters, and Zines
    www.libdex.com/journals.html
    A listing of roughly 125 publications related to the LIS world. Entries
    are organized alphabetically by title, many include several-word an-
    notations to indicate audience or publishing organization, and all are

linked to websites. A good starting point from which to explore information resources for the subjects you'd like to learn more about.

Library-Oriented Lists & Electronic Serials
http://liblists.wrlc.org
A directory of hundreds of LIS-related lists, searchable by title, subject, or keyword. Entries provide name of the list, subject, website URL, and subscribing information. Monitoring electronic discussion lists is one of the most effective professional development tools available, and this resource makes it easy to find just the list to address your area of interest.

Library Weblogs
www.libdex.com/weblogs.html#us
A directory of briefly annotated links for library blogs in the United States and other countries. For another LIS blog directory of more than 150 weblogs, see the listing at the Open Directory (http://dmoz.org) by searching Reference > Libraries > Library and Information Science > Weblogs.

Nationally Recognized NCATE-AASL Reviewed & Approved School Library Media Education Programs
www.ala.org/ala/aasl/aasleducation/schoollibrarymed/
ncateaaslreviewed.htm
Directory of and links to the thirty-two reviewed and approved school library media education programs. To limit to those offering some distance education component, go to the ALA accredited LIS programs page (www.ala.org/Template.cfm?Section=lisdirb) and search by the limiting criteria of school library media program and your distance ed option of interest.

OCLC Learning Library Partnership (LLP)
www.oclc.org/education
Business skills offered online, with a focus on competencies of value to all professionals. OCLC is partnering with the "For Dummies" publisher, Business Skills Videos, Mindleaders (IT courses), and Harvard Business School to deliver multiple online training and continuing ed options.

OLMS Training Skills Support Site
www.arl.org/training/ilcso/index.html
The intent of this site is to support academic librarians responsible for developing training programs, but it also has useful information for those wanting to gain a better understanding of the learning process (especially their own). See especially the two articles under "Adult Learning."

Web Junction Learning Center
http://webjunction.org
An "online community of libraries and other agencies sharing knowledge and experience to provide the broadest public access to information technology," Web Junction is a clearinghouse of information and best practices shared among U.S. and Canadian librarians. From a professional education standpoint, however, Web Junction's value is that it provides access to online courses and training that support LIS professional development. At the time of this writing, soon to launch was E-Learning Clearinghouse, a database of online education programs

and courses offered by ALA accredited graduate schools, community colleges and regional service providers.

Notes

1.   Grace Anne DeCandido, "Ten Graces for New Librarians," Commencement Address for the School of Information Science and Policy, SUNY/Albany, May 19, 1996, accessed at www.well.com/user/ladyhawk/albany.html on November 1, 2005.

2.   *Competencies for Information Professionals of the 21st Century.* Rev. ed. Special Libraries Association, June 2003. Accessed at www.sla.org/content/learn/comp2003/index.cfm on June 24, 2005.

3.   Mary Ellen Bates, "The Newly Minted MLS: What Do We Need to Know Today?" *Searcher*, 6(5) (May 1998), 31.

4.   Deborah S. Grealy and Barbara A. Greenman, "Special Librarians Set New Standard for Academe," *Information Outlook*, 2(8) (August 1998), 18.

5.   Chris Olson, "Brand Touchpoints," *Information Outlook*, 7(11) (November 2003), 38.

8
Thriving on Change

It's not the strongest of the species who survive,
nor the most intelligent, but the ones most
responsive to change.
—Charles Darwin

In careers as in life, change brings opportunity. In fact, if you have a good understanding of who you are and what you may want to achieve (which you do by now!), change can be a tremendous ally.

In 1934, Austro-American economist Joseph Schumpeter published his landmark study of entrepreneurship, *Theory of Economic Development: An Inquiry into Profits, Capital, Credit, Interest and the Business Cycle* (Harvard University Press). Although economists of the day generally dismissed any role for entrepreneurship as a major macroeconomic influence, Schumpeter asserted that periods of technological innovation and the entrepreneurial activities associated with them created "waves of creative destruction." Old ways of doing things were swept away, but were replaced by dynamic new processes and solutions, not to mention businesses and industries.

Well, yes, change *does* brings disruption, confusion, uncertainty, and often a sense of loss. No wonder it's so easy to default to our "duck and cover" response—if I ignore it, it just *might* go away. By now, however, most of us have realized that's probably not the most effective coping strategy, and many of us have learned to take a different approach. Like so many things, that involves reframing—specifically, reframing what change can mean in our lives.

If we take Schumpeter's vantage point, change offers opportunities where none previously existed. The trick is to learn how to spot them, and then how to align your skills with those opportunities. As Mary Ellen Bates has suggested, "learn to think like an entrepreneur," and that bit of wisdom applies whether you're employed or an independent.

Before you begin this chapter, take out your career journal and think back through moments of major change in your career. Note them in your journal, and we'll come back to them in a bit.

Positioning for Opportunity

It has been said that good luck is the result of preparedness meeting opportunity. Good career luck is no different: if you systematically prepare for the opportunities that changes in the profession create, then you're in a much better to position to recognize and respond to them.

A lot of this is simply training yourself to be aware of the world around you, but with an eye toward circumstances that could benefit from what you know, or know how to do. It also helps to think through some basic approaches to monitoring your environment that will help you target opportunities that most closely align with your individual goals.

As you start exploring your own changing landscape, think about the following approaches to help organize your process.

Understand what to look for. A number of business experts, economists, and futurists have weighed in on which change categories are most likely to produce economic opportunity, including management thought leader Peter Drucker in his *Innovation and Entrepreneurship* (Collins, 1993). Arguing that opportunities for change could be categorized and then monitored, he identified emerging trends, technology advances, changes in established processes, and changes in what he termed "industry and market structures" among other defining events or trends that brought about opportunity.

William Bridges, author of *Jobshift*: *How to Propser in a Workplace Without Jobs* (Perseus, 1995) and expert on change and transitions, included among his hit list a roadblock or a bottleneck, a shortage or limitation, or a chronic weakness. He also suggested that any interface between groups having different values, languages, or outlooks would necessitate new solutions.

Do any of these resonate in the library and information worlds? Consider—

- downsizing and layoffs at all types of libraries
- outsourcing of key operational functions
- the Internet's ongoing morphing
- new information and communications technologies
- disintermediation between user and information resource, i.e., "the Google effect," where users connect directly with information without intervention from librarians or other information professionals
- digitization of information resources, and "born digital" publishing
- perception/expectation of 24/7 accessibility of information
- the internationalization of information
- the aging of the profession
- organizations recognizing the value of information (if not always of the information center)

Okay, time to practice your change-framing skills. Take out your career journal and write down as many examples of the following types of change as you can identify in your own professional environment:

An unmet market (or organization) need

Example(s): _____

Upcoming or anticipated events (regulatory, demographic, technology-based) or trends that will necessitate new solutions

Example(s): _____

A product, service, or process in need of improvement (keeping in mind that process innovation—or simply figuring out how to do something better—can be as valuable as a product or service innovation)

Example(s): _____

These may apply as well to opportunities related to your current employer, industry, or community as they do to starting a new business. (Needless to say, some organizations are more responsive to new ideas than are others.)

Once you've identified all the changes you can think of, put your notes aside for a moment; we'll return to them momentarily.

- the prominence of individual, alternative information feeds through blogs, etc.

- emerging constituencies, for example, home schoolers, charter schools, adult/online learners, and ESL patrons

- the merging landscapes of the education, information, communications, and entertainment industries

- changing expectations of what a library is—and does—in the world

What opportunities do these changes represent? A recent article in *Library Journal* described how the Ann Arbor (MI) public library launched its innovative new website—made up of seven blogs. (New product.)[1] Although fewer corporations are investing in corporate libraries, more and more are embedding their information pros in functional teams, where they are key assets. (New role.) Although more users can access information directly, this has created a stronger teaching/coaching role for librarians than ever before. (New service.) Outsourcing information functions creates a need for freelancers and independents to step in on a project basis. (New business.)

In fact, each one of the changes noted above either has or will create opportunities within the profession—ones new and different from those we're comfortable with, but opportunities nevertheless.

Target your areas to monitor. There are three places to monitor for change: in your own environment, in that of the constituencies served by your organization or business, and in the world at large. For example, your own environment might be public libraries, and its constituencies a community of seniors, young adults, home schoolers, entrepreneurs, adult learners, and book club members.

Or your own environment might be the corporate library of an aerospace engineering firm, and its constituencies defense contractors, research and development (R&D) firms, government agencies, and regulators.

Or your environment might be an academic library, serving constituencies of traditional undergraduate students, graduate students, nontraditional students, full-time and adjunct faculty, and possibly alumni.

Or perhaps your environment is that of an information broker, and the constituencies you serve will be local small businesses, or law firms specializing in environmental issues, or high-tech start-ups in the biotech arena.

The point is that changes to the environments of your constituencies will have as much impact on your professional life as changes specific to your immediate environment. So it only makes sense to pay as much attention to what's going on in *their* lives as in yours. Changes there can be as likely to produce opportunity for you as those at your fingertips.

Beyond that, be aware of the world at large. Just because iPods started out as cool toys for early adopters and adolescents doesn't mean they're not going to end up playing a major role in how we deliver reference services. Keep your mind open to taking that creative leap of imagination, and look for connections—especially for those *outside* the LIS profession that may become solutions *within* it.

Set up a monitoring process. Staying attuned to changes in your world and others' involves monitoring information, looking for specific types of "signifiers," and thinking creatively about possible impacts and opportunities. Your primary tool is an environmental scan, or an ongoing, broad-ranging monitoring of emerging information in targeted disciplines as well as "outside the box."

Think about identifying context: extrapolating meaning and possibility from emerging patterns. As noted, your environmental scan should include resources both inside and outside of the LIS profession. But as part of your scan, look for information about new vocabulary, technology issues, and developments in your areas of specialization; about emerging trends and patterns; about disruptive ideas and technologies and events; about doors that are closing as well as those just opening.

Then take it to the next level. Based on the information and trend data you gather, extrapolate where those trends and ideas and disruptions might lead. Who will need what you can do—or what you'll soon know how to do? What position or role can you create that may not yet have a name or description? And what will you do to stay ahead of this curve?

Where to look? Periodicals, print and online, generally form the basis of an environmental scan, but blogs have added a new and often very useful type of information feed. Conferences are always a great source of emerging trends and technologies; even if you can't attend, many of the presentations will be available online after the event. Special "trends" issues of business publications are a great source of forecasts for key technologies, regulatory issues, potential international impacts, demographic trends, and other market influences; analyst reports when available are also valuable for their analysis and forecasts. Another source of trend indicators is professional

Take It Up a Level—Practice Building Scenarios

Scenarios are possible outcomes, based on specific circumstances. Scenario building is extrapolating various possible futures from stipulated sets of circumstances. Basically, what you're looking for is the range of possible outcomes, and then what changes and/or opportunities those may drive.

Let's go back to the change examples you wrote down earlier in your career journal, or you can use any of the following as "change events:

- An extremely large number of senior librarians are nearing retirement age

- Many next-gen librarians coming into the profession are having a difficult time finding full-time positions in their desired area of work

- The LIS profession is going to need to quickly train managers and leaders to step into key roles in all types of libraries to replace retirees

- Online learning is becoming increasingly effective and available

- Personal communications technologies (e.g., handhelds) continue to drive disruptive—but also enabling—changes

These are just a few data points we can identify within the profession; now let's throw in some variables. For example, assume that economies either improve (delivering additional funding) or worsen (further funding cuts). Or assume that older librarians start retiring early, or choose not to retire until much later.

For each change event you've noted, think through and describe several possible outcomes for what these various futures mean for your career. What opportunities might they present? Also, if circumstances improve, what choices *and actions* will that drive? If they worsen, what choices then?

One of your goals in building scenarios around these data points is to establish if/then options for yourself, so that no matter what happens, you're not completely blindsided. (In terms of today's workplace, the old advice to "expect the best, plan for the worst" has new resonance.) But the point of going through this exercise is also to make sure that you're in position to respond quickly when opportunities do arise, because you've already been visualizing your moves for just such an occasion.

As you go through the exercise of building scenarios based on the information you have available today, try also to think about how many different possible outcomes they might really indicate. Also, keep in mind Amara's Law (from Roy Amara, founding member of the Institute for the Future), which states that we tend to overestimate the impact of change in the short run and underestimate it in the long run.

In Peter Schwarz's classic work on scenario planning, *Art of the Long View* (Doubleday Currency, 1991), he makes the point that only by exploring possible futures will organizations be able to prepare or position for them, either from a defensive or opportunistic position. The same goes for you. By thinking about potential futures, you give yourself the intellectual space to consider alternative career strategies and responses. You also ensure yourself the maximum amount of flexibility among your choices.

associations, which often do annual forecasts on issues of interest to their membership.

What's the best way to get into this habit? Practice, practice, practice. Read the local business journal with a goal of identifying three potential employers or clients and the strategic contribution your skills could make to their organizations. Cruise *Library Journal* with a goal of picking the top five innovative ideas or programs or products. When you attend conferences, look for cutting-edge programs that address emerging challenges in your area of specialization.

Anticipate the future. Take a look at the publications that do annual forecasts, including business titles, science and tech publications, and social-science and futures-oriented issues like *The Futurist*. Explore their predictions, and try to identify a threat and an opportunity for information professionals in as many specific forecasts as possible. How might you—and the profession—position for each? Build scenarios: if this outcome happened, what would it mean to me? Do I think it likely? How would I position my career to prepare for this?

Read job postings, look for changing parameters for traditional jobs, and new positions with possibilities for LIS professionals. Where there's a match between your skills and an unusual position, think through what makes this type of work valuable to the employer, then consider for whom else it would be valuable as well. Can you pitch this role to other potential employers, or this service to potential clients?

Read for questions as well as answers. Perhaps the most important questions are "what impacts might this have," and "upon whom?" Look for changes happening in the profession, in the communities you serve, in your target constituencies or industry (if in corporate), and in the market of your target industry. Look for who needs your skills but doesn't know it yet.

As you scan your environment, consider how your education agenda will help position you for the changes you see. Does your environmental scan turn up more strengths than weaknesses, more opportunities than threats? If so, you know you're on the right track.

Make opportunity work for you. Go back to the change events, possible outcomes, and positioning strategies you identified. As you consider these circumstances, think about aligning your skill set with them to see where there's a match. Do you have technical skills and industry knowledge that make you the best person to create a new, networked market-research process for your employer? Does your knowledge of languages position you to create outreach programs for a new immigrant community? Does your track record working with local nonprofits make you the perfect person to head up the new social innovation center? Could your knowledge of South America and international business information resources perfectly suit you to join the company's launch team working on introduction of its new product in Brazil?

The purpose of paying attention to these types of circumstances is to help you think about which ones might offer you an opportunity to create something new—a service, product, program, solution, or position—that takes you in the direction of your career goals. Whether you aspire to a traditional, nontraditional, or independent path, or even an eclectic combination of all three, being able to identify the opportunity in change helps move you toward that future.

Reading Outside the Box

Most of us read the key professional journals to stay current, but it's equally important to range afield into non-LIS, cutting-edge information resources to learn about emerging technologies, areas of convergence, demographic or market trends, etc. The best way to counter insularity in any profession is to engage with ideas and events outside of it, and the easiest way to do this is to seek out a diverse range of alternate sources.

In additional to your regular LIS journals, consider hitting the library once a month and briefly scanning—

- one general source (e.g., *Time, Newsweek, U.S. News & World Report*)

- one business source (e.g., *Forbes, Fortune, Business Week,* the local business journal)

- one management source (e.g., *Harvard Business Review, Strategy & Business*)

- one international source (e.g., *World Press Review, The Economist*)

- two opposing political sources (e.g., *American Prospect, National Review, New Republic, Weekly Standard, Commentary*)

- one source on business technology impacts (e.g., *Technology Review, Wired, Business 2.0*)

- two social issues/community sources (e.g., *Utne, Futurist, Future Survey*)

- one career development source (e.g., *Fast Company*)

- at least one discipline-specific title in an area that interests you (e.g., *Cable and Broadcasting, Training & Development, Journal of Marketing Research*)

(Keep in mind that many of the titles you choose to scan will also have their current articles available on their websites, which makes it easier to stay current via some quick lunch-hour online scanning.)

Also, consider the vast number of blogs that are now providing cutting-edge information as well as alternative viewpoints. A good blog can energize your thinking and push you to reframe your assumptions— just the thing for channeling your inner change agent.

What to scan for? Look for ideas, trends, patterns, or issues that may impact your practice area or the interests of your constituencies, be they patrons, customers, clients, or colleagues. But also keep an eye out for changes that may impact your career goals. Is something happening that might make your skills in high demand—or highly obsolete? Have recent technology advances created a new opportunity for an information specialist with a sci/tech skill set such as yours? Has an article on activist librarians in *Utne* sparked an idea for a new career direction for you? The world is full of fascinating information that can enrich your imagination and engender new career thinking, if you take the time to look.

Creating Your Change Strategies

You gain strength, courage, and confidence by every experience in which you stop and look fear in the face. You must do the thing you think you cannot do ... you learn by living.

—Eleanor Roosevelt

Most of us associate change with loss; understandably so. Change disrupts our familiar routines and answers and patterns. Change can create chaos in our ordered lives, and destroy the easy flow we've come to rely on. It brings on that winning combination of "loss of the familiar" and "fear of the unknown," often with the inspiring subtext of "your job is on the line." Easy to see why change so often elicits our duck-and-cover response.

During change, we're often going into unknown territory where we basically don't have a clue what we're doing. We're all familiar with the phrase "comfort zone," and we know that one of the challenges of change is that it pushes us out of our comfort zones. But most LIS professionals set very high performance standards for themselves, so the more important issue is that change pushes us beyond our *competency zones.*

When you're used to generally feeling like you know what you're doing, willfully going into a situation where you feel clueless is not usually an opportunity that most of us jump at. However, when you're facing change, this is often exactly what you *must* be able to do in order to take advantage of those opportunities. To quote Hellen Keller, "avoiding danger is no safer in the long run than outright exposure. Life is either a daring adventure or nothing at all."

In fact, your ability to approach change from a positive perspective is critical to the success of your efforts to grow your career over a span of years and decades. For most of us, our ability to move from old change responses to new ones is probably along the two-steps-forward-one-step-back continuum—some days you'll be on top of your game, other days beneath it. But consistently making the effort to approach change from a position of confidence rather than fear is key to building the career you're capable of.

Are there strategies you can put in place to diffuse the intimidation factor of being in unfamiliar territory? Are there ways to become more comfortable with the risk-taking that new opportunities entail? Are there coping strategies that will help the desire for gain outweigh the fear of loss? Actually, there are many. For starters, consider the following approaches:

Embrace *beginner's mind*, and get comfortable with not knowing. When you're an adult and you're used to being good at your job, you're also used to a high level of competency. Having to start all over again, to be in a place where you don't know what you're doing, can be unnerving at best. Yet this is exactly where change frequently lands us.

Without a willingness to move out of our competency zones, we can't grow. If we can't grow, we can't adapt to change, can't take what choreographer Agnes De Mille called "leap after leap in the dark." Instead, we need to get beyond our initial embarrassment at not knowing in order to reach the openness, lack of ego, and humility that defines *beginner's mind.* Only then can we position for the opportunity inherent in the changes around us.

Develop a sense of adventure. Okay, so most of us are probably not going to rush right out and take up sky diving. But we could probably stand to cultivate a bit more openness to life, and this is just the opportunity change offers us.

Yes, it's easier and less disruptive to stay with the familiar, to say no thanks, to avoid the unknown. But if we never take a flyer, if we never cultivate a sense of adventure, then life becomes pretty predictable pretty early on, and our souls become old and tired well before our bodies (or professional abilities) do. Change provides the adventure of new opportunities if we but have the courage to embrace it.

Work on being more open to opportunities for growth. Often the older we get, and the more we've experienced, the easier it is to say no. But what if instead our knee-jerk response was "what the heck, let's try it and see what we can make happen?" Not "we already tried that and it didn't work," but "what can we do differently to change the outcome?"

Albert Einstein pointed out that an apt definition of insanity is doing the same thing over and over again and expecting different outcomes. Why not open up to change and see what happens? Respect your need for security, but push yourself outward when you can. Baby steps are still steps forward.

Move your own cheese. One way to do just that, to push yourself outward, is to actively initiate change in your life so that you create a sense of familiarity with your own personal change process. Whether it's something like changing your morning routine or where you go on vacation or how you celebrate the holidays or where you live, making changes that *you* have initiated allows you to create a change process that supports you through transitional periods in your life.

 Do you need to mourn the loss of familiar routines before you can enjoy a new situation? Is there some ritual of letting go of the old and committing to the new that is meaningful to you? Do you need to involve friends to support you through change decisions? Or, like me, do you need to read every book ever published on a given change you're contemplating before you take the leap? Whatever your individual change process is, it helps immensely for you to become familiar with it in a safe environment, i.e., one that you have created, before you have changes thrust upon you from the outside.

We all have different ways of coping with change; if you start initiating changes now and begin to develop an understanding of what your most effective strategies are, it makes it less likely that changes coming at you externally will derail you.

Honor your sense of humor. Learn to laugh at yourself and not take yourself so seriously. Librarians have never been known for their raucous sense of humor—in fact, we tend to take anything related to librarianship *extremely* seriously. This may also tend to make us also take *ourselves* very seriously, which is a real negative when it comes to embracing change.

If you can laugh at things, life and relationships flow more easily, change is less threatening, and you don't get as bogged down in making sure you're in control of the world. When life seems to be spiraling out of control, laughter can be the thing that saves our sanity and keeps us centered.

Get used to letting go. One of the toughest things about change in your professional life is that it often entails the loss of something you've become attached to. It can be relationships you've come to enjoy, work you've developed an expertise in, a paycheck you've relied on. But the reality is, things change, and your only healthy option here is to accept that and not take it personally.

I read somewhere that in the Afghan language, the verb "to cling" is the same as the verb "to die." Yet for most of us, it's simply part of our natures to want to keep close to us those things we've come to care about. Unfortunately, it is the nature of the world that change will often result in their loss. We can be angry and bitter about this, or we can recognize and understand the immutable flow of life, and of our professional lives, and simply accept it.

Be patient with the unfolding, rather than rushing to closure. Okay, how many of us read the last few pages of the mystery before we start the book? How many of us want to close in on a decision before all the options have been put on the table? How many of us start filling in the test answers before we've finished reading the instructions? How many of us are still trying to figure out how to have the patience to be "in the moment" rather than planning for the conclusion?

Change is, among other things, an extended process that unfolds in its own time, as do our reactions to the changes we're confronting. It can be frustrating for those who want to quickly move to resolution—okay, my life has changed drastically, I will give myself three days to process my emotions around this, and then everything will be "back to normal." Needless to say, this strategy rarely works in real life. Instead, if we're lucky, we finally begin to understand that rushing through life and insisting on controlling its outcomes is counterproductive—it takes away the flow of moments that need time to develop into wisdom and clarity.

Develop your strategies for dealing with chaos. One of the most interesting points that Alvin Toffler made more than thirty years ago in *Future Shock* was that the people who dealt most successfully with ongoing and chaotic change in their lives always had some corner of calm and order that anchored them.

It might be a ritual like spending all morning on Sundays reading the *New York Times*. For someone else it might be having a cup of tea at 4:00 every afternoon. For others it might be a yoga or meditation practice adhered to faithfully every day. But the point is to have some routine or ritual or space that is consistent, orderly, and sustaining. That way, as chaos swirls around you, you can remain as grounded as possible.

Let go of perfection. Anyone who has ever taught a class of library students has seen the debilitating effects of perfectionism writ large. I don't know if it's hardwired into our profession or we develop it as we go along, but we all seem to be so focused on doing a perfect job of whatever we're doing that we often have no energy or initiative left over for any broader perspective. Change is especially unnerving for perfectionists because by its very nature it means we have to do something new, which we don't yet know how to do, so we can't be perfect at it.

We *have* to be willing to fail, to be wrong, to make mistakes without losing our sense of self esteem. It's simply the only way we will ever be able to move forward with the world. Writer Anne Lamott says it best: "perfectionism is the voice of the oppressor, the enemy of the people. It will keep you cramped and insane your whole life."

Learn your risk-taking style. Initiating change always entails a level of risk. I'm not talking about life-threatening stuff like bungee jumping here, I'm talking about the really important things—your job, your self-esteem, your mortgage, or perhaps even more distressing, the respect of your colleagues.

Some of us find the easiest way to take a risk is by simply closing our eyes and leaping off the cliff. Others will want to have prepared ten contingency plans for every possible negative outcome. Others, and I count myself among them, will practically research something to death until they are sure that the risk they are taking is an *informed* one, that they have weighed every single piece of information in order to minimize the potential downsides associated with a given action.

Whatever your risk-taking style is, it will help you manage your fears around change if you have explored and understood how you most comfortably or effectively deal with it.

Invest yourself in the process, not the outcome. Yes, there is the whole Zen thing about the journey being more important than the destination, and on our more enlightened days, many of us can totally connect with that approach. However, there's also a very practical reason to look at our professional lives this way—very few of us control the money, which means that we also don't control the outcomes.

Instead, focus on the work itself, and how you can grow professionally from it. Establish your personal learning agenda and a set of goals for yourself—for example, work on your management or team-building skills, focus on practicing process innovation, or identify some other skill that you want to develop or improve. That way, no matter what the long-term outcome of your work, you will have accomplished your *own* goals. You'll never control the outcomes; too many variables. But if you invest yourself in what you learn/connect with/build during the process, the outcome becomes almost a minor part of the equation.

Feel the fear, but keep moving forward. I have never gone into a new situation where I was responsible for the success of a venture without being flat-out terrified. And since every job I've taken for the past twenty years was something that I'd never done before—and several of them something that *no one* had ever done before and I was essentially making them up as I went along—that's a lot of being flat-out terrified.

But if we let ourselves be limited by our fears, that means we never give ourselves the opportunity to expand beyond what we can do comfortably today. Change and the unknown may scare the daylights out of us, but we can make a decision that we're just not willing to let that stop us. The reality is, fear doesn't go away. But we can learn to manage it, so on a good day it's not debilitating, and on a great day we can harness its energy to take us to exhilarating heights of accomplishment.

Develop an expectation of personal resiliency. Change is going to bring a lot of setbacks with it. We are going to mess up, fall down, and just generally flail about as we try to figure things out. Life's messy that way. But you can make a decision that you can retrench, recover, and move forward. You can know that you're smart, capable, and *important* to your communities, so you need to show up with your best stuff every day, even on those days when you have no clue what you're doing.

If we can commit to resiliency rather than wasting our energies on perfectionism, then change can become our tool rather than our nemesis. Where are you going to put your energy? Better to learn to navigate change than waste time and lose focus by fighting it.

If you decide that you are the type of person who finds a way to grow in any situation, you will be. This is a combination of frame, attitude, and will. It can become a matter of principle to us that although setbacks may detour or distract us, they will never defeat or derail us.

We don't have a choice about whether or not to accept change, or deal with it, or be touched by it. Our only choice is in how we respond—will we take the initiative to lead the opportunities embedded in the changes hitting us, or will we let others determine our options? Will we deal positively, assertively, *confidently* with change —or be clobbered by it? The alternative may not be death, but very possibly it's worse—it's marginalization, where our contributions are no longer needed or valued. For those of us in the LIS profession, the fear should not be of failure, but of invisibility.

Looking for opportunity in change is not meant to deny the fact that in a dynamic—okay, chaotic—environment, there will be some serious dislocation going on. People lose their jobs when things change, and there's not much we can do to stop it. What we can do instead is to assume this may happen, and be prepared for it. That portfolio you were working on? One of its purposes is to remind you to be prepared for disappearing jobs. That way, rather than being stuck in neutral, you can focus *your* energy on moving forward with change.

I get up. I walk. I fall down. Meanwhile I keep dancing.

—Hillel

Resources

Books

Drucker, Peter. *Innovation and Entrepreneurship.* Collins, 1993. 288 pp. ISBN 0887306187.
Renowned management consultant and author Drucker suggests that rather than innovation or entrepreneurship being serendipitous, the familiar "lightbulb going on," these opportunities can instead be systematically developed. He identifies seven circumstances that enable innovative opportunities, many of which have applicability to the LIS environment.

Kelley, Kevin. *New Rules for the New Economy: 10 Radical Strategies for a Connected World.* 179 pp. Penguin Books, 1999. ISBN 014028060X.
A number of authors have become known for their interpretation and analysis of emerging trends, forecasting their long-term impact. John

Naisbitt and Alvin Toffler led the way, and Kevin Kelley has picked up the torch with a number of engaging titles like *New Rules for the New Economy*, which looks at what our networked world will mean for economies, industries, and individuals. Kelly is one of the thought-leaders to monitor (articles and books) as you scan the broader environment. It's a great way to expand the types of ideas you're exposed to.

Lerner, Harriet. *Fear and Other Uninvited Guests: Tackling the Anxiety, Fear, and Shame That Keep Us from Optimal Living and Loving*. HarperCollins, 2004. 256 pp. ISBN 0060081570.
Lerner calls anxiety, fear, and shame "the big three that muck up our lives." Anxiety and fear can also do a number on our careers. Her book helps you understand the underpinnings of these damaging emotions, while also providing excellent counsel for overcoming them. Unlike that found in many self-help books, Lerner's writing is never glib; instead she a voice of steady support and encouragement.

Lindgren, Mats and Hans Bandhold. *Scenario Planning: The Link Between Future and Strategy*. Palgrave Macmillan, 2003. 240 pp. ISBN 0333993179.
Scenario Planning translates the seminal work done by Peter Schwartz in *Art of the Long View* into its practical application. Focus is on aligning scenario planning with business decision making. A good primer on the application of scenario planning (which can also present interesting career opportunities for info pros).

Popcorn, Faith and Lys Marigold. *Clicking: 17 Trends that Drive Your Business—and Your Life*. Collins, 1998. 480 pp. ISBN 0887308570.
The *Popcorn Report* (Collins, 1992) launched its author into the forefront of consumer trend forecasting (remember "cocooning?"), and *Clicking* updates her prognostications through the late nineties. Although now somewhat out of date, these types of trend forecasts can be useful resources for thinking about potential impacts (and career opportunities). Popcorn's most recent trend forecast is *EVEolution: Understanding Women – Eight Essential Truths that Work in Your Business and Your Life* (Hyperion, 2001).

Schwartz, Peter. *The Art of the Long View: Planning for the Future in an Uncertain World*. Currency, 1996. 288 pp. ISBN 0385267320.
The seminal work on scenario planning, Schwartz's book explains how his employer, Royal Dutch Shell, was able to respond effectively (and profitably) to the oil crisis of the seventies because of the scenario planning they had engaged in prior to it. Schwartz explains the theory underlying scenario planning and its strategic role in business decision making as well as its broader applications.

Periodicals

In addition to the key LIS publications, an environmental scan should also take in several resources outside the LIS community. Some good places to start:

Business 2.0. Business 2.0 Media, Inc., 2001– . Monthly. ISSN 1538-1730. www/business2.com
A great resource for tracking trends in the business world. Peter Schwartz is a regular contributor, as are several other business,

economic, and futures thought leaders. Past articles can be accessed at the website, some for free.

Future Survey. World Future Society, 1979– . Monthly. ISSN 0190-3241.
www.wfs.org/fsurv.htm
The World Future Society (WFS) does an imaginative job of identifying where emerging trends and technologies may lead in the next ten, twenty, or thirty years. This monthly publication provides abstracts of "books, articles and reports concerning forecasts, trends, and ideas about the future," then extrapolates key themes and issues among them. (Check the website for access to a number of these.) WFS also publishes *The Futurist*, a bimonthly "clearinghouse of ideas" and feature articles.

MIT's Technology Review. Massachusetts Institute of Technology, 1899– . Bimonthly. ISSN 1096-3715.
www.technologyreview.com
A fascinating tour of technology advances (and impacts) in the areas of biotech/healthcare, business, computing, energy, nanotechnology, security, software, telecommunications and the Internet, and transportation. Articles are archived at the website, and browsable by category or searchable by keywords.

Wired. Wired USA, 1993– . Monthly. ISSN 1059-1028.
www.wired.com
Hip, happening, and annoyingly hard to read, *Wired* is also a fascinating hit-or-miss source of information on emerging trends, technologies, and opportunities. Check the website for archived back issues, a news archive of stories organized under the headings technology, culture, business, and politics, and a growing collection of special-interest blogs.

Articles

Abrams, Stephen. "32 Tips to Inspire Innovation for You and Your Library," *Sirsi OneSource Newsletter*, July, September, and October 2005
http://stephenslighthouse.sirsi.com/archives/2005/10/32_tips_
part_3_1.html
Abrams is one of the industry's most perceptive thought leaders, and this two-part article brings together his ideas of how libraries can remain innovative in today's "Web-enabled (web-dominated) world of information service and delivery." Anything by Abrams is usually an interesting read, but these two articles should be required reading for anyone contemplating a career in any type of library. The author not only identifies opportunities, but then addresses both the solutions and attitudes necessary to respond.

Crowley, Bill. "Save Professionalism," *Library Journal*, vol. 130, no. 14 (September 1, 2005), pp. 46–48.
Whether or not you agree with Crowley's argument, this thought-provoking article provides an excellent starting point for discussions about the appropriate role of public libraries in an information-rich democratic society. Stating that "the public library cannot compete in the information marketplace," Crowley goes on to suggest public libraries must return to their "roots in education." The article's conclusions have import not only for the profession, but also for the career

opportunities it may offer. A good example of futures thinking within the profession.

"Rejuvenating Your Career" issue, *Info Career Trends*, May 2002
www.lisjobs.com/newsletter/archives.htm
A collection of articles written by LIS practitioners on topics including dealing with change, preparing for job transitions, and ways to put more energy into our careers. See also the May 2001 issue, "Changing Careers."

Strouse, Roger. "The Changing Face of Content Users and the Impact on Information Providers," *Online*, vol. 28, no. 5 (September/October 2004), pp. 27–32.
Much of the futures work for the LIS community comes from research and surveys done by highly respected industry analyst Outsell. This article, based on Outsell findings, explores the future impact of increasing independence among information users, and new roles this will necessitate for LIS professionals.

Watstein, Sarah Barbara. "Scenario Planning for the Future of Reference: Five White Papers Posit the Future and Raise the Bar for Us All," *Reference Services Review*, vol. 31, no. 1 (March 2003), pp. 36–38.
Based on five papers presented at the Reference and User Services Association's (RUSA) program at the 2002 American Library Association's Annual Conference, this article examines the scenario-planning process each exemplifies, with suggestions about their applicability for the entire LIS community.

Associations and Organizations

Outsell, Inc.
www.outsellinc.com
Outsell is the leading information industry analyst, and produces much of the research and analysis that vendors use to position their future strategy. The company also makes a substantial amount of its findings available to the LIS profession, either through white papers, articles, or conference presentations. At its website, sign up for Outsell-Now, an e-mailed update of industry news, and check out the Complimentary Downloads (see especially "FutureFacts: Information Industry Outlook").

World Future Society
www.wfs.org
Founded in 1966, WFS draws its 25,000 members from more than eighty countries. Its mission is to provide a clearinghouse for ideas about how social and technologic developments will shape the future. Many of these are *highly* imaginative, but are great for sparking "what if" thinking. Check "Forecasts" at the website for *"Top 10 Forecasts from Outlook 2005."*

Online Resources

The Continuous Environmental Scan: Where Do You Get All Your Ideas?
http://blogs.salon.com/0002007/2005/04/25.html#a1123
From David Pollard, posted at his website, How to Save the World. He identifies nine steps to set up a continuous environmental scan,

including "know how you learn," "determine your information universe," "discover infomediaries," and "tap into the stuff inside your organization." A smart, practical, and realistic approach to setting up a personal (or organization-wide) environmental scan.

The Future of Libraries: Beginning the Great Transformation
www.davinciinstitute.com/page.php?ID=120
From futurist Thomas Frey of the Colorado-based DaVinci Institute, this paper identifies ten trends that will affect development of "the next generation" of libraries, as well as providing four recommendations for developing successful roles. An interesting prognostication from someone outside the profession.

Pew Internet and American Life Project
www.pewinternet.org/
Funded by the Pew Charitable Trusts and an initiative of the Pew Research Center, the *Pew Internet and American Life Project* researches the impact of the Internet on various aspects of our lives. The reports of most interest to information professionals (and the ones most frequently quoted in the press) are the ones under the headings "Internet Revolution" and "Technology & Media Use." The reports are data- and statistics-rich, but also interpret findings in a meaningful way so that they can easily be incorporated into scenarios.

Special Issues
www.specialissues.com
Special issues of magazines can be an especially valuable source of data for environmental scans and scenario-building. The Special Issues database includes industry outlooks, overviews, or surveys; statistical issues; and annual forecasts, among other topics. In addition, the database notes additional website content related to the specific special issue. Not a free service, but for those doing serious or broad-based environmental scanning, a very valuable resource.

2003 Environmental Scan: Pattern Recognition
www.oclc.org/reports/escan/
A fascinating overview of trends "impacting OCLC, libraries, museums, archives, and other allied organizations, both now and in the future." Especially useful for LIS professionals in traditional areas of librarianship.

Note

1. Brian Kenney, "Ann Arbor's Web Site Maximizes Blogging Software," *Library Journal*, 130(14) (September 1, 2005), 27.

9
Creating Your Career Map

To venture causes anxiety. Not to venture is to lose oneself.

—Soren Kierkegaard

You've self-assessed, scoped out the professional options, reframed your skill sets, and expanded your knowledge horizons. But how do you get from where your career stands today and where you want to be in the future? How do you get from here to there?

You create a strategy.

According to *Webster's Ninth,* strategy is "the art of devising or employing plans or strategems toward a goal." It's the plan you put together that aligns your goals with the realities of your life. It's where you change the question from "can I?" to "how will I?"

Based on the Greek *strategos* ("the art of the general"), your strategy is what puts you in charge of outcomes, and your *tactics* are the action items you undertake to execute your strategy. Your strategies and tactics are what you use to achieve your goals.

Goals, strategies, tactics. If thought through carefully, these three elements can enable you to move forward methodically and consistently toward the career you want. They also will help you create your personal career agenda—targeted outcomes that shape how you approach assignments, projects, classes, and possible job opportunities. The most effective way to put together your action plan is to create a career map that captures those goals, strategies, and tactics within a timeline of execution.

The purpose of a career map is not to lock you into a grid of predetermined actions, but to 1) get you to commit to yourself in writing that you can and will take positive steps to create the career you want, and 2) start you thinking about where you'd like to go and what you'd like to accomplish, so that when opportunities arise, you have a guide against which to judge them. For those stuck in unrewarding jobs, a career map can be a way to keep you investing your energies and time in positive future opportunities rather than wasting both being mired in the negative energy of your current workplace.

Depending on what format works best for you, your career map might be an outline of goals/strategies/tactics, or a multicolored visual graphic of key goals and radiating strategies and tactics. Perhaps a written narrative that describes your action plan better suits you, or a detailed flowchart, or a project management grid. The idea is simply to create some sort of document or graphic that establishes what you plan to accomplish, how, and within what timeframe.

For example, you might decide that as part of your career agenda within three years you want to have written a book on working with non-traditional college students. You would figure out what you needed to complete that goal, for example a comprehensive literature search or interviews or surveys you'd need to undertake, and then identify how and when you would go about doing that. Maybe you want to take a stronger leadership role in your profession—your career map would chart how you would do that, for example running for office in a professional organization, and when you planned to do that.

So grab your career journal and all those notes you've been making. Run away from home for a weekend, take a mental health day, do whatever it takes to carve out some space for yourself, and start organizing your thoughts. If you're going to be an LIS professional for the next several decades, putting together your career map will be a small investment that pays you great dividends.

Career Map Components

Career maps are as different as the individuals compiling them, but generally will build on all of the work you've done so far.

To recap, these areas have included:

Exploring personal preferences. Essentially, what work might you want to do, and how might you want to do it? *Might* is the operative word here because sometimes these answers will only clarify themselves through several years (or more) of experimenting with options and then paying close attention to your responses.

Your career map will help you identify things you can do to test your reactions to work environments, types of work, and similar preferences. Look for or create opportunities to try out various options without having to actually commit to them. Volunteering can be especially valuable here.

Considering career choices. Traditional, nontraditional, independent, or some combination or sequence of them all?

Once you've identified career paths of potential interest, your career map is the place you'll note what activities you'll participate in to find out more about them. Will you shadow a practitioner, request an informational interview (in person or via e-mail), do volunteer work, read descriptions of this type of work, join a professional association and listen to members' war stories, join an electronic discussion group and see what issues are being discussed? How will you learn more about the possible downsides of your potential career choices? If you're considering the independent path, how will you find out more about the market for your services?

Working on projects. Reframing your career from the portfolio perspective not only allowed you to see your professional strengths and accomplishments, it also highlighted professional "gaps," areas where you'll want to build expertise or a track record of increasing responsibility.

Your career map is the place for you to record what types of projects you'll seek out, and why. Will you up your visibility, learn a new skill, add higher levels of managerial responsibility to your portfolio, work with an outstanding colleague, bridge to a new professional opportunity, position yourself with a new constituency?

Learning. When you did your learning agenda in Chapter 7, you identified new areas of knowledge you wanted to master, and how you would accomplish that.

Will it be formal or informal learning? Perhaps you're not certain; in that case, this part of your career map may focus on exploring and evaluating learning options. Also, how will you explore your most effective learning style(s)?

Gaining visibility, creating your professional presence. True, making the effort to align who you are—your values, your abilities, your smarts, and your passions—with how the world perceives you may seem like hype. But the reality is, either consciously or by default, we define how the world sees us.

What actions will you take to gain visibility within or outside of the LIS profession? To establish your professional value to colleagues and potential employers/clients? To demonstrate expertise, or innovative thinking, or strategic initiative? Your career map is where you'll set the direction.

Building contacts. As we've seen, building a community of colleagues will strengthen not only your career options, but also your ongoing enjoyment of your career.

In your career map, you'll get specific about how you'll expand your professional connections, if this is a priority for you. Will those relationships be within or outside of the LIS field? How will you help others in your community of colleagues?

Experimenting with your change process. You're determined to turn change from a threat to an ally... here's where you create the strategy to make good on that commitment.

How will you try out your best approaches for dealing with change? What techniques will you use? Will you read books about the psychology of change? Experiment with one small change a week, a day, or a month? What changes will you try?

Strengthening your risk-taking muscle. We looked at the fact that supporting your change frame is your ability and willingness to take risks. By holding you accountable, your career map will help push you in the right direction.

What risks will you take, so you can start getting comfortable with your ability to "feel the fear and do it anyway?" What risks will support the direction you want your career to go? Big steps or baby ones, the goal is familiarizing yourself with how you react to risk, and coaching yourself through it. The more often you do it, the less intimidating it becomes.

Building your information base. You're an information pro—you do information. So keeping on top of it is one of the most important skills you'll have. We've explored a number of options; your career map is where you'll get specific.

How will you identify the information you'll need to gather regarding your intended or potential career paths, and how will you gather/monitor it? What magazines will you subscribe to, what electronic discussion lists join? Will you monitor blogs, and if so, which ones and why? Will you join professional associations, attend conferences, identify and read a core collection of books on your topic? Keep in mind, your information base will probably reflect two areas: information about the profession or type of job you're interested in, and the knowledge necessary to perform the job.

Assembling Your Career Map

To pull your career map together, first go back and review the notes, comments, and questions you've entered in your career journal. You should find ideas and actions to explore—now is the time to decide *how* you will explore.

To get started, you'll need to start by asking yourself those three key questions: what are my goals, what strategies will I use to reach my goals, and what tactics will I use to execute my strategies? Then, based on your answers to these questions, you'll need to take it a couple of steps further to flesh out your plan.

Step 1: Identify your goals. Whether for the next year or three or five, what do you need to accomplish to make progress toward your career goals? Consider the following possible goals to get you started, and complete the statements to reflect your personal circumstances:

- Explore these three options

  _____

- Develop an expertise in

  _____

- Find out whether I want to be/do

  _____

- Try out these three new skills

  _____

- Move to Seattle and

  _____

- Get a job doing

  _____

- Find out more about

  _____

- Increase my income by

  _____

- Learn more about _____ as a
  possible career choice

- Other goals

  _____

Keep in mind that exploring is as valid a goal as deciding or acting, but if you're exploring, your focus will be on documenting your findings, whether personal preferences (I took a leadership position, how did that feel?) or information (there are a total of XX private-practice medical clinics in this region that could use my cool new consumer medical pathfinders).

Step 2: Identify your strategies. Strategies are broad-brush approaches for achieving a goal, such as increasing knowledge, positioning for increased visibility, or expanding skill sets. Say, for example, you have as a goal to purchase a home in the next year. Your strategies might include preparing your personal finances, researching local neighborhoods, and investigating the home-buying process to understand what to expect.

Now you try it. Return to the goals you listed in your career journal, and then for each, come up with at least three strategies that will help you achieve it. If you can't come up with any strategies, brainstorm with a friend or colleague to help get the thought processes going. Your focus is on solutions, on getting from here to there, in a realistic fashion.

Step 3: Decide on your tactics or actions within these strategies. If goals are what you hope to accomplish and strategies are the approaches you will use to do so, then tactics are the action items supporting your strategies. You'll want to think carefully about the tactics you'll use to support each strategy; otherwise your strategies (and your goals) are simply wishful thinking. Also, at the tactical level, you'll want to attach timelines to your actions—what will you do, and by when will you do it? This ensures accountability, so you can easily know if you are on track . . . or still sitting at the station.

Let's go back to that house-purchase goal, to your three strategies of prepping your finances, researching local neighborhoods, and investigating the home-buying process, and how you might line this out. Your approach might look something like the one shown in Figure 9.1.

Now you try it. You've identified your goals and strategies in Steps 1 and 2, here is where you set your marching orders. What actions will you take, and when? Lay out your plans in your career journal in whatever format works best for you, whether in an outline, project management approach, graphic with circles, boxes, links, and arrows, or some other creative rendering.

Step 4: Identify what processes you'll need to establish. Following an action plan necessitates setting up a system or process for sticking to your plan. As our often-neglected treadmills and rowing machines testify, if you don't allocate regular time to do something, it's probably not going to happen. So when you look at your career map, decide when you're going to schedule in "career time." A useful approach here is to never let Monday show up without having noted at least one career-related action item to complete that week. Create processes to integrate your career-map actions into your daily life; if you can't get to them at work over your lunch hour, plan

Strategy	Tactics
**Prepare my personal finances	Request and review my credit file from the three major
	credit bureaus next week; correct any errors
	Set up and follow a schedule for paying off my credit card balance over the next three months
	Create a budget that reflects my projected monthly mortgage payment, and start living within those budget constraints within two months
Research local neighborhoods	Contact local Board of Realtors within next four weeks for information they may have available
	Start checking out homes Saturday mornings for sale in various neighborhoods to get a sense of prices
	Compile a "pro-and-con" sheet to note benefits and disadvantages of each neighborhood
Investigate home-buying process	Check with my local public library for recent books on how to purchase a home as I get closer to the move
	Ask friends who've already been through the house-buying process to give me pointers
	Work with my real estate agent to put together a hit-list of questions, documents, and action items I need to start working on—schedule a working lunch for next month

to execute at home. Your career map can be a great tool for getting unstuck: come up with one thing you can do for at least an hour a week, and you'll be moving toward the future you want.

Step 5: Find out what resources are available to you. Generally, your resources will include time (as in free time to devote to your action items), people (including colleagues on and off the job), your employer (who may offer training, tuition reimbursement, mentoring programs, support for conference attendance, and portfolio-expanding project opportunities), and, if you're a student, your degree program. Approached strategically, most LIS programs offer outstanding opportunities for professional growth, self-exploration, portfolio-building, and career positioning, in addition to the coursework learning opportunities.

Step 6: Decide how you'll handle obstacles to your plans. Whether looking at goals, strategies, or tactics, it's best to assume that life will intervene and play havoc with your best laid plans. For most of us, people come first, whether family or friends, and life in all its glory is nothing if not messy. So knowing that your plans will be disrupted, displaced, and hijacked on a regular basis—and planning for it—will help you see these events as detours, not derailments.

There are lots of ways to deal with interruptions. If time or scheduling is an issue (when isn't it?), scale back your plans for the time being. Instead of trying to follow through on all your strategies and tactics, focus on just one. Rather than writing four hours a week, write for two. Instead of pursuing a second master's degree, read books on your topic of interest or subscribe to a print or online publication you can read over your lunch hour until you're able to start your coursework. If volunteering to edit the organization newsletter is not feasible given other time commitments, volunteer to write an article now and then for the newsletter.

If financial constraints delay a goal of moving to New York and landing your dream job in a special library, simply switch your focus for the moment. Use the time to build skills and credentials that will up your value to potential employers when you eventually do arrive. See if there are ways to connect with special librarians there to get a better sense of the local job market in advance of your arrival. Consider joining the New York chapter of SLA while you're waiting for the opportunity to move.

If personal commitments to family and friends mean those to your career are temporarily put on the back burner, decide whether to take a time-out for the moment or simply scale back but continue to move forward with your goals more slowly. If the latter, be adamant about scheduling in time for your career-development activities so you don't completely lose your forward momentum.

If, on the other hand, you decide what you really need is a time-out, it helps to have a trigger firmly established in your mind for when you will reengage with your career activities. Is it when your youngest child starts kindergarten? When your friend has gotten through the breakup crazies? When your partner or spouse has landed a job? When you've finished preparing your mom's taxes?

The key point here is to realize that those we love will *always* need our time and attention, and human nature being what it is, they'll also be extremely good at laying claim to our every spare minute. If you want to pursue your career goals, it's critical to make a commitment to yourself of time, energy, and attention. If others are less than supportive of the time you're now spending focused on your own goals, that's understandable—but not a reason to stop your forward progress. Solicit their support, but know you can move forward without it.

Sample Career Maps

Below are very brief examples of one-year career maps for three different circumstances: someone who's currently in a dysfunctional job situation, but for family reasons needs to stay in it for at least another year; someone who wants to establish and grow a freelance business as a patent researcher; and someone who wants to secure a job as the business librarian for an academic library on the West Coast.

Staying Put in Current Job

Goal   Find a way to stay in current job without making myself (and everyone else around me) miserable

Strategies

1. Maintain a positive attitude

2. Gain a better understanding of possible job options to consider next

3. Develop a successful exit strategy to have in place for when I leave current employer

Tactics

1. Maintain a positive attitude

   - Look for positive ways to rechannel frustration (for example, target a new skill I can learn on the job)—try out one approach per week

   - Find ways to cope with dysfunctional colleague—read two books about workplace personality dynamics and practice what I learn

   - Examine how my own actions may contribute to a poor working relationship—ask a trusted colleague or co-worker to *gently* critique my interpersonal skills

   - Explore ways to improve attitude on job—spend at least three lunch hours per week focused on my career map action items, which will help me shift my energy away from anger and instead invest it in a great future

2. Understand job options

   - Identify and monitor LIS career resources (for example, read the monthly *Info Career Trends* newsletter, *Library Journal's* online career site, the articles at LIScareer.com, and the career blog *Beyond the Job*)

   - Tap my colleague community for advice and counsel—try to attend as many local meetings of my professional associations as possible; let key members know I'm exploring job options, and ask them for suggestions

   - Learn more about specific types of jobs—check out at least five job postings every week for descriptions of job responsibilities, requisite skills, and education levels

3. Create exit strategy

   - Make preparations to leave on a positive note—for example, make sure all documentation for my position is in order, including files and process notes; create written hand-off instructions for the person who replaces me

   - Make sure I've maximized my job's learning opportunities—determine my employer's tuition reimbursement, training, and career-attendance policies, and spend the next year focusing on skill expansion

   - Start positioning for visibility—depending on what environment I want to be working in, consider writing an article on an emerging topic for an appropriate local or state publication within the next six months

Becoming a Patent Researcher

Goal   Launch my business as a freelance patent researcher within three years

Strategies

1. Understand the potential market opportunity

2. Become an expert patent researcher

3. Become a knowledgeable businessperson

Tactics

1. Understand the market opportunity

   • Decide whether to be generalist or specialist (this will determine type and size of market opportunity)
   • Based on decision above, identify at least ten potential clients (local and/or national)
   • Segment my market (who, among potential clients, will actually be likely to use my service? What are their key drivers? Who in the organization makes the purchase decision? How will I market to them?)
   • Identify my competition (how many, how active, possible collaboration opportunity?)

2. Become an expert patent searcher

   • Identify courses and/or books on patent research; attend classes if possible (check for online courses, preconference workshops, and association webinars as possible options), read books over the next three to six months
   • Become familiar with all resources and tools necessary for patent searching (print, online, government, commercial, etc.)—master one each month
   • Practice using these tools, preferably as a voluntary project for a client (check with local business incubator or small business development centers for possible clients)
   • Join all professional communities related to patent research (look for associations, special interest groups, communities of practice, electronic discussion groups, etc.)

3. Become a knowledgeable businessperson

   • Determine optimal business structure (solo, network, business with employees; sole proprietor, partnership, incorporated?)
   • Do research necessary to set up office infrastructure (location, admin support, telecommunications, office technology)
   • Develop marketing/branding/positioning resources and tools (website, brochure, stationary, elevator speech, etc.) within next three months
   • Establish financial expectations and relationships (budget, financial forecast, accountant, banker, etc.)
   • Write business plan (and ask others whose business judgment I trust to review and comment) within next three months

Securing Academic Library Position

Goal   Secure job as the business librarian for a West Coast academic library

Strategies

1. Understand what the job market looks like in my target areas
2. Determine whether there are areas of professional expertise I need to bulk up
3. Start building professional connections in region

Tactics

1. Understand the job market

   • Identify and monitor information resources on academic job market for California, Oregon, and Washington on weekly basis
   • Identify all higher education institutions in target areas and set up process to monitor for library job openings (keep in mind that those near schools with LIS programs will probably be inundated with job applicants) within next four weeks
   • Check out ALA, ARL, and *Library Journal* salary surveys to determine salary expectations, especially regional variations

2. Determine requisite areas of professional expertise

   • E-mail several academic business librarians at institutions outside my target area and ask them about key skills for a competitive advantage in the hiring process—complete within six to eight weeks
   • Review job postings every Sunday afternoon and compare to my current skill set; do I have a skills gap?
   • See whether there are any projects I could take on in my current position that would make me a more attractive job candidate for a potential employer
   • Do a literature search to identify articles on current and future job skills for academic business librarians, read appropriate ones, and develop education map to address skills gap

3. Start building connections

   • Join electronic discussion groups specific to my target area within next two weeks; monitor regularly and contribute my knowledge/expertise when appropriate
   • Join ALA's Business Reference and Services Section (BRASS) and establish contact with members working in West Coast academic libraries
   • Consider scheduling a road trip for the spring or summer to visit some of the institutions and living areas that may be of interest

These three strategy maps present only a few of the strategies and tactics you might use if pursuing the goals above on a real-life basis, but they can give you an idea of how goals, strategies, and tactics work together to support progress toward your career targets.

In the meantime, don't forget that it isn't necessary for a goal to be a specific achievement; it may be simply gaining a better understanding of something important to you, or clarifying an upcoming decision, or qualifying an opportunity on the horizon.

Setting Agendas

In order to turn your career map into a document that takes you toward the career you dream of, it's important to always have your agenda in place. Whether you're a student in a grad program, an LIS professional just starting out on a new job, a seasoned practitioner wanting to move into a new career phase, or someone who simply wants to grow in an existing job, having a career agenda helps you align key aspects of your situation with the goals you've set for yourself.

Your agenda grows out of the career map you've created, and focuses on what goals you have for whatever situation you're in. There may be skills that you want to improve or pick up, a type of project you'd like to add to your portfolio, someone you'd like to build a relationship with, or visibility you'd like to gain. The purpose of your agenda is to align your individual professional goals with the organizational goals of your employer so that both advance simultaneously.

For example, assume you've been working as the company intranet coordinator, and you've just been asked to explore options for setting up an enterprise-wide content management system. This is an area where you have no expertise, but you're interested in growing in this direction. For the company, your goals may include doing a needs assessment, creating a request for proposals, evaluating potential software solutions, acquiring the right product, and putting it in place.

Depending on your career goals, you might decide that *your* agenda throughout this process would include—

- Raising your visibility throughout the organization by targeting key executives for personal interviews during the needs-assessment process

- Reading up on how to do great requests for proposals (RFPs) and then asking others who've done them previously for tips and feedback on your draft, so you can build this as a new skill area

- Creating a process template for evaluating RFP responses, which you'll add to your portfolio

- Developing an expertise in project management by taking vendor training in a leading project management software platform, which you then use to implement your CM project

- Building your leadership skills by bringing together a multidepartmental, collaborative team to support the introduction of the CM solution throughout the organization

Or say you're a student, going through an MLIS grad program. The school's agenda will be delivered through a well-thought-through curriculum of courses and learning opportunities designed to help ensure that you graduate with a solid LIS knowledge base. But while you want to fully engage with your courses, you can also use your graduate studies as an opportunity to advance your career agenda as well. Some possibilities are—

- Using your courses to try out various processes for dealing with change, for risk-taking
- Experimenting with the different learning styles to determine which one (or combination) works best for you
- Working on your writing skills to improve this important professional capability; asking for specific feedback on your writing from your professors
- Developing an expertise in working on and leading group and/or virtual project teams
- Using assignments for self-assessment: do you prefer leading or being a team member on a group project? Working with student colleagues or on your own? Standing up and speaking to your class or being class secretary? Research or technology or management courses?
- Getting to know your professors and letting them get to know you and your interests to start building your professional community
- Demonstrating (or developing) leadership skills by getting involved with the student group or by organizing special programs
- Following up with guest speakers for expert career advicing
- Using your assignments to research companies, employers, or career paths of interest to you

The idea is to honor your obligations to your employer (or graduate program) but at the same time look for opportunities that support your career goals, as identified in your career map.

This strategy can be especially helpful if you're in a job that isn't a good match for you but is also one you can't leave for the time being. While honoring your obligations to your current employer, you can be looking for opportunities to learn new skills, meet new people, or spend your lunch hours researching new opportunities. Push the boundaries of your position by volunteering for projects outside your defined job, by exploring ways to improve existing processes within your job, or by exploring knowledge outside your skill area by tapping colleagues' expertise. You'll be able to invest your energy in the opportunities of the future rather than the frustrations of the day.

Putting Your Career Map in Play

As you've created your career map, you've focused on items that are actionable—that is, realistic and measurable. You've been specific about your action items (identify three potential employers, interview five colleagues, monitor these three blogs...). The very concreteness of your plan is what will ensure that you're accountable to yourself.

Keep in mind, however, that it's also important to take into consideration your life circumstances and your individual personality. In other words, don't volunteer to head up the programs committee if you're never able to make it to the monthly membership meetings. Don't take on a project-management role if deadlines bring on panic attacks. And if your mother-in-law has just moved in for a three-month stay, expect that there may be a few time-outs in your upcoming schedule, and cut yourself some slack.

Focus on yourself, and the things that you can control. If your goal is to change your boss's behavior from clueless to enlightened, it's simply not going to happen. But if instead your goal is to find techniques for working with your boss in a way that helps you move toward your professional goals rather than staying mired in anger and resentment, *that's* an outcome you can control.

Don't get discouraged if you don't achieve your goals on the first pass, if you're not making forward progress as quickly as you'd anticipated. Don't interpret this as failure, but rather use it as valuable information, an opportunity to figure out why you missed your marks. This isn't, by the way, a failure, it's simply real life showing up. Don't feel derailed; instead, plot your strategy for recognizing and handling similar situations successfully the next time they come around.

What if you decide you don't like where your career map is taking you? Congratulations! You've just gained invaluable insight that allowed you to avoid a painful career choice, and you can now shift direction to explore a different opportunity or career path that may be a better match with your interests and aspirations.

Most often in your career choices you'll be striving for progress, not perfection. The reality is, there is no perfectly "right" job or career path. There are multiple choices and opportunities to contribute, grow, and learn, and your career map will help you shape those choices in a way that most closely complements who you are, and what you envision for your career.

Using Your Career Map to Achieve Your Goals

A career map should be a useful tool for you rather than simply an exercise in daydreaming. It can be a framework within which to evaluate new opportunities—for example, does that possible new job you're considering take you toward or away from the career you want? It can be a roadmap of actions to take to move closer to your goals on a daily, weekly, or monthly basis. It can remind you what to do next when you've been "missing in action" from your career path for a while due to circumstances beyond your control.

Tailored to and reflective of your dreams and aspirations, your career map should not be seen as an inflexible plan but rather as a pathway. You'll still want to be opportunistic—you don't want to not respond to a terrific job or project offer simply because you didn't have it listed in your plans. Instead, consider your career map to be a blueprint that can be tweaked to fit both your life's circumstances and emerging professional interests.

A career map is where you not only document your dreams, you also prove to yourself that they are achievable. It's how you set yourself up for success rather than failure, as you let small steps build momentum for you.

Asking the Critical Question

What is your definition of success?

The answer to this question will underly all of your goals and strategies and tactics, yet it's one we rarely stop to think about. Mostly we unconsciously mirror the expectations and value frames handed down to us by family, influential friends, the profession, and often society at large, without realizing they may not actually fit us at all.

Our culture tends to define success in terms of financial standing and professional status—how high are you on the ladder? But that doesn't need to be your definition. In a world of constant change, the real criteria for judging success might be that we were able to overcome our fears in order to contribute at our highest potential. It might be that you chose to stay and engage rather than go into "duck and cover" mode. It might be that you created a product or a service or a solution that sparked others' imaginations, and they took your ideas to a new level. It might be that you worked every day to use your skills to make someone's life a bit better, using the new tools and technologies at your disposal even though they had initially confused you.

To some extent, you may find that your answers to the self-assessment questions in Chapter 2 tell you how much you value the traditional signifiers of success in our society: pay, title, and status. Generally speaking, people who go into the LIS profession aren't usually targeting stratospheric salaries or the high-flying jobs that bring fame and fortune, although it *is* possible to earn some pretty high incomes by taking your LIS degree in nontraditional directions. If this is an important component of career success for you, then it should figure strongly in your career map.

If working for socially responsible organizations where you can make a positive difference in peoples' lives is one of your key success criteria, then you'll probably want to focus your career goals on public library or nonprofit work, or on creating an independent path that supports this. And if your definition of career success includes the ability to continue working—and contributing—well into your golden years, then ongoing education is likely to figure *very large* in your career map.

The other reason to think through your personal definition of success is that if you only use the benchmarks of others, you may discount extraordinary successes you achieve along the journey. If, for example, one of you success components is to have made a positive contribution to the vitality of your local professional community, then the time you spend mentoring that younger colleague is, in fact, an expression of your ongoing success.

How to think about success criteria? One way to frame the question is to apply the same approach used by psychologist Abraham Maslow in his famous "Hierarchy of Needs" pyramid. His premise was that at the bottom of the pyramid were our most basic human needs—that is, physiological needs such as food and water—followed up the pyramid by safety needs, belonging and love needs, the need to know and understand, aesthetic needs, and self-actualization, which was defined as finding self-fulfillment and realizing one's potential. (At the very top of the pyramid was "transcendence," at which point, we can assume, career success is probably no longer an issue....)

Applying this same approach to your career aspirations, what are your core expectations and needs? For most of us, the bottom rung is a job that pays a living wage, uses the skills we've trained for, and doesn't make us crazy. But what about the next tier? Is it that you have an opportunity to contribute to your organization at a strategic level? Or that your career now offers a wealth of learning opportunities? Or that the work you do allows you to increasingly invest time and energy in a second aspiration such as writing or participating in international bike races? At each new tier, the assumption is that you have met the previous goal and can now move onto the next level of self-defined success.

When going through this process, it's helpful to consider what would signify to you that you had reached "self-fulfillment and realizing one's potential" within the context of your career. For example, during one of my ongoing debates with myself about what I wanted my career to be about, I decided to see if I could come up with a professional mission statement. This would be something that defined for me what my purpose would be, and what contribution I could, I hoped, make.

The statement I finally settled on was "to turn information into a tool for individuals, communities, and organizations to grow, learn, and achieve their goals." Based on that commitment, self-actualization for me would be that because of my unique knowledge and skills, I was able to contribute ideas and resources and solutions where they might not have existed had I not tried. Based on this commitment, I created and teach a course in the University of Denver LIS program in career alternatives, on which this book is based.

In fact, none of my success "tiers" have anything to do with titles or salary or job status; they have rather to do with impact. Have I been able to make a difference in peoples' lives? Have I been able to devise and execute innovative solutions? Have I been willing to learn the things that would enable new opportunities instead of falling back on familiar, but increasingly limited, competencies? These success criteria are meaningful to me, but may look like nothing so much as pretty minor goals for others whose values differ from mine.

That's why, when creating your own career map, it's important you understand that what's meaningful to you is unique to your values and aspirations—and deserves your full honor and commitment. Your spouse, parents, co-workers, or neighbors may not share your view of success if it doesn't involve a six-figure salary or a corner office, but that's their issue, not yours. Your challenge is simply to honor, respect, and pursue your vision with all the passion and energy you can deliver.

Resources

Books

Bryan, Mark and Julia Cameron. *The Artist's Way at Work: Riding the Dragon.* Harper, 1999. 304 pp. ISBN 0688166350.
> An extension of the ideas found in Cameron's wildly popular *The Artist's Way* (Tarcher, 2002), . . . *at Work* continues to espouse the benefits of creative expression as a way of connecting with your authentic self. Central to this process is the free-form, stream-of-consciousness journaling the authors recommend first thing every morning. This is a great way to connect with goals, issues, and ideas that will eventually find their way into your career strategy.

Cairo, Jim. *Motivation and Goal-Setting: How to Set and Achieve Goals and Inspire Others.* Career Press, 1998. 128 pp. ISBN 1564143643.
> Putting together your career map is the first half of the equation; actually *doing* the things you've committed to is the second. If you're struggling with the implementation piece, Cairo's book will deliver strategies and tips that can help you figure out how to get—and stay—motivated.

Covey, Stephen R. *Seven Habits of Highly Effective People.* Free Press, 1989. 358 pp. ISBN 0671663984.

The book that launched the Covey phenomena and marketing juggernaut. It lays out a thoughtful, methodical, and disciplined approach to aligning your life with the values and goals you've committed to. Covey manages to avoid the usual glibness and hype of self-help books and instead asks you to seriously consider where your life is today, and what efforts you will undertake to change it for the better. Provides a valuable framework for thinking about what career actions you'll undertake—and how they can support broader life goals—in the coming months and years.

Helgesen, Sally. *Thriving in 24/7: Six Strategies for Taming the New World of Work.* Free Press, 2001. 272 pp. ISBN 0684873036.
From the author of *The Female Advantage: Women's Ways of Leadership* (Doubleday, 1995), *Thriving in 24/7* identifies strategies for taking control of our lives—great for helping navigate the challenges you face when putting your career map into action. Helgesen's message is engaging and insightful, but even better, it's highly practical.

Lichtenberg, Ronna. *Pitch Like a Girl: How a Woman Can Be Herself and Still Succeed.* Rodale Books, 2005. 256 pp. ISBN 1594860092.
A realistic, supportive guide to understanding, acknowledging, and showcasing your competencies for women. Lichtenberg makes the point that most women, regardless of their level of accomplishment, tend to undervalue themselves and their skills. *Pitch Like a Girl* provides practical approaches and techniques for overcoming our self-defeating tendencies, and instead playing to—and getting paid for—our strengths. Includes key points and action items to incorporate in your career map whether you're a woman or a man.

Morgenstern, Julie. *Time Management from the Inside Out.* 2nd ed. Owl Books, 2004. 304 pp. ISBN 0805075909.
There are a number of excellent time-management books out there, but Morgenstern's is particularly interesting because she bases her recommendations not on changing your personality to fit a "one-size-fits-all" system imposed by some expert, but on structuring your approach to more effective time management around your values and personal/emotional priorities. An excellent tool for figuring out a realistic time commitment in terms of your career development strategies.

Scholten, Diane M. *Be Your Own Life Coach.* Penguin, 2004. 144 pp. ISBN 0142196274.
One of a dozens of career self-coaching books currently available, Sholten's is especially useful for its visualization exercises and suggestions about laying out career goals by creating a collage of meaningful pictures or images. An effective approach for those individuals who would benefit from a more visual approach than outlining or journaling.

Toms, Michael and Justine Willis Toms. *True Work: Doing What You Love and Loving What You Do.* Harmony/Bell Tower, 1999. 208 pp. ISBN 0609802127.
True Work takes a spiritual approach to discovering and pursuing your true vocation, wrapping its "how-to" message in the equally important "why-to." This can be an especially helpful resource for those wanting to ensure that any career strategy they put in place reflects an equally strong commitment to spiritual values.

Articles

Johnson, Timothy J. "Making it to the Major Leagues: Career Movement Between Library and Archival Professions and from Small College to Large University Libraries," *Library Trends*, vol. 50, no. 4 (March 1, 2002), pp. 614–630.
An interesting case study of the steps involved in transitioning among library environments, with an exploration of the impact of professional education, career planning, and involvement with professional associations on career opportunities.

Montgomery, Denise L. "Happily Ever After: Plateauing as a Means for Long-Term Career Satisfaction," *Library Trends*, vol. 50, no. 4 (March 2002), pp. 702–716.
A fascinating article on a topic not usually addressed in the professional literature—career plateauing. Citing leading authors on this topic, Montgomery explores the impact of plateauing on both the individual and the organization, then identifies strategies for getting unstuck.

Topper, Elisa F. "Test Careers with Information Interviews," *American Libraries*, vol. 34, no. 9, (October 2003), p. 74.
A brief but useful overview of information interviews, including benefits, etiquette, and a list of potential questions to ask. Especially useful for those who have informational interviews as part of their career development strategies.

Online Resources

A Librarian Without a Library: Staying Professionally Active While Unemployed
www.liscareer.com/shontz_activeunemployment.htm
A practical hit-list of action items for those who find themselves taking a temporary (from several months to several years) leave from their LIS careers. From the prolific Priscilla K. Shontz, and part of her LIScareer website.

Career Planning
www.liscareer.com/careerplanning.htm
Part of the LIScareer.com Library & Information Science Professional's Career Development Center, this is a collection of articles by LIS professionals on career choices, alternative careers, setting career goals, and other useful topics. Lots of good strategy ideas.

Building Your Career
www.lisjobs.com/newsletter/archives2003.htm
From the May 2003 issue of *Info Career Trends* newsletter, these five articles (plus recommended online resources) focus on strategies for moving through your career toward areas of opportunity.

10
Taking Charge of Your Career

*Twenty years from now you will be more
disappointed by the things you didn't do than by
the ones you did do. So throw off the bowlines,
sail away from the safe harbor. Catch the
tradewinds in your sails. Explore. Dream.
Discover.*

—Mark Twain

Years ago, Mary Catherine Bateson, daughter of anthropologists Margaret
Mead and Gregory Bateson and a respected writer and cultural anthropologist in her own right, wrote a book called *Composing a Life*. The book seemed
intriguing not just because of its excellent reviews, but also because the idea
of a "composed" life seemed so amazing, with its connotations of order and
purposefulness and control. It seemed almost *mythical*, given the realities
all of us deal with on a daily basis.

The book was engaging, inspiring, and beautifully written, weaving the
life stories of five notable women into a tapestry of survival and achievement. But it was evident that these women weren't so much composing their
lives as *improvising* them, as is perhaps the case for most of us, men and
women. We improvise—create solutions on the fly—because life so rarely
slows down long enough for us to methodically compose our answers to its
challenges.

Instead, the circumstances of our professional careers frequently require us to deal with change or get run over by it. In the interests of not
becoming road-kill, we work on our improvisational tap-dancing skills. And

like most physical skills, how you think about your moves, how you visualize your actions, and how you perceive your environment determine how effectively you execute in real life.

So far, we've considered our strengths in terms of key practice-area skills (such as the ability to do research, or catalog, or create systems networks) and key professional skills and competencies (such as the ability to manage effectively, communicate well, manage projects, or lead teams). These are important considerations and will take you a long way toward realizing your career dreams.

However, there is another critical competency that determines how easily you navigate the ups and downs of a typical career. This competency is as much about attitude as actions, and it's a key determinant in how resilient your career will be. This competency is self-leadership—how honestly you approach your career, how you react to circumstances around you, and what you expect of yourself.

Self-Leadership

Everyone is necessarily the hero of his own life story.

—John Barth

If you think back about the various competencies we discussed earlier, you'll find that many of them are based on making choices. You can choose whether or not to explore who you are, to improve your ability to take risks, to respond to change, to position for opportunity. French writer Albert Camus stated that life is the sum of our choices; so, too, are our careers.

We can *choose* to become leaders in our own lives. Our ability to do so successfully, however, is to a large extent determined by how we approach the idea of locus of control.

The essence of self-leadership, the concept of *locus of control* is based on work done by social learning theorist Julian Rotter during the sixties. Essentially, if you have an *external* locus of control you tend to believe, and behave as if, others control the outcomes of your life. If you have an *internal* control locus you tend to believe, and behave as if, your own actions drive the results and outcomes of your life.

Generally, all of us frame our life events in ways that comfort us. It's how we explain to ourselves the stories of our lives. Someone with an external frame or locus of control attributes his or her circumstances to outside influences, for example, a parent, luck (good or bad), a supportive or unsupportive work environment. For someone with an external locus of control, life seems out of control because it is—there's no way to control all the external forces that seem to be able to dictate what happens—or doesn't—in our lives. The result can be a sense of helplessness about the future and its opportunities, as well as an inability to commit to the work necessary for creating the career you want.

Having an internal locus of control, however, shifts responsibility for your circumstances to your own choices—basically, *your* decisions and actions and efforts drive the majority of the outcomes of your life. Although having total responsibility for those results—good and bad—can be a bit daunting, the really *good* news is that if you focus on your ability to drive your own outcomes, all of a sudden life gets much more interesting. And so does your career.

What does an external versus an internal locus of control look like in your career?

Think about which of these responses are most likely to help you move forward to the job or career you want:

I'm unhappy in my job because—

> I work for an unfeeling idiot, *again*!

> My workplace isn't supportive, so I need to figure out ways to meet my own professional needs.

Finding a better job is a matter of—

> Really, *really* good luck.

> Persistent effort, lots of research, and ongoing colleague connections.

My friends always seem to get better jobs than I do because—

> Life is unfair.

> I've been spending all my time hanging out in karaoke bars singing "I Love Rock and Roll," and they've been taking web design classes.

Getting more education and broadening my skill set will—

> Only be worth it if there's a guaranteed job with a 50 percent salary increase as a result.

> Continue to open up new career options for me.

I can shape my career so it is rewarding to me because—

> I deserve a break today.

> I'm willing to make the effort to plan my goals and objectives and execute my strategies.

Pretty clear which is an internal and which an external locus of control?

Although psychologists point out that we all exhibit a range of behaviors between external and internal locuses of control, and that internal is not always a better option than external, when it comes to building the career you want, internal is definitely better. If you understand that your career is in fact based on choices that you control, then your possibilities are endless. It's the difference between inertia and action, between victim and victor, between stuck and successful. It's the difference between learning from your mistakes or denying them—and being doomed to repeat them over and over. It's the difference between the career that employers say you can have, and the career you create for yourself through your own efforts.

A key indicator of external locus-of-control thinking is language, the words you use to describe the way things are going in your life. On our bad days, most of us have occasionally been heard to mutter these familiar, self-defeating phrases—

- I deserve to get paid more
- I work so hard, I should be treated with more respect
- I spent two tough years in graduate schools, I have a right to a good job

- I deserve the best opportunities because of my job seniority

- I assumed promotion would be based on superior skills (i.e., mine)

All of these phrases are based on a misconception, which is that the unspoken contract with the rest of the world we have in our heads has somehow been agreed to by the other party.

Librarians *do* deserve to get paid more. Relying on advanced professional skills, they provide an invaluable service for the communities within which they work. However, the reality is that compensation and societal value are not always (or even often) linked, and salaries for traditional librarians are unlikely to increase substantially unless we can figure out a way to turn librarianship into a national sport involving some sort of ball.

Hard work *should* be deserving of respect, but in real life the two are only ocassionally linked together. The general public bases respect on all sorts of criteria, but rarely on the values we think should be key. If you want someone to respect you based on hard work, you have to be doing the kind of hard work *they* think is valuable —and very few people have a sufficient understanding of what librarians do to be impressed by how hard we work.

Yep, after getting through those tough years in graduate school, it would be nice to land a good, full-time job with opportunities commensurate with your skills. But feeling like you're *entitled* to one will only set you up for a terrible sense of frustration and betrayal, making it difficult to sustain the positive energy necessary to finally land a job.

The problem is that words like *deserve, should, right, expect,* and *assumed* all set us up for self-defeating mindsets that keep us stuck in place, wasting our energy on how things *should be* rather than on how they *are.* It's human nature to vent, but when all your energy is being channeled in that direction on an ongoing basis, you've got none left over for more useful things—like tracking down a great new job. You're stalled in the ineffectiveness of external locus-of-control thinking.

Instead, consider these statements:

- I'm unhappy in my job; what am I going to do to change things?

- I'm not growing in my career; what steps can I take to move forward?

- I'd like to be making more money; what options can I identify for this, and which ones will I choose to pursue?

- I'm bored with my job; what things can I do to reengage and bring fresh energy to my responsibilities?

- My boss is extremely difficult to work for; what are my choices for responding to this short-term and long-term, and which ones will I choose?

- I need to determine what I want from my career, and then figure out ways to achieve it.

Each of these statements reflects an internal locus of control, a willingness to take responsibility for your own outcomes and a belief that you can successfully do so. An assumption that external forces control you may keep you stalled in miserable situations. Becoming instead the leader in your own life lets you find—or create—what you need.

In terms of career planning, a self-leadership approach means you identify the problem, explore how you're contributing to it (if that's the case), accept reality (the only thing you can control is yourself, your actions, and
reactions), and come up with your strategy for creating a different outcome. Or it means targeting an opportunity, creating a plan for achieving it,
making a commitment to yourself to follow through on your plan, and then
doing it.

Getting Unstuck

How many times have you been party to one of those "all the reasons I
can't move forward" conversations? You know, the one where everybody tries
to come up with helpful suggestions for one of your companions, only to be
continually rebuffed with reasons why any and all solutions are impossible?

It's just human nature to focus on all the obstacles we're sure will
keep us from doing anything about our deplorable circumstances. When it
comes to our careers, there are all sorts of different ways we can feel "stuck."
Among the recurring themes are—

- I'm a new mom and I'm going to be out of the workforce for awhile—I
  know my career's just going to stagnate

- I think I know what I might like to do, but I don't know if I'd like the
  work

- We just bought a new house and I can't afford to leave my job for at
  least a year

- I really want to become an independent, but don't have the money to
  do it

- I don't get any support from family or friends in terms of career
  growth

- Making these kinds of changes or taking this kind of initiative is just
  too daunting, overwhelming

- I'm not good at brainstorming, so I can't come up with any good ideas

- I feel guilty taking time to focus on my own needs

- I'm not smart/creative/confident enough to push my career goals

- It's too scary to make major changes

- I'm too old to waste time pursuing a different career, even if I think
  I'd love it

- I don't know where to start

- I don't know what I'd need to know to succeed

- All my career "energy" is going into grad school

Even though the basic circumstances of a situation may, in fact, be exactly
as stated—for example, a new mom will be out of the workforce for awhile—
it doesn't necessarily follow that one's career is going to be damaged. Instead, you can practice shifting into a self-leadership stance and come up

with take-charge solutions for each of the obstacles identified. Here are some examples:

Obstacle: I'm a new mom and I'm going to be out of the workforce for awhile— my career's just going to stagnate

Take-charge solution: Figure out ways to stay visible, stay connected, and stay current

Possible action items:

- Stay active in local professional groups by volunteering—keeps you visible, networked, and on top of industry news
- Read at least one professional publication monthly to stay current
- Sign up for electronic discussion lists in your area of interest to stay current
- Go online and research trends in your area of expertise
- See if you can do freelance or project work for colleagues or local organizations—creates visibility, ongoing professional engagement, portfolio building
- Monitor job listing sites so you can see where skill sets are heading, and identify areas you may need to refresh when you're ready to return to the job market
- Assess online learning opportunities that will allow you to continue to grow your skills without interfering with your parenting commitments
- Target a couple of areas where you can differentiate your skills by developing areas of specialization (second language, trends in the biometrics industry, nonprofit website development)
- Work on your research skills by doing Internet or database (if free access is available through your local library) research on topics of professional interest to you
- Work on your writing skills by turning that research into an article for a publication (print or online)—creates visibility, bulks up your portfolio

Obstacle: I think I know what I might want to do, but I don't know if I'd like the work

Take-charge solution: Get the information you need to make that decision

Possible action items:

- Identify resources related to the career path that interests you, including books, electronic discussion lists, periodicals, blogs, associations, etc.
- Sign up for the key discussion lists and blogs, consider joining the appropriate associations, check out online articles from the periodicals, and read at least one of the books to get a sense of roles and responsibilities, issues, etc.

- Do informational interviews with several people locally who are in a position similar to the one you're interested in
- Shadow a librarian or information professional in this type of job to understand what their day looks like
- Research emerging issues in your practice area to identify how the characteristics of this job might change and determine whether or not that appeals to you
- Check out LIS job postings to get a sense of the roles and responsibilities involved in the position, with an eye toward whether or not these align with your self-assessment findings
- Consider what other professional options might also offer the type of work you enjoy doing; for example, someone who loves reference work might also enjoy running public outreach programs (public interaction) or being a competitive intelligence specialist (research)
- Seek out a part-time (evenings, weekends, or freelance) position that would allow you to try out the role without leaving your current job

Obstacle: Some of my family members and friends aren't very supportive of my interest in career growth—especially when it takes time away from them—so I'm concerned about finding time to pursue the career goals I've identified

Take-charge solution: Let yourself assume a leadership role in your own life, and believe in your right to do so

Possible action items:

- Understand that sometimes those in your inner circle—friends and family—are dealing with their own fear issues and feeling threatened by your changes, so they may have a tough time being supportive
- Understand that *knowing* this shouldn't mean *accepting* it; if you lack support, become your own best cheerleader
- Find colleagues and friends who understand how important professional growth is to you, and ask them to become your brain-trust
- Stay focused on forward progress (not perfection); if you have to fight for time to focus on your career goals, then celebrate every successful effort, even if it's only an hour a week
- Start building a community of colleagues that reinforce your passion for your career and your enthusiasm for new challenges
- Start journaling; create a private space for you to write down your dreams, ideas, goals, fears, favorite quotes, and anything else that lets you stay centered and supported on your career path
- Put together a personal portfolio—document the things you've learned over the past two or ten or twenty years, the successful projects you've worked on, the ways you've contributed to others' lives, with a focus on proving your value and ability to yourself so you'll need less encouragement from others

- Create success opportunities for yourself, no matter how small: think of a useful or interesting information project, create an execution plan, and complete it; this will help you prove to yourself your competence and ability, and start documenting a track record of initiative and success for you to rely on

- On a day when you are feeling frightened or frustrated or unsupported, remember that your happiness is worth the effort, and that you are capable of creating that happiness

Every one of the obstacles students raised can be addressed with this type of solutions thinking. Taking a leadership role in your life doesn't mean that obstacles go away, but it *does* mean that you won't let them derail you. Instead, you'll be able to identify the circumstances holding you back, and then come up with a collection of solutions to try. Some may work, some may not, but the bottom line is: you'll be the one in charge, so you can keep trying out solutions until you find the one that works for you.

Now you try it.

What are some obstacles that you feel are keeping you from moving forward with your agenda? Is it people, money, emotional issues, time constraints? Whatever they are, write them down in your career journal and then shift your approach from one of "feeling stuck" to one of solutions.

Reframe your response as an affirmative, take-charge one, then identify and write down possible action items to resolve the issue. As you do so, make sure your locus of control is internal, rather than external. One of the most important characteristics of self-leadership is to realistically recognize what you can't control, what you can, and then to target your energies on the latter.

Why is this so critical? Because throughout your career, whether or not you move forward is based not on your ability to change others' responses, but on your ability to change your own.

To a great extent, this commitment to taking control of your career trajectory is the end goal of all the effort you've been putting into you career journal. What we've been trying to unearth is what you want in a career, so that you can then plot a strategy for achieving that end. The good news is that the "achieving that end" part is completely up to you.

Taking Charge When You're a Student

Sometimes, being a grad student feels like your choices are completely driven by other people's agendas. But with a bit of thought and planning, you'll be able to use your time in your MLIS program to build the foundation for the brilliant career to follow. Consider these points:

- Use your practicum and/or internships to try out work environments and types of work, while also building new skills that add to your portfolio

- Take classes outside the LIS program not only to gain broader knowledge but also to build a network of contacts beyond your immediate LIS professional community

- Whenever possible, shape your assignments to focus on learning more about topics or industries you're interested in, or to give you an opportunity to do a volunteer project for a potential employer, or to build portfolio pieces—aim to "multipurpose" your course assignments whever you can

- Use your student status to learn from professionals—the world is usually very responsive to student questions, so don't hesitate to follow up with guest speakers, contact industry thought leaders for their insights, or connect with individuals whose work or thinking you admire, whether local or distant

- Build faculty and student colleague relationships as the beginning of your professional community

- Stop saying (and thinking) "I can't do that," and trust yourself enough to instead go with "I'm not good at that—yet"

- Become an advocate for your own learning—as you engage with each new course, begin by determining what things *you* want to learn, which may be in addition to what the course offers

- Invest your time and efforts in learning that is valuable to your career goals rather than in getting straight A's

- Understand that graduate school is not an end in itself, but simply an important building block in a decades-long career

Freedom to Choose

Freedom is actually a much bigger game than power. Power is about what you can control. Freedom is about what you can unleash.
—Harriet Rubin

We alone choose how we frame reality. As Martin Seligman pointed out in *Learned Optimism* (Knopf, 1991), how you explain to yourself why the events of your life have happened—your explanatory style—to a great degree determines whether or not you feel able to shape life's outcomes.

In the LIS profession, we have the option to decide which stories to embrace: the ones where your opportunities are already defined and determined for you within a set range of expectations, or the ones where you're tap-dancing as fast as you can to bring your incredible skills into an increasing range of information spaces. Your stories can be about what the world did or didn't do for you, or about what you did for yourself and for others.

If we rethink information work, we can blow away boundaries that say "that's not what we do," and instead with confidence say "I think I'd like to explore that." Rethinking information work frees you to improvise your responses, to create careers based on saying yes to opportunity and seeing where it leads. It's what allows you to have a career of no limits, one where you alone define the universe of opportunities. It's what leads to a resilient career, a lifetime of professional independence.

You now possess strategies, tactics, and tools, as well as a career journal rich in ideas and potential pathways. You've mapped an action plan to move you from today's circumstances to tomorrow's opportunities.

You're part of one of the smartest, most passionate, most supportive professional communities in existence. You work with the two most important resources of the twenty-first century—information and knowledge. You have a skill set whose applicability across all types of organizations, industries, and communities is limited only by your imagination.

You are poised for a terrific career as an LIS professional. What choices will you make?

Resources

Books

Brooks, Donna and Lynn Brooks. *Seven Secrets of Successful Women: Success Strategies of the Women Who Have Made It—And How You Can Follow Their Lead.* McGraw-Hill, 1999. 274 pp. ISBN 0071342648.
The premise of this book is that if you understand organizational behavior, you'll be equipped to make better choices when dealing with office (or library) relationships. Most graduates of MLIS programs get little coaching around organizational behavior (also known as office politics), so titles like these can be a quick primer on how to survive and thrive in the workplace. The seven secrets: find a mentor, increase your visibility, develop a solid network, brush up on your communication skills, strike a balance between work and personal lives, be willing to take risks when appropriate, and understand the internal politics of your organization. These strategies apply across all organizations (including libraries), and are equally appropriate for men and women.

Csikszentmihalyi, Mihaly. *Finding Flow: The Psychology of Engagement with Everyday Life.* Basic Books, 1998. 144 pp. ISBN 0465024114.
Based on the groundbreaking ideas expressed by Csikszentmihalyi in his earlier work *Flow, the Psychology of Optimal Experience* (Harper & Row, 1990), this work focuses on how to find "optimal experience" in our everyday lives, including our work lives. The key is finding work that challenges us "with tasks that require a high degree of skill and commitment" to actively shape our engagements rather than passively accepting whatever tasks present themselves. An interesting approach to thinking about our relationship with the work that we do, and what we expect from it.

Lubit, Roy H. *Coping with Toxic Managers, Subordinates . . . And Other Difficult People: Using Emotional Intelligence to Survive and Prosper.* Financial Times/Prentice Hall, 2003. 272 pp. ISBN 0131409956.
Sometimes the best career move we can make at the moment is to stay right where we are, despite a less than healthy work environment. In that case, it helps to develop a positive strategy for dealing with bosses and co-workers who are making you crazy. Lubit identifies five toxic personality types—narcissistic, unethical, aggressive, rigid, and impaired—then, building on Daniel Goleman's work with emotional intelligence, suggests ways to both understand and cope with these

individuals. An especially good resource for helping you take charge of dysfunctional work interactions rather than letting them control you.

Maddi, Salvatore R. and Deborah M. Khoshaba. *Resilience at Work: How to Succeed No Matter What Life Throws at You.* American Management Association, 2005. 213 pp. ISBN 0814472605.

Maddi and Khoshaba equate resilience with "hardiness," or the ability to survive if not thrive despite stressful circumstances. Emphasizing that resilience is a skill that can be learned, the authors focus on information, motivational insights, processes, and tools to help readers master this important capability.

Miller, John B. *QBQ! The Question Behind the Question: Practicing Personal Accountability in Work and in Life.* Putnam, 2004. 128 pp. ISBN 0399152334.

Miller considers the question behind the question to be "what can I do to improve this situation?" His theme of personal accountability is woven through stories and advice which may be old hat to those who've practiced internal locus of control for years, but his down-to-earth coaching will be useful for those just starting down this path.

Seligman, Martin E. *Learned Optimism: How to Change Your Mind and Your Life.* Free Press, 1998. 336 pp. ISBN 0671019112.

Seligman has studied optimism, pessimism, and such related issues as learned helplessness and the effect of explanatory style (the way you explain outcomes and events in your life to yourself) for decades. In *Learned Optimism*, he asserts that people can learn to develop an attitude of optimism even if it isn't their default mindset, and then proceeds to offer information and insights to help readers do just that.

Sher, Barbara. *It's Only Too Late if You Don't Start Now: How to Create Your Second Life After 40.* Dell, 1999. 352 pp. ISBN 0440507189.

Sher has written many books on creating your best life (see also *I Could Do Anything If I Only Knew What it Was* in the Chapter 2 Resources section), but this one specifically targets those wondering if it's still possible—or even worth the effort—once we hit middle age. Sher's resounding answer—*yes!* An inspirational resource for those coming into the LIS profession as a second or later-in-life career.

Siebert, Al. *The Resiliency Advantage.* Berrett-Koehler, 2005. 225 pp. ISBN 1576753298.

Resiliency may be one of the most important career skills you can master: since life will always provide moments of adversity, our ability to bounce back determines our ability to keep growing both personally and professionally. Siebert helps readers understand the critical value of resiliency, then provides practical information to help them achieve it. An important complement to self-leadership.

Articles

Coutu, Diane L. "How Resilience Works," *Harvard Business Review*, vol. 80, no. 5 (May 2002), pp. 46–52.

Based on organization behavior research and numerous interviews with human resource professionals, Coutu's article identifies three characteristics found in resilient individuals: (1) an ability to understand and accept reality; (2) an ability to find meaning in aspects of one's personal and professional life; and (3) an ability to improvise as circumstances change.

Drucker, Peter. "Managing Oneself," *Harvard Business Review*, vol. 83, no. 1 (January 2005), pp. 100–109.
Intended for all knowledge workers, this classic article expands on Drucker's assertion that "success in the knowledge economy comes to those who know themselves—their strengths, their values, and how they best perform." Although not specifically focused on information professionals, Drucker's take on the information economy and those who will work in it has relevance to all in our profession.

Waterman, Jr., Robert H., Judith A Waterman, and Betsy A. Collard. "Toward a Career-Resilient Workforce," *Harvard Business Review,* vol. 72, no. 4 (July/August 94), pp. 87–96.
According to the authors, career resilience should be a responsibility shared by both employee and employer. If both parties work to enhance the individual's employability inside *and* outside of the organization, the result will be a workforce of increased value to the employer, and an employee who grows more confident in his or her ability to contribute at a high professional level. Although the article is dated, its concepts continue to resonate in today's workplace.

Online Resources

How to Be a Leader in Your Field: A Guide for Students in Professional Schools
http://polaris.gseis.ucla.edu/pagre/leader.html
Philip E. Agre, an associate professor of information studies at UCLA, has written what he describes as "detailed instructions for students on the process of becoming an intellectual leader in your profession." Excellent, thoughtful, and practical advice that will serve you well during both your graduate school tenure and your subsequent career.

Appendix A
Special Interest Groups

Membership in professional organizations can be an effective way to extend the reach of your professional community, especially if you join one of the many special interest groups (SIGs) hosted by the major associations. Looked at this way, ALA, SLA, and other LIS organizations offer a rich and varied community of communities, at least one of which may align with your interests.

SIGs are an excellent way to connect with others who share your professional interests, to learn more about a specific practice area, and to create a personal connection within what can often feel like an overwhelmingly large and somewhat distant organization. SIGs are also a great place to start volunteering, and begin building a national community of colleagues.

Depending on the structure and activities of SIGs, they may be called sections, roundtables, discussion groups, caucuses, forums, or special interest groups. Almost all of the SIGS also have electronic discussion groups that address their topic area or several of its subtopics. Also, new special interest groups are formed on a regular basis, so be sure to check with the association to see if new ones have been added since this list was compiled.

American Library Association

www.ala.org

Divisions

American Association of School Libraries (AASL)
www.ala.org/aaslhomeTemplate.cfm?Section=aasl

Sections

Educators of Library Media Specialists Section (ELMSS)

Independent Schools Section (ISS)

Supervisors Section (SPVS)

Association for Library Collections & Technical Services (ALCTS)
www.ala.org/ALCTSTemplate.cfm?Section=alcts

Interest Groups

Catalog Form & Function

Electronic Resources

Networked Resources & Metadata

Publisher/Vendor Library Relations

Association for Library Service to Children (ALSC)
www.ala.org/ALSCTemplate.cfm?Section=alsc

Discussion Groups

Children and Technology

Children's Books

Children's Collection Management in Public Libraries

Managing Children's Services

Preschool Services

Public Library-School Partnership

Storytelling

Teaching Children's Literature

Association of College & Research Libraries (ACRL)
www.ala.org/ACRLTemplate.cfm?Section=acrl

Sections

African American Studies Librarians (AFAS)

Anthropology and Sociology (ANSS)

Arts

Asian, African, and Middle Eastern (AAMES)

College Libraries (CLS)

Community and Junior College Libraries (CJCLS)

Distance Learning (DLS)

Education and Behavioral Sciences (EBSS)

Instruction (IS)

Law and Political Science (LPSS)

Literatures in English (LES)

Rare Books and Manuscripts (RBMS)

Science and Technology (STS)

Slavic and East European (SEES)

University Libraries (ULS)

Western European Studies (WESS)

Women's Studies (WSS)

Association of Specialized and Cooperative Library Agencies (ASCLA)
www.ala.org/ASCLAMAINTemplate.cfm?Section=ascla

Sections

Independent Librarian's Exchange (ILEX)

Interlibrary Cooperation & Networking (ICAN)

Libraries Serving Special Populations (LSSPS)

State Library Agency (SLAS)

Library Administration and Management Association (LAMA)
www.ala.org/lamahometemplate.cfm?Section=lama

Sections

Buildings and Equipment (BES)

Fundraising and Financial Development (FRFDS)

Human Resources (HRS)

Library Organization and Management (LOMS)

Measurement, Assessment, and Evaluation (MAES)

Public Relations and Marketing (PRMS)

Systems and Services (SASS)

Library & Information Technology Association (LITA)
www.ala.org/LITAMAINTemplate.cfm?Section=lita

Special Interest Groups

Authority Control in the Online Environment (with ALCTS)

Digital Library Technologies

Distance Learning

Electronic Publishing/Electronic Journals

Emerging Technologies

Heads of Library Technology

Human/Machine Interface

Imagineering

Internet Portals

Internet Resources

JPEG 2000 in Archives and Libraries

Library Consortia Automated Systems

MARC Formats (with ALCTS)

Personal Computing

Open Source Systems

RFID Technology

Secure Systems and Services

Standards

Technical Services Workstations (with ALCTS)

Technology & the Arts

Public Library Association (PLA)
www.ala.org/PLAHomeTemplate.cfm?Section=pla

Clusters

Issues and Concerns Cluster

Intellectual Freedom

International Relations

Legislation

Library Confidentiality

Public Policy in Public Libraries

Recruitment of Public Librarians

Research and Statistics

Workload Measures and Staffing Patterns

Library Development Cluster

Branch Libraries

Marketing Public Libraries

Metropolitan Libraries

Practical Applications of Technology in Public Libraries

Public Library Systems

Rural Library Services

Small and Medium-Sized Libraries

Technology in Public Libraries

Library Services Cluster

Adult Continuing and Independent Learning Services

Basic Education and Literacy Resources and Services

Career and Business Services

Cataloging Needs of Public Libraries

Collection Management

Community Information Services

Readers' Advisory

Services to Preschool Children and Their Caregivers

Services to Teenagers and Their Caregivers

Reference and User Services Association (RUSA)
www.ala.org/RUSAMAINTemplate.cfm?Section=rusa

Sections

Business Reference and Services (BRASS)

Collection Development and Evaluation (CODES)

History Librarians

Machine-Assisted Reference (MARS)

Reference Services (RSS)

Sharing and Transforming Access to Resources (STARS)

Young Adult Library Services Association (YALSA)
www.ala.org/yalsaTemplate.cfm?Section=yalsa

Roundtables

Continuing Library Education Network and Exchange (CLENERT)

Ethnic and Multicultural Information Exchange (EMIERT)

Exhibits (ERT)

Federal and Armed Forces Libraries (FAFLRT)

Gay, Lesbian, Bisexual, Transgendered (GLBTRT)

Government Documents (GODORT)

Intellectual Freedom (IFRT)

International Relations (IRRT)

Library History (LHRT)

Library Instruction (LIRT)

Library Research (LRRT)

Library Support Staff Interests (LSSIRT)

Map and Geography (MAGERT)

New Members (NMRT)

Social Responsibilities (SRRT)

Staff Organizations (SORT)

Video (VRT)

American Society of Information Science and Technology (ASIS&T)

www.asis.org/AboutASIS/asis-sigs.html

Special Interest Groups

Arts & Humanities (AH)

Bioinformatics (BIO)

Blogs, Wikis, Podcasting (BWP)

Classification Research (CR)

Critical Issues (CRIT)

Digital Libraries (DL)

Education for Information Science (ED)

History & Foundations of Information Science (HFIS)

Human-Computer Interaction (HCI)

Information Architecture (IA)

Information Analysis & Evaluation (IAE)

Information Needs, Seeking and Use (USE)

Information Policy (IFP)

International Information Issues (III)

Knowledge Management (KM)

Library Technologies (LT) *formerly Library Automation and Networks (LAN)*

Management (MGT)

Medical Informatics (MED)

Metrics (MET)

Scientific & Technical Information Systems (STI)

Technology, Information, & Society (TIS)

Visualization, Images & Sound (VIS)

Special Library Association (SLA)

www.sla.org

Caucuses

Archival & Preservation

Association Information Services

Baseball

Gay & Lesbian Issues

Information Futurists

International Information Exchange

Labor Issues

Natural History

Nontraditional Careers

Retired Members

Women's Issues

Communities of Practice

Biomedical & Life Sciences

Cataloging

Chemistry

Information Literacy Committee

Competencies

Competitive Intelligence

Emerging Leaders Network

Government Information Section

Government Libraries

Information Systems Section

Information Technology

Insurance, Risk Management & Employee Benefits

Medical Section / Biomedical & Life Sciences

Military Librarians

Risk Management Network

Solo Librarians

Technical Services Section

Terrorism/Homeland Security

Webmaster Section

Divisions

Biomedical & Life Sciences (DBIO)

    Medical Section

Business & Finance

College & University Business Libraries

Corporate Information Centers

Financial Institutions

Investment Services

Private Equity

Chemistry
Competitive Intelligence
Education
Engineering
    Aerospace
Environment & Resource Management
    Forestry
Food, Age, & Nutrition
Government Information Division
Information Technology (DITE)

    Communications

    Digital Content

    Government Information

    Information Systems

    Technology Services

    Virtual Libraries

    Webmaster

Insurance & Employee Benefits
Legal
Leadership & Management

    Consulting

    Knowledge Management

    Marketing

Materials Research & Management
Military Librarians
Museums, Arts, & Humanities
News
Petroleum & Energy
Pharmaceutical & Health Technology
Physics—Astronomy—Mathematics
Sciences—Technology
Social Science

    Geography & Map

    International Relations

    Nonprofit Sector

    Public Policy

Solo Librarians
Transportation

Ethnic Group Organizations

American Indian Library Association
www.nativeculturelinks.com/aila.html

Asian / Pacific American Librarians Association
www.apalaweb.org/

Black Caucus
www.bcala.org/

Chinese American Librarians Association
www.cala-web.org

REFORMA
www.reforma.org

Appendix B
Employment Resources

LIS Employment Sites and Resources

In addition to the resources listed below, keep in mind that almost all of the LIS professional organizations (and many of their special interest groups) offer job postings, as do several of the MLIS programs and nearly all of the state libraries.

ALA Career Leads Online

www.ala.org/ala/education/empopps/careerleadsb/careerleadsonline.htm
Jobs listed by title, library, and location; organized by date posted. Postings are those appearing in *American Libraries*, plus others posted specifically to the Hot Jobs Online website. Check archives for job postings from earlier issues of *American Libraries*. While on the site, check out the "Working Knowledge" columns, also archived on the site and full of practical career tips.

JINFO: Jobs in Information

www.jinfo.com
Online clearinghouse of job listings, from the same team that produces the U.K.-based FreePint site. Search by keyword, sector (academic, corporate, or public), country (including U.K. region or U.S. state), hours (full- or part-time), duration (contract, permanent, temporary, work experience), and minimum–maximum salary expectation. At the website, sign up for the e-newsletter to receive a twice-monthly update of career tips and the most recently posted job listing.

Jobs for Information Professionals

http://web.syr.edu/~jryan/infopro/jobs.html
Part of Joe Ryan's "Information Resources for Information Professionals" directory, the section on jobs aggregates links of use to LIS job hunters under such areas as Guides, Trends, Top Companies, Job Prep, Job Postings, Salary Information, etc. An extremely broad-ranging (okay, eclectic) collection of sources, with something on almost every aspect of the profession, although most postings are from 2000 or earlier.

Jobs in Library and Information Technology

www.lita.org/jobs/postings.html
This site, offered by the Library & Information Technology Association (LITA), organizes its job postings by region (northeastern, southern, midwestern, western, and outside the United States). Not an extensive list, but useful and current.

LIBJOBS: Employment Mailing List for LIS Professionals

www.ifla.org/II/lists/libjobs.htm
From the International Federation of Library Associations and Institutions (IFLA), LIBJOBS is "an Internet mailing list for employment opportunities for librarians and information professionals." The site includes a browsable archive from mid-1995 forward. Check website for instructions on signing up for the list.

Libjobs.com

www.libjobs.com/
Post your resume (or resumes—up to five), and/or search job postings by keyword, category (e.g., administration, information services, reference, sales, and training), employer, location, and date. A commercial site maintained by WebClarity Software, Inc., the job listings here are for public, academic, and school library positions. See also the "Career Tools" section for recommended career tools and resources.

Library Job Hunting (Ann's Place)

www.geocities.com/aer_mcr/libjob/
Clearinghouse of links to sites that post job openings, organized by geographic region (United States and Canada, United Kingdom and Ireland, Australia and New Zealand). Especially useful for its inclusion of job posting sites hosted by the major LIS associations. See also "Other Job Information" for mostly LIS-based articles and resources (a couple from Monster.com) in the categories of advice, resume-writing, cover letters, interviews, thank-you letters, letters of resignation, networking, and relocation information. Apparently not updated for several years, but most of the links were still active as of this review.

Library Job Listings

www.coe.missouri.edu/~career/library.html
Created to support students in the University of Missouri-Columbia's LIS program, this listing of a couple dozen briefly annotated job lists includes resources focused on library-specific jobs as well as those in higher education, K-12, and international teaching opportunities.

Library Job Postings on the Internet

www.libraryjobpostings.org/
Created and maintained by Sarah L. Johnson, this site offers perhaps the most extensive coverage of job information available. Resources are organized by categories such as type of library or job (academic; archives/records management, school, special, federal); placement services; individual library sites; and sites listing all positions types/all locations. A "clickable" map allows you to search by region or nation. Current and comprehensive, a great resource.

Library Journal Job Zone

www.libraryjournal.com/community/891/Careers/42799.html
Search jobs by category (academic libraries, children's/young adult, management, public libraries, technical). Postings include title, company/ organization, location, and job description, often including salary.

Lisjobs.com—Jobs for Librarians and Information Professionals

www.lisjobs.com/
A key resource. Rachel Singer Gordon covers every aspect of working in the LIS profession, and her site includes job and resume postings, a listing of jobs both by state and nationwide, non-U.S. jobs, advice from practitioners, and the invaluable newsletter, *Info Career Trends*. Sign up now, then go back and read every issue in the archive—especially if you're a student!

Employment Firms

C. Berger Group (CBG)

www.cberger.com
A nationwide contract-services firm for "clients from academic, not-for-profit, public, business, educational, government, and industrial organizations including many Fortune 500 companies." CBG also recruits qualified individuals for positions within those same organizations.

InfoCurrent

www.infocurrent.com
InfoCurrent specializes in library and records management staffing, on both a project and permanent basis. At the website, check Job Categories for a listing of the types of positions being filled.

Library Associates

www.libraryassociates.com/index.php
Library Associates describes itself as "an information-focused organization dedicated to providing outstanding staffing and information management solutions to libraries, corporations, archives, museums, academia, hospitals, law firms and government agencies."

General Job Listing Sites

An important part of exploring how many different ways your LIS skills might be applied is to understand how they match up with non-LIS jobs. The sites below provide plenty of jobs to explore; try running some of the job titles listed in Chapter 4 in their search engines to see what you find.

Careerbuilder

www.careerbuilder.com
Find jobs, set up job alerts, post a resume, explore by location of job type within category (for example, college, human resources, information technology, nonprofit). Other search options include searching by company, by industry, in Spanish, and by international jobs. Register for e-mailed job opening alerts.

Monster.com

www.monster.com
Similar in scope to Careerbuilder, Monster's primary focus is job listings and resume posting, but it has also branched out with education partners, career networking, and career advice message boards. If you're *really* interested in career exploration, consider signing up for Monster Career News, their online e-newsletter.

The Riley Guide

www.rileyguide.com
The Riley Guide doesn't post jobs itself but links to hundreds of sites that do (unannotated, listed alphabetically). In addition, it also lists all sorts of career "how-to" resources on topics like "business etiquette," "changing careers," and "internships, fellowships, and work exchange programs." An extensive, content-rich, very useful career tool.

Appendix C
Current Awareness Resources

Listed below are some of the most popular current awareness resources, although this is by no means a comprehensive or exhaustive list. Rather, consider this a starting point from which to launch your exploration of the profession and its information tools, but one that you will then build on and tailor to your own interests as you identify them.

Almost all of the resources listed below have daily or weekly blogs and/or newsfeeds, so it's easy to monitor emerging trends and information resources by aggregating them into a single information feed.

Keeping Current with the Profession

beSpacific

www.bespacific.com/
This site from Sabrina I. Pacifici provides "accurate, focused law and technology news." Brief daily postings cover such topics as RSS fees, copyright issues, privacy, the impact of the Patriot Act, etc. Previous issues are archived at the website.

Current Cites

http://lists.webjunction.org/currentcites/
From digital information guru Roy Tennant, the monthly Current Cites is an "annotated bibliography of selected articles, books, and digital documents on information technology." Check the website for searchable, browsable archives.

Librarian.net

www.librarian.net/about
A fascinating, engaging blog from Jessamyn West, who describes herself as "a user-oriented librarian when I'm working at a library, and a library activist when I am not. My passion presently is mucking about in the intersection of libraries, technology and politics and describing what I find there," which aptly describes the content of her online observations. The site includes a searchable archive of links and related information.

Library Journal Headlines

www.libraryjournal.com/index.asp?layout=Learn_RSS
Sign up for blogs on breaking news, infotech news, book news, tech news, and "in the bookroom."

LISNews

www.lisnews.com
Librarian Blake Carver and his assistants pull together excerpted news stories of relevance to LIS professionals, especially those involved in LIS technologies. Search the online archives by author, topic, section (academic, books, interviews, etc.), or date.

Peter Scott's Library Blog

http://blog.xrefer.com/
Scot's blog covers new information on databases, conferences, services, software, vendors, and emerging issues in the LIS profession. Keyword searchable, or browse archives going back to February 2003. On the website, see also links grouped under the headings of public library, academic, school, and special library blogs.

The Shifted Librarian

www.theshiftedlibrarian.com/
From tech whiz and self-described "information maven" Jenny Levine, the Shifted Librarian covers an eclectic mix of LIS issues, technologies, and cool tools. A great way to monitor what's going on, and what tech implications you're going to want to be thinking about if you're not already.

Steven Bell's Keeping Up Web Page

http://staff.philau.edu/bells/keepup/
What do you need to keep up with? Bell's site will help you keep up with resources for: librarians, information technologists, instructional technologists, academic librarians, business librarians, Internet searching and search engines, higher education, web technology and design, computing and PC technology, cool web sites, general technology and innovation, online training and distance education, and web page change detection services.

Keeping Current with Information Resources

Docuticker

www.docuticker.com/
Docuticker provides daily updates of "new reports from government agencies, ngo's [nongovernment organizations], think tanks, and other groups." Sample topics have included postings on international studies on prekindergarten education, trends, and impacts of broadband in the Latino community, U.S. tsunami preparedness, and the World Health Report 2005. From the same team that creates Resource Shelf (see below).

Ex Libris

http://marylaine.com/exlibris/

A weekly posting of LIS-focused articles by reference librarian Marylaine Block, as well as occasional guest contributors. Block is also known as the author of "Neat New Stuff," a compilation of recommended new websites. Students exploring career options may also want to check the website for Block's archive of "guru" interviews.

FreePint

www.freepint.com
A terrific collection of information, resources, and career advice dispensed through the FreePint newsletter. Check the website for more than 350 archived newsletter articles, and wander through some 28,000 questions and answers in the FreePint Bar. A great resource and fun to read, as well.

Law Library Resource Xchange (LLRX)

www.llrx.com/
Although targeting legal researchers and librarians, LLRX provides coverage of basic Internet research strategies and resources valuable to all LIS professionals. Updated twice monthly; subscribe at the website for e-mailed updates.

Librarian's Index to the Internet

www.lii.org
An exceptionally well-organized, authoritative directory of librarian-vetted and annotated web resources. Organized by topic within broad categories such as Arts & Humanities, Business, Media, Science, and Society & Social Science, among others. A key resource.

Reference Reviews

http://reviews.gale.com/
From publisher Thompson/Gale, Reference Reviews brings together reviews by Peter Jasco (online and CD-ROM products), John R. M. Lawrence (books), Blanche Woolls and David Loetscher (K-12 print reference materials), and more than 500 archived reviews, including Jim Rettig's highly regarded *Rettig on Reference* columns.

Research Buzz

www.researchbuzz.com
One of the oldest (est. 1998) and best resources for Internet research. Author Tara Calishain covers all aspects of "search engines, new data managing software, browser technology, large compendiums of information, Web directories," all from the perspective of their usefulness to reference librarians. Past entries are searchable by keyword.

Resource Shelf

www.resourceshelf.com/
Gary Price's Resource Shelf includes coverage of such "resources" as new websites, search engine news, info industry announcements, emerging issues in the LIS world, and similarly useful and broad-ranging information. A key resource.

The Scout Report

http://scout.wisc.edu/Reports/ScoutReport/Current/
Part of the Internet Scout Project and published since 1994, the weekly Scout Report identifies and annotates outstanding, authoritative Internet-based resources. Check the website for searchable archives of past reviews. A key resource.

SearchEngineWatch

http://searchenginewatch.com/
The key resource on Internet search tools, strategies, and players, from search engine gurus Danny Sullivan and Chris Sherman (of "invisible web" fame). The focus of this site is to help maximize search engines for marketing purposes, but it is equally valuable for LIS professionals who use the Internet for research.

Index

About the Author

G. KIM DORITY, adjunct faculty at University of Denver's graduate library school, teaches courses in *Information Entrepreneurship* and *Career Alternatives for Library Science Students and Professionals.* Formerly, she led the team that designed and created Jones e-global library, an online library for students and other researchers, and was corporate librarian for Jones International. In addition, she served as Interim Assistant Director for DU's graduate library school. A long-standing *ARBA* reviewer, Kim authored two editions of *Guide to Reference Books*, as well as numerous journal articles.

The *RIW* Website

The resources in this book will be maintained through the book's website, accessed at www.rethinkinginformationwork.com. Please check the website for corrected URLs, resources added as they become available, and additional resource sections. You may also want to check out the monthly column on alternative career paths for LIS professionals.

Please send any questions you may have, comments about the book, or suggestions for resources or career-related topics you would like to see covered in the site's resource section or columns to kimdority@ rethinkinginformationwork.com.